Gowns

How to Make the Wedding Dress of Your Dreams

Susan E. Andriks

Edited by Pati Palmer

Design by Linda Wisner
Illustrations by Jeannette Schilling,
Kate Pryka and Diane Russell
Photography by Pati Palmer
Styling and Sewing by Marta Alto
Technical edit by Alicyn Wright
Final Edit by Barbara Weiland

Palmer/Pletsch Publishing

Dedication

I would like to dedicate this book to my husband, Steve, for his love, support, and absolute patience throughout this endeavor; and to the memory of my mother, Kathryn Graves Zink, from whom I inherited the "sewing gene."

Acknowledgements

I would like to acknowledge Gail Brown and Karen Dillon, the authors of the original Palmer/Pletsch Book, *Sew A Beautiful Wedding*. Their work was the inspiration for this book and it is incorporated here. I would also like to thank Pati Palmer and Palmer/Pletsch Associates for the opportunity to rewrite and expand their book.

Also, thanks to Marta Alto for sewing the gowns for the Fit chapter and the chapter on "Exciting Possibilities;" to Sheila Adams and Cindy Palmer for being the models; to The McCall Pattern Company for use of their beautiful bridal photography; to Alicyn Wright for her beautiful designs for The McCall Pattern Company and her technical input; to Susan Khalje, for her blessing on this project and the inspiration she has given us through her book **Bridal Couture**; and to Carla J. Peery for the creative samples she did for this book. Thanks to Jeannette Schilling for the photo of her parents on their wedding day that appears on the Table of Contents page.

Cover painting by Diane Russell

Copyright © 2000 by Palmer/Pletsch Incorporated

Library of Congress Catalog Card Number: 99-085795

Published by Palmer/Pletsch Publishing, P.O. Box 12046, Portland, OR 97212-0046. U.S.A.

Printed by RR Donnelly & Sons Company, U.S.A.

ISBN 0-935278-51-6

Table of Contents

About the Author 4

INTRODUCTION 4

CHAPTER 1 5
Who Will Sew It?

CHAPTER 2 6
Choose Your Gown Style

CHAPTER 3 19
Designing Your Gown

CHAPTER 4 25
The Big Picture

CHAPTER 5 29
Fitting Real Brides

CHAPTER 6 40
The Exciting Possibilities

CHAPTER 7 56
Bridal Fabric

CHAPTER 8 60
Bridal Sewing Basics

CHAPTER 9 69
Sewing Special Fabrics

CHAPTER 10 77
All About Lace

CHAPTER 11 89
A Bridal Gown
from Start to Finish

CHAPTER 12 90
Shaping the Bodice

CHAPTER 13 95
Bodice Construction Basics

CHAPTER 14 97
Necklines & Collars

CHAPTER 15 111
Closures

CHAPTER 16 115
Sleeves

CHAPTER 17 125
Skirt Basics

CHAPTER 18 133
Hems

CHAPTER 19 137
Trains & Bustling

CHAPTER 20 141
Slips

CHAPTER 21 144
Headpieces, Hats & Veils

CHAPTER 22 154
Finishing Touches

Resources and
Metric Conversion Chart 155
Index 156-157
Palmer/Pletsch Products 158-160

About the Author

Susan Andriks comes from a long line of crafters; her mother and aunts all sewed and did handiwork. Kay Hardy, a "how-to" author whose books were published during the 1930s, '40s and '50s, married Susan's grandfather. Her work included an early McCall's publication, *A Treasury of Needlecraft*. Ms. Hardy also wrote home decorating articles for many women's magazines during her career.

Susan learned to sew in her 7th grade Home Economics class. Her first project—a simple cotton skirt—started her on the path to sewing her own wardrobe. Constant compliments from co-workers on her sewing prompted Susan to begin sewing for the public in the early '80s.

After moving to New Hampshire in 1989, custom sewing and teaching became Susan's part-time business. When the majority of her customers turned out to be brides who could not find what they wanted in ready-to-wear, Susan's focus gravitated toward this market. Experimentation and extensive research helped her in this new endeavor. To further her education, Susan took a year-long professional dressmaking course in 1992, offered at a local fabric shop. She also studied costume techniques with Susan Khalje, whose couture book, *Bridal Couture*, she recommends for further reading. In 1998 Susan fulfilled a long-held dream and opened a custom dressmaking studio where she creates bridal and special occasion dresses, teaches sewing classes, and writes about sewing and sewing-related topics.

Susan lives in Canterbury, New Hampshire, with her husband, Steve and her parrot, Alex. She is an active member of the American Sewing Guild, and is a member of P.A.C.C. (Professional Association of Custom Clothiers).

©1997 Katie Dow Photography

Introduction

When I started sewing bridal gowns, I discovered I had more questions than answers. The first Palmer/Pletsch bridal book, *Sew A Beautiful Wedding*, published in 1980, provided many of the answers, but in the years since it was written, machines and materials available to the home sewer have changed quite a bit.

This revised, updated, and expanded book answers questions about bridal sewing that aren't readily answered in other currently available references and expands on the information provided on pattern guidesheets. It was written for the home sewer who wants to create her own very special gown and for professional dressmakers who want to enhance their knowledge and add new skills to their bridal sewing repertoire.

You have many options—whether you're making your own gown or having it made—and you may begin to think you have too many decisions. This book is designed to help you make some of those decisions and to help inspire you to create the wedding gown of your dreams. If you are a professional dressmaker, you'll find many *Dressmaker's Tips* designed to give you specific information on dealing with customers and helping them make the many decisions about their gown. They also will help you with the business side of your custom sewing service. There's an example below.

So, before you take scissors to fabric, read the entire book. It will help you avoid costly mistakes.

Happy Sewing!

Susan E Andriks

Tip for a Dressmaker

Remember, "the customer is always right." You will, on occasion, need to summon all of your tact and diplomacy to steer your customer away from a style that is very unflattering to her. Try to convince her to go with a style that you know is better for her without actually saying "the style you've picked is totally wrong for you!" It's a difficult position to be in, but you'll be doing yourself and the customer a favor. If she gets negative feedback from her family, she (and they) may blame you, the designer, forgetting that the choice was hers.

CHAPTER 1

Who Will Sew It?

Sewing Your Own Gown

Sewing your own wedding gown is not as difficult as it may seem—there are some techniques to learn about the fabrics that you'll use, some special ideas on how to work with lace, and directions for putting it all together. That's the basis for this book. It's organized to help you design, create, and sew your own wedding gown, offering ideas, tips, and techniques designed to make the whole process as fun, as memorable, and as easy as possible.

Your gown is **the most** important part of the wedding (aside from the groom, of course!). It will be the focal point of your wedding photos, you'll spend most of your wedding day in it, and it is what you'll remember most when you look at your wedding album. **Don't compromise on what you want.**

There are many reasons for making your own wedding gown. One of them may be that you hope to save money over a comparable or much more expensive ready-to-wear garment. Sometimes this is possible, but not always. With outlet shopping flourishing across the country, the fabrics you choose could very well cost more than a ready-made gown.

Custom sewing has many advantages over purchasing ready-to-wear. Aside from the pride of creating your special gown yourself, you'll have a memory that you'll cherish. You'll get *exactly* what you want in a style that suits you and a fabric that you love, all complemented with your choice of trim and accessories. The gown will fit to perfection, you will have fun, and people won't believe that you actually made your beautiful gown yourself.

Using a Dressmaker

When you enlist a dressmaker to create your gown, you get most of the advantages of sewing your own dress—you can have exactly what you want and the dressmaker can sew part or all of the gowns and accessories for the wedding party.

If you get in over your head making your own wedding gown, you can call a professional dressmaker to bail you out. You may also decide that your skills are not up to the task of making your gown or you may want to have your attendants' gowns made if they don't sew and you don't have time to do it all yourself. To find a dressmaker, begin by checking with your local fabric store, ask friends for references, or call the Professional Association of Custom Clothiers' executive director at 541/772-4119. for the name of the nearest chapter president who can give you names of dressmakers specializing in bridal sewing in your area. Some dressmakers also advertise in the local newspaper or the Yellow Pages.

Not matter how you find a dressmaker, be sure to interview her before hiring her to make your gown. Before you call, prepare a list of questions: Does she handle wedding gowns? Is that her specialty? How much lead time does she need? Does she work by appointment only? Her answers to your questions should give you an idea of her working style. If you feel comfortable talking with her on the phone, make an appointment to meet with her to discuss your gown.

If you are calling her in a panic because you're halfway through making your gown and are stuck, she should be sympathetic—but be prepared that she may not be able to fit you into her schedule if time is short. If she cannot complete the gown for you, she may be willing to give you some pointers for a consulting fee.

Before enlisting the dressmaker's service, check her work for quality. She should have a portfolio she can show you and possibly some samples you can examine. At your meeting, explain what you want. Take along photos or sketches, if you can, as well as an idea of the type of fabric you envision.

The dressmaker should be able to give you an estimate for the cost of making your gown, but don't expect one while you wait. She will probably need time to determine how extensive any necessary pattern changes will be, the availability and cost of your fabric, and the difficulty of the style of the gown you've chosen. Her estimate will be based on the design you both discussed—any changes you want as the dress takes shape will affect the final price. She should discuss this with you at the time you place a deposit for your gown.

You get what you pay for, so don't shop based on price. You must be comfortable with your dressmaker and you must be confident in her ability to handle the job. Having a professional dressmaker make your wedding gown can and should be a rewarding and enjoyable experience. Choosing your dressmaker carefully is the key to success.

CHAPTER 2

Choose Your Gown Style

Once you've become engaged and have set the date for your wedding, your thoughts will naturally turn to the focal point of the wedding day: your gown. You, your groom, and your family should discuss the type of wedding you'll have: formal, semi-formal, or casual; day or evening; the number of attendants and guests; the list is a long one. The gown style you choose should relate to the formality of your wedding. For example, a trainless gown with a "garden/country look" worn without a headpiece would *not* be appropriate for a formal evening wedding. Do remember, however, that most gown types can be made more or less formal depending on your choice of fabric, trim, and accessories.

When you begin to design your gown, you may already know what you want it to look like. Before you buy the fabric and lace, however, it's important to do your homework.

♦ Look through bridal magazines. Let your imagination run wild. After all, you aren't worrying about price at this point. You may find that you like the sleeves of one gown, the bodice of another, and the neckline on yet another. Cut out the pictures, cut the pieces apart, and play "paper dolls." Glue the pieces together to see if all the parts work together to create a pleasing design.

♦ Visit bridal shops with a friend or relative—but take only one person as too many opinions only muddy the choices. Try on several styles of gowns. Be critical, just as you would be with any piece of clothing. Look for styles that are flattering to your figure type and fit the image of what you want to look like on your special day. Make note of the styles and details that flatter you most. Don't feel guilty about doing this. You may actually find the perfect dress that fits and opt to buy it instead of making your gown. Of course, that will make the shop very happy.

♦ If yours is not a traditional wedding, look for design ideas elsewhere. For example, you may find a look you really love in the evening wear department.

One more thought: There are no hard-and-fast rules of etiquette for brides. In days past, brides didn't wear formal white gowns and veils, invite hundreds of people, or toss a bouquet. Times, attitudes, and brides have changed. Your choice of a wedding gown is up to you, your fiancé, and perhaps your families. Many second-time brides prefer a simple ceremony and wear a colored contemporary gown. Some choose a simple headpiece or none at all. They often have only one attendant and only a few guests. Others take the opportunity to have a full, formal wedding because, for one reason or another, they missed it their first time around or chose the "less is more" route and want a more elaborate celebration this time around. Remember that it's your day, and try not to allow "peer pressure" decide for you!

Wedding Gown Types

Wedding gowns can be characterized as classic/traditional, romantic, Victorian, contemporary, garden/country, and country/western—to name the most popular types. The size of your wedding party (and guest list), the location (church or outdoors, for example), and the time of your ceremony are all factors that help define which type of gown is best for your wedding. Illustrated on the following pages are the various gown types; the best fabrics, lace, and trims to use; and sample gowns to give you some ideas. Any of these types are appropriate for a formal or semi-formal wedding. It's your choice of fabric that will make the difference.

Color examples of some of the exciting possibilities appear on pages 40-48. See "Designing Your Gown" (pages 19-24) for design details such as necklines, waistlines, sleeves, and trains.

Tip for a Dressmaker

Often, designing a gown with a client is as much a process of elimination as it is anything else. Guide your client with questions like: Which styles do you particularly like and which do you definitely stay away from? Is there a design feature you've always admired? Make sketches as you and your client talk. Before you know it, a gown will appear before your very eyes.

Romantic

"Picture-book" styling typified by a full, swirling skirt adorned with ruffles and ribbons; fitted bodice with elaborate sleeve detail; shaped neckline; puffed sleeves; soft veil, picture hat, and parasols.

Suggested Fabrics

Antique lace
Brocade
Crepe
Domestic, all over lace yardage
Imported laces
Moiré
Peau de soie
*Satin—light- and medium-
    weight*
Sheers—soft or crisp
Silks
Taffeta

Trims

Pleated ruffles
Ruffled flounces
*Lace appliqués
    and edging*
Openwork

Classic/Traditional

Clean, simple lines; re-embroidered lace and beading in the bodice and sleeve areas; generally long-sleeved; chapel, cathedral, or sweep train and veil.

Suggested Fabrics

Brocade
Crepe
Faille
Peau de Soie
Re-embroidered lace
Satin—especially heavy bridal satin
Sheers—soft or crisp
Silks—shantung, silk satin
Taffeta

Trims

Beading
Lace appliqués
  and edging

Victorian

Lots and lots of lace, beading, ruffles, and pintucks; usually has a high collar or a V neckline, often with a lace cape or a collar of lace; tea- or floor-length skirt, with or without a train; frequently with an underslip of silk or satin covered with additional layers of beaded, all over lace; long sleeves with fullness at the shoulders.

Suggested Fabrics

All over lace
Challis
Charmeuse
Cotton batiste
(for underskirt)
Guipure lace
Satin
Sheers—soft or filmy
Silk—lightweight
Venice lace

Trims

Alençon or Venise edgings
Beaded lace

Contemporary

Soft, refined fabric textures in late-afternoon or evening clothes styling; straight silhouette; may be a short dress; may have a jacket; the look can be very dramatic, highlighted with a one-flower bouquet or a close-fitting headpiece with no veil.

Suggested Fabrics

Challis
Crepe
Pleated fabrics
Sheers—soft or filmy
Silk—crepe de chine, charmeuse
Silkies

Trims

Lace
Metallic or
 beaded accents

Country/Western

*Reminiscent of "prairie dresses;"
shaped neckline; long sleeves; fitted
waistline; tea-length skirt, usually with a
handkerchief hem; yoke with fringe and
additional fringe trim around the hem.*

Suggested Fabrics

*All over lace
Crepe-back satin
Faille
Satin gabardine
Satin—midweight
Silk satin*

Trims

*Beaded lace
Fringe*

Garden/Country

Simplified styling in crisp fabrics; dainty tucks and trim detail; fitted bodice; sleeveless to long-sleeved; may not have a train or veil; headpiece can be simply a flower wreath.

Suggested Fabrics

Batiste
Broadcloth
Cotton laces
Embroidered fabrics
English net
Eyelet
Gauze
Gingham
Lawn
Linen
Polished cotton

Trims

Beading lace
Crocheted lace
Eyelet trim
Ribbon

Figure-Flattering Styles

Recommendations

Choosing the most flattering style for you is one of the most important planning decisions you will make. It will be the most influential factor in your photos—the only visual memory of your wedding day. It's best to choose the lines and styles that you know are flattering to your figure. Now is not the time to try something radically different or out of character for you. To make your job easier, read the style recommendations for specific heights and proportions in the following section. For more information, refer to **Looking Good** (see page 158).

NOTE: If a style term is unfamiliar, see pages 19-22.

Slender/Short

LOOK FOR simple, straight design lines and fabrics that give the illusion of height.

- Silhouettes with long, vertical lines to add height—A-line, princess, straight. Remove some fullness in a too-full skirt style.

- Simple, uncluttered styles

- Designs that draw the eye upward—bodice or neckline detail with lace, beading or trim

- High necklines or long, narrow V or U shapes

- Long, straight sleeves

- Vertical decoration, such as lace, at center front; pintucked front bodice panels to create the illusion of height

- Soft, fluid fabrics—sheers, gauze, supple brocade, soft satin, silk satin, lightweight satin, soft lace, crepe

- Delicate, higher-heeled shoes

- A shorter than cathedral-length (page 24) train that won't overwhelm your body

- Fingertip or longer veil with edges defined with rolled-hem edging, binding, or trim to create vertical lines

- A high headpiece to add height. Avoid an overly full one however, as this will add unnecessary width and could overpower a small person.

AVOID design lines and fabrics that make your figure appear shorter and wider.

- Too-full sleeves, i.e., very exaggerated puffed or large bell sleeves

- Gathered, tiered skirt; a deep hem ruffle

- Heavy lace fabric or trim or very crisp, stiff fabrics (heavy bridal satin, taffeta) that overpower your size

- Heavily textured fabrics such as linen, heavy cotton lace, damask, or velvet; large-scale prints

- Big flowers; large bouquets

Full-Figured/Short

LOOK FOR design lines and fabrics that make the figure look longer and leaner.

- Vertical silhouette lines: A-line, princess, and straight

- Fit that skims the body and is never too tight. A well-fitting bra helps!

- Slender sleeves. Long, fitted are best. For a hot-weather wedding, consider sleeves from sheer organza or lace.

- Scoop, V, keyhole, or surplice neckline

- Fluid fabrics with a dull finish—soft sheers, crepe, dull-luster satin, silk satin. Shiny fabrics *add* visual pounds; dull or matte finishes *detract* from size. Check the wrong side of regular bridal satins—some have just the soft patina you want!

- A high headpiece with fingertip or longer veil without trimmed veil edges to avoid unnecessary width

- Small to medium-sized bouquet

AVOID design lines that draw the eye horizontally across the figure or fabrics that are bulky or clingy.

- Bouffant or tiered silhouettes and very full veils

- Large-scale prints

- Heavily textured fabrics such as velvet, quilted looks, heavily beaded and heavily re-embroidered laces

- Shiny fabrics

- Lace trims at hemline (unless very narrow), tiers, ruffles

- Ruffled necklines

- Cathedral-length trains

Average/Average

Lucky you! Most styles flatter you. When choosing a gown, concentrate on your figure challenges. To best show off your shape, choose a basque or dropped waistline. You can also wear a fitted princess style.

Full-Figured/Average

LOOK FOR continuous vertical design lines and smooth, fluid fabrics that minimize the figure.

- Silhouettes that direct attention to the face—princess, A-line and straight; an empire waist to camouflage a thicker waistline if you have one

- Dresses that fall smoothly and gently over the hips and are not tight

- Scoop, V, keyhole (with or without Queen Anne collar), sweetheart, scalloped, or surplice neckline

- Headpiece that provides height to balance body size

- Soft fluid fabric—crepe, sheers, antique satin with a dull finish, silk satin, peau de soie

- Any length train—but not one that is excessively full

- An all-lace sleeve or one with a lace upper and a sheer lower portion to help hide full upper arms

- Oversized shoulders and sleeves with details to broaden shoulders and make you look less rectangular in shape

AVOID choppy horizontal design lines or fabrics that add weight.

- Huge or very tiny prints

- Heavily beaded lace, velvet, velveteen, heavy brocade, and very heavy bridal satin; shiny fabrics

- Round necklines that add roundness to your face

Full-Figured/Tall

LOOK FOR design lines and fabrics that make the figure look more slender.

- A-line, straight, or princess silhouettes, especially those with an empire waist that hide the midriff

- Soft fabrics—crepe, peau de soie, silk

- Scoop, V, keyhole, or high, Victorian style

AVOID designs that are out of scale with your size and fabrics and that add weight to the figure.

- Short, puffed, leg-o-mutton, or very full bishop sleeves

- Cinched waists and cummerbunds

- Clingy fabrics

- Very shiny or bulky fabrics including heavy laces

Slender/Tall

You have a model's figure so most styles are flattering. However, if you are concerned with your height in relation to your groom's, you may want to appear shorter. If you are exceedingly thin, you may want to add fullness.

LOOK FOR design lines that run around the body and textured fabrics that make the figure appear fuller.

- Details extending beyond the silhouette

- Bulky, bunchy silhouette lines; very full skirts; straight-line silhouette *if* the lines are soft, i.e., a blouson bodice

- Curved rather than straight lines

- A-line styles with trim and appliques around the body

- Full, horizontal draping across the bust or hipline

- Off-the-shoulder effects; peplum at waist or on the hips

- Full, long, or three-quarter-length sleeves; cooler sheer organza or lace sleeves for hot weather

- Heavy, re-embroidered lace, peau de soie, velvet, satin, heavy bridal satin, fabrics with shiny surfaces

- Any length train—including the fullest sweep style

- Long, full veils and short headpieces

- Bustle-back slip

- Low-heeled shoes

AVOID design lines and fabrics that overemphasize your height and your thinness.

- Very straight gowns

- Very tailored looks

- A blush-length veil that looks too short for your height

Queen Size

If you are heavier than full figured, a size 18+, or if you think you could lose 50 or more pounds, you are in this category. (Also see NOTE below.)

LOOK FOR clean, simple design lines that play down your size and figure. Bring the focus to your face! Choose fabrics that just skim the body contours.

- Princess lines, A-line, or straight-line silhouettes

- Straight or fitted sleeves, but not too tight

- A trim fit—not too tight or too loose

- Any length train

- Fine lace for neckline, bodice, and hem trim

- Off-white or pastel; bright white reflects the most light, which makes the figure appear larger.

- Lower neckline—scoop, camisole, keyhole, sweetheart, V, surplice

- A simple veil with not too much fullness, for example a lovely lace mantilla

- The layered look done with lightweight fabrics such as chiffon or organza, perhaps with the last layer being lightweight lace

NOTE: Adapt large or women's size dress patterns. A number of bridal and attendant gowns are now available in sizes up to 32W.

AVOID busy design lines and bulky fabrics that add weight to the figure.

- A "too-tight" fit
- Very clingy fabrics
- Gathers, ruffles, or trims that encircle the body
- Fabrics with dramatic texture or sheen like satin, taffeta, plush velvet, heavy lace
- Very high, tight-fitting necklines such as Gibson, mandarin, and cowl
- A very full train or veil

Specific Figure Challenges

Sloping Shoulders

LOOK FOR shoulder/bodice details that make the shoulders look more square.

- Horizontal design lines through the shoulder and neckline area, including square necklines, circular or square yokes, and camisoles

- Any silhouette that gives the illusion of a slimmer waistline to make the shoulders look proportionately broader

- Soft shoulder pads

- Full, shoulder-length hair style or veil

AVOID styles that over-expose or emphasize your shoulder slope.

- Sleeveless, halter or strapless style gowns. It can be difficult to balance the width of your skirt with no sleeves or difficult to keep straps up. Spaghetti straps may fall off your shoulders.

- Raglan sleeves

- High necklines that bring attention to sloping shoulders (not all do)

Broad Shoulders

While broad shoulders are not always considered a figure challenge, you can create the illusion of a narrower shoulder with:

- Oval or V necklines
- Raglan sleeves
- Flared peplums

Full Bust

LOOK FOR styles that make the bust look smaller and in balance with the rest of your figure. Be sure to wear a well-fitted bra.

♦ A smooth (not tight) fit through the bodice area

♦ Off-the-shoulder, portrait, and V necklines. Full-busted women *can* wear off-the-shoulder styles—with some careful "engineering" of the underlayers of the gown.

♦ Flat lace such as Cluny, Lyon, Schiffli, or all over Venice. Try individual lace appliqués on smoother fabrics, taking care to position them away from the full bust.

♦ Fitted sleeves

♦ Softly draped bodices

♦ Soft flare in skirts to give the illusion of curves below the waist; details in skirt to draw the eye away from the bust

♦ Sloping waistline, such as a dropped V waist

AVOID styles and fabrics that add weight or draw more attention to the bust.

♦ Heavy, re-embroidered lace in an all over pattern

♦ Napped, ultra-shiny fabrics

♦ Full sleeves that add width across the bustline and make it look larger; also short sleeves or sleeves ending at your bust level—they visually widen your bust

♦ Cinched natural waistlines

♦ Empire lines that are fitted just under the bust

♦ Superfluous details at the neckline or bustline—ruffles, pleats, shirring

♦ *Very* low necklines

♦ Victorian, Gibson, and other puffed sleeve styles

Tip for a Dressmaker

Often one shoulder will be lower than the other. In a gown with sleeves, you can correct this visually by using two different sized shoulder pads. Experiment during a fitting with the customer until her shoulders look balanced.

Small Bustline

LOOK FOR styles and fabrics that will add visual dimension to the bustline.

♦ Heavy, beaded laces to add fullness to the bodice where needed

♦ Large collars, ruffles, roses, and bows around the neckline

♦ Soft front fullness—gathers or pin tucks for example

♦ A defined natural waistline to help make the bust, in contrast, look larger (avoid if your waist is large)

♦ Square or jewel necklines as well as yokes and camisoles to help make bustline look larger

♦ Full sleeves such as leg-o-mutton, puffed, Victorian, and Gibson to add fullness to the bodice area

♦ Full or elaborate veils and headpieces for added width across the figure

AVOID styles that make your bust look flat and small (especially if the rest of your body isn't).

♦ Filmy, soft fabrics across the bustline area

♦ Tight-fitting bodices without any attention-getting details

♦ Overly tailored bodices

♦ Very full skirts that can make the bustline look too small proportionately unless balanced by bodice width (shoulder ruffles, yokes, etc.)

Short Neck

LOOK FOR styles that will make your neck appear longer.

♦ An upswept hairstyle if hair is long to keep it away from face and neck

♦ A higher headpiece for the illusion of a longer neck

♦ Scoop, surplice, V, and keyhole necklines

AVOID styles that cover up the neck, making it appear even shorter.

♦ High or jewel necklines or stand-up collars such as the Victorian style

♦ Hairstyles that cover up the neck

Full Tummy/ No Waist Definition

LOOK FOR design lines that focus the eye away from the tummy area if it is full or prominent.

- ◆ Details positioned away from the center front

- ◆ Skirt fullness that camouflages a full tummy

- ◆ A sloping waistline (higher or lower than the normal waistline). An empire line in which the skirt flows from below the bust into an A-line skirt minimizes the waist and helps create a long, lean silhouette.

- ◆ Flat tucks rather than puffy gathers at the hip area

- ◆ Details above the waistline, including neckline and headpiece details

- ◆ Fabrics that have body without bulk—heavy crepe, light-weight lace, antique satin, silk shantung, peau de soie

AVOID styles that reveal or highlight the tummy area.

- ◆ Natural waistlines; they reveal a full tummy or heavy midriff.

- ◆ Any garment that fits too closely in the waist

- ◆ Full or bell sleeves; they add width to the waist and tummy areas.

Short-Waisted

LOOK FOR

- ◆ Long torso lines with the bodice extending into the hip area, Basque, for example

- ◆ V necklines

- ◆ Normal length bodice at sides coming to a point in the front/back

- ◆ Narrow, center panel in the bodice

Long-Waisted

LOOK FOR

- ◆ Wrapped and blouson bodice styles

- ◆ Natural waistlines, not dropped; raised waistlines such as Empire, to visually shorten the waist

- ◆ Shoulder yokes

- ◆ Vertical lines in the skirt

Wide/Full Hips/Thighs

LOOK FOR long, narrow silhouettes. When fitted properly they will add height and subtract from hip and thigh width. Eliminate some of the fullness in fuller skirt styles.

- ◆ Soft fullness in the skirt

- ◆ Gathers positioned just in front of or just behind the sides (you can adjust the positioning of fullness in gathered and pleated styles)

- ◆ Shallow skirt yokes

- ◆ Elongated bodices attached to skirts with controlled fullness—if waist is small

- ◆ Bodice emphasis at the shoulder

AVOID

- ◆ Extra fullness in skirts at the side seams; bustles

- ◆ Large bows or other trims at the back that add visual fullness

Narrow Hips

LOOK FOR

- ◆ Wide center panel in skirt

- ◆ Hip yokes

- ◆ Full, gathered skirts

- ◆ Large bows or detailing in back

CHAPTER 3

Designing Your Gown

First, draw your dream wedding gown. You can't draw? Don't despair. Using tracing paper, trace the silhouette you want from the front and back of our "traceable bride" below and on page 20. Then choose and trace your neckline, sleeve, bodice, and skirt styles (pages 20-22) onto the traced bride. For additional design details and embellishments, see "*The Exciting Possibilities*," page 40. Remember that the back of your gown should be beautiful—the entire wedding party will be seen more from the back than the front.

Also, decide on the length you want your dress to be. Popular lengths include:

Hi-lo. The hemline falls to the mid-calf in front and to the floor in the back. It is more dramatic if the hemline is to the knee in the front.

Street. The hemline just covers the knee.

Ballerina. The hemline falls to just above the ankles.

Floor. The hemline falls from ½" to 1½" from the floor.

After you have made your design decisions, find a pattern that is closest to your drawing or combine several patterns. The pattern companies offer a lot of variety and you're sure to find one or more that will work to create the dress of your dreams.

The style of the dress will also determine the types of fabrics you will want to use. Chapter 7 (page 56) will guide you through those choices.

Tip for a Dressmaker

Buy a magnifying glass. It will come in very handy when a bride brings you a magazine photo. Details are clearer and easier to identify, making it easier to select the pattern or patterns to use.

The Traceable Bride (or bridesmaid)

To design your gown, trace this figure, and the back view on page 20, following the lines of your desired silhouette, then turn to the next pages to add design details.

Traceable veils are on page 149.

Traceable Waistlines

Dropped
2"-3" below natural waist

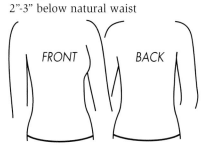

Dropped/Hip Length
4" below natural waist

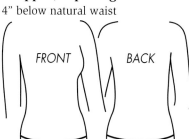

Basque
4"-5" below natural waist

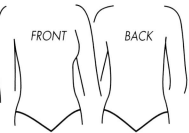

Natural V

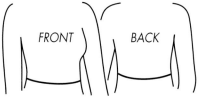

Sloping Waistline
Raised in front and sloping to just above the natural waistline in back

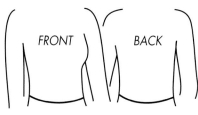

Raised Waistline
Halfway between bustline and natural waistline

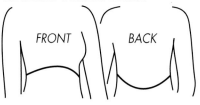

Natural/Fitted

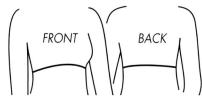

Empire
Just below bustline

The Back of the Traceable Bride

Trace the back of your desired silhouette.

NOTE: Remember that the back and front must flow together, that is, you shouldn't have princess seaming in the front that comes from the shoulder and princess seams that start at the armhole in the back. Likewise, if the gown has darts in the front, there are usually darts in the back.

Princess line inner seaming
Straight-line
A-line
Princess
Bouffant

20

Traceable Necklines

Jewel
Use Basic Back #1.

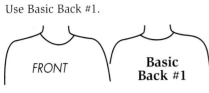

FRONT   **Basic Back #1**

Scoop
Use Basic Back #2.

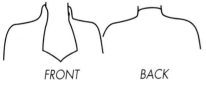

FRONT   **Basic Back #2**

Square

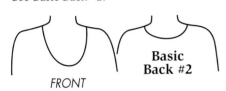

FRONT   BACK

Sweetheart

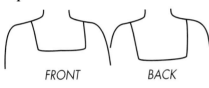

FRONT   BACK

Sweetheart with Queen Anne

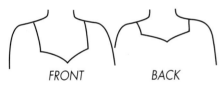

FRONT   BACK

Wide Scoop with Ruffle

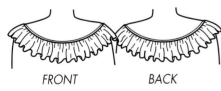

FRONT   BACK

Bertha Collar

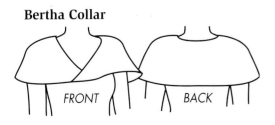

FRONT   BACK

Keyhole with Queen Anne Collar

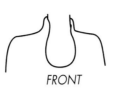

FRONT

BACK

Camisole

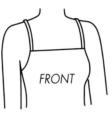

FRONT

BACK

Halter

FRONT

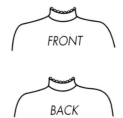

BACK

Victorian

FRONT

BACK

Keyhole
Use basic back #1.   **Surplice**
Use basic back #2.

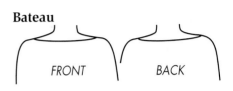

FRONT   FRONT

Bateau

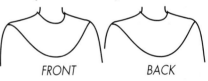

FRONT   BACK

Strapless

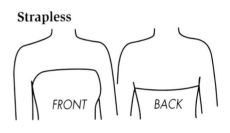

FRONT   BACK

Yoke (with illusion)

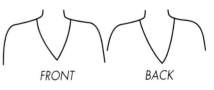

FRONT   BACK

V (May use Basic Back #2.)

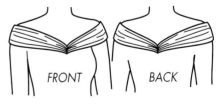

FRONT   BACK

Off-the-Shoulder

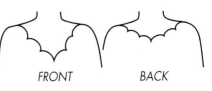

FRONT   BACK

Scalloped

FRONT   BACK

Traceable Sleeves

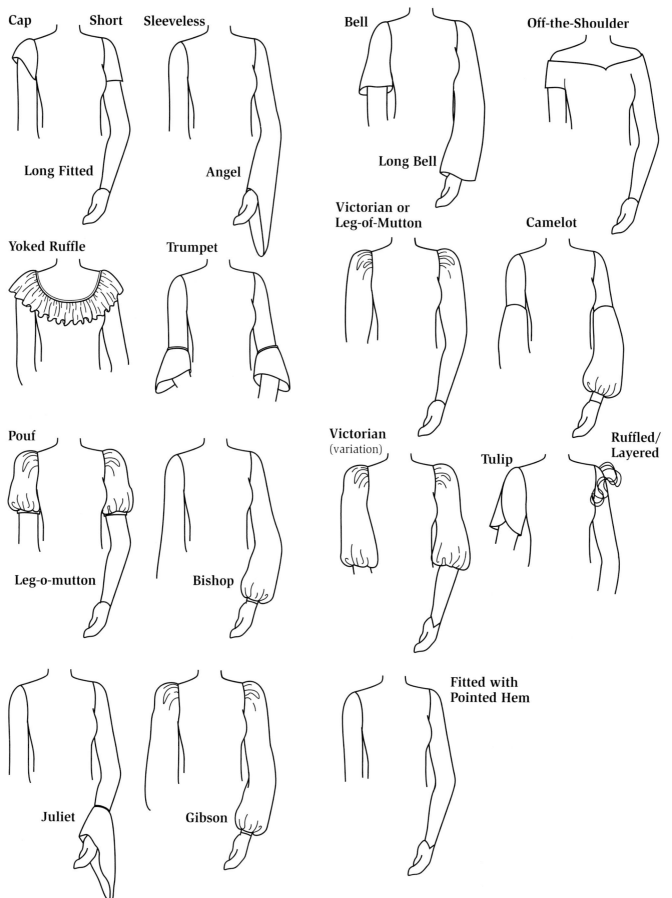

Cap   Short   Sleeveless

Long Fitted   Angel

Bell   Off-the-Shoulder

Long Bell

Yoked Ruffle   Trumpet

Victorian or
Leg-of-Mutton   Camelot

Pouf   Bishop

Leg-o-mutton

Victorian
(variation)   Tulip   Ruffled/
Layered

Juliet   Gibson

Fitted with
Pointed Hem

Translating Your Ideas Into a Pattern

After sketching your gown design, you are ready to find your pattern(s). If you cannot find the design elements you want in the bridal section, remember to try the evening wear and dress sections of the catalog, too.

Try to find a pattern that matches your sketched gown as closely as possible. This will limit both the number and complexity of the pattern changes that you'll need to make.

Look for one pattern that has the lines that form the *exterior lines* of your gown. Compare the seam-lines of your sketch to the line drawing in the pattern catalog. Then look for patterns that have or are close to some of the other details you want. Begin with the bodice and look for the most important design detail (an unusual neckline, for instance).

◆ How is the bodice shaped? Is the shaping done with seams or darts?

◆ If the bodice has princess seams, do they start at the shoulder or the armhole?

◆ Is the waistline normal, empire, low, pointed, shaped, or raised?

◆ What neckline does the gown have? Victorian, sweetheart, V, off-the-shoulder, or strapless? (Re-drawing necklines on a pattern is easy.)

NOTE: You may need to use your imagination to "design" the back of a gown you saw in a magazine. Most photos show only one side or the other; both front and back are rarely pictured for one gown. The line drawing on the pattern envelope or guidesheet will help.

Look for the sleeves next. Are they long or short, full or fitted, etc.? Basic sleeve shapes are relatively easy to spot.

◆ If the sleeve in your photo has several layers, try to determine the shape of the innermost layer.

◆ Does the sleeve have a lace overlay? The sleeve pattern should be roomy enough to allow for two layers of fabric—in other words, not too fitted.

◆ If the sleeve is lace, does it have an underlining? You can use any sleeve pattern for this—just look for the sleeve style you want.

◆ Is the sleeve puffed with a lot of fullness? You may need to adjust the fullness to your size (less fullness for a petite; more fullness for small shoulders, etc.).

◆ Compare the armhole shape on the bodice pattern you've chosen with the sleeve pattern you find on another bodice. They must be the same—you cannot sew a raglan sleeve into a fitted armscye, for example. For set-in sleeves, trace the armhole from its corresponding front and back bodice pattern pieces onto the bodice you have chosen, if it had a different sleeve style.

Finally, search for the skirt and back details.

◆ Does the gown have a full skirt or a narrow one?

◆ How many layers does the skirt have? Is the fabric appliquéd with lace or is it lace over another layer of fabric?

◆ What kind of train does the gown have—or what kind of train would you like to have?

◆ If you have selected a dropped, shaped waist, find a pattern for a skirt that's attached to a similar style bodice. It will be easier than changing the waistline seam on the skirt from a natural one to a V shape, for example.

◆ Check the bottom width of the skirt on the back of the pattern envelope. To get a visual idea of how full the skirt is, cut a piece of string to the length stated on the pattern and arrange it on the floor in a circle; adjust as needed for the desired fullness.

Tip for a Dressmaker

Your local fabric store may sell you (at a nominal charge) their out-of-date pattern catalogs. These are very helpful when meeting clients in your home/shop. Be careful not to use books that are too dated—one season is enough—or you may find that the pattern your client has finally picked has been discontinued! Try the Alicyn Exclusives website (www.sewbridal.com) where out-of-print bridal patterns are available, giving the seamstress additional choices.

♦ If the skirt you want has two or more layers and you want additional layers of tulle, organza, or lace, you can cut them all at once. A full skirt can have lining, petticoat net, skirt fabric, and four layers of tulle, so this saves time. (This is easier if all fabrics are the same width.) See "Skirt Basics," beginning on page 125.

♦ The back of your gown should be beautiful since the entire wedding party will be seen more from the back than the front during the ceremony. That's why trains, bows, lace appliqués, and veils adorn the back of most ready-to-wear gowns. Some patterns don't have back interest so consider adding some or choosing a more decorative headpiece or hairdo. Since long hair can hide the back of your gown and detract from a consistent look for your party, consider wearing your hair up and suggesting that your attendants do so as well. For back neckline design ideas, see page 21.

Trains

Trains and bridal veils definitely give your gown back interest. The different types and lengths of trains shown here can be worn with or without a veil. (See "Veils" on page 148.)

For formal weddings, long veils and sweep-, chapel-, or cathedral-length trains are recommended. Extended trains are part of the gown design. The more common detachable trains are separate from the gown and attached at the waist.

A "watteau" is a train attached to the shoulders of the gown.

Detachable train attaches at waist.

A popular contemporary look is to wear a short dress (knee length or shorter) with a long, detachable train.

Sweep Length
This is a short train that barely sweeps the floor. It is usually 8" to 10" longer in back than the front and doesn't bustle.

Chapel Length
The back of the dress is 12" to 18" longer longer than the dress front. The train can be a part of the dress (extended) or detachable.

Cathedral Length
The back is 20" to 72" longer than the dress front. The train can be extended or detachable.

CHAPTER 4

The Big Picture

Your wedding is like the set of a play. To have it look aesthetically pleasing, you need to make decisions about the wedding color scheme and decor.

Color For the Bride

All shades of white—true white, ivory, candlelight, and cream—are the most popular choices for brides. Throughout history, white has been considered a sacred symbol of purity and joy, but it wasn't until Anne of Brittany married Louis XII that white was established as the traditional bridal color. Prior to that, red, as a symbol of gaiety, was the norm. The Spanish carried on a tradition of black wedding gowns and early American women wore their best dress, regardless of color.

Softened white shades are more flattering to most lighter-skinned brides while the starkness of true white is worn best by brides with darker skin tones. If you have your heart set on a *white-white* gown, try the fabric next to your face. You may look great in it! Different fabric textures in white may be more or less flattering to your face and figure. Satin, for example, reflects the most light and visually enlarges the area in which it is worn, while a textured lace absorbs light, helping to minimize size.

Pastel tints such as soft yellows, blues, pinks, mauves, and grays are appropriate for all types of weddings and may be more flattering than stark white or off-white. Underlining a white sheer or lace fabric with a pastel adds a hint of color.

For more casual weddings, particularly those categorized as Contemporary or Garden/Country Look (see pages 11 and 13), think about colors and/or prints. The wedding gown of one of my first clients had a bodice of polished cotton to coordinate with a full skirt and short puffed sleeves made from a Waverly® chintz home decorating print. A third coordinating striped fabric was used for a center front inset in the skirt. It was perfect for her outdoor wedding held in a beautiful setting near a pond.

Ask these questions about your color choices:

1. Will this color flatter my skin tone and figure?

2. How will the color choice blend with the bridesmaids' attire and the flowers?

3. Can I find trims and laces to blend or match? Even whites can be difficult to match. (See page 155 for a resource for dyeing to match.)

Bridesmaids' Color and Style

At one time it was customary to have the entire wedding party dress alike to disguise the bride and groom from potential enemies. That tradition has evolved to one of costumed attendants who assist before, during, and after the wedding. They are usually the couple's near and dear friends or relatives.

Color and style choices for the attendants are the basis for a truly beautiful wedding and photographs. Above all, the bride and groom are the focus for the wedding and shouldn't be outdone by the bridesmaids or ushers. Beware of a look that shouts "too much, too loud, too-overdone."

Attendants' dresses often have the same feeling as the bride's gown but they don't have to be an exact copy. Choosing a style that will flatter every attendant can be a real challenge since attendants come in all sizes and shapes—and they all want to look their very best.

Like decorating schemes, wedding color schemes fall in and out of favor. Look through current bridal magazines for ideas on current colors if you are at a loss. In addition, some fabrics are more appropriate for a particular season of the year. See the chart on page 57 for more information on appropriate fabrics.

Use the following checklist to make it easier to choose the color and/or print and the style for your attendants' gowns.

♦ Decide on the number of attendants. A bold print or color might be great for one but overpower the bride when worn by eight. Also consider the size or size range of the attendants. Muted or darker shades minimize a fuller figure.

♦ Try a range of colors in light to dark or an actual rainbow of colors—another popular choice. Make sure that the range blends comfortably to avoid visual confusion. Also, make sure the largest figure is not dressed in the most eye-catching color.

- Don't make design and fabric decisions by committee. Choose two or three styles and show them to your attendants to get their opinions and ideas. Ultimately, you must make the decision.

- Be flexible but don't compromise your own desires. Lots of unhappiness can result from disputes over pattern and fabric choices. You can usually minimize conflict if you pay for part or all of the costs of the bridesmaids' gowns.

- Coordinate the bridesmaid and usher attire to the flower scheme. How will your color choices blend with the wedding photo backdrop—the church, chapel, house, garden?

NOTE: If you are having your bridesmaids' dresses custom made, have them all made by the same person so all the dresses look alike. Using the same dressmaker also ensures that all the fabrics will be pretreated the same so they will all look the same and react to cleaning in the same way. Double-check the final look, fit, and hems of gowns at least one week before the wedding to allow time to make any necessary adjustments. Weight changes can wreak havoc with a perfect fit!

Style Convertibility

While most brides think of their gowns as heirlooms, some brides (and most bridesmaids) would like to get more wear out of their wedding attire.

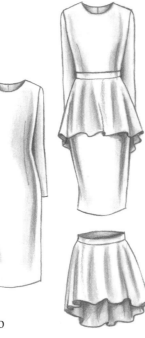

You may want a wedding gown that converts to a more comfortable reception/dancing dress by removing a train. Or, you and your attendants may want to be able to adapt your gowns to daytime dresses with some simple sewing.

Think about convertibility as you plan the wedding costumes. For example, you can make lace trim removable by attaching it with a basting stitch—as long as stitch marks won't show after removing the lace for a less formal look. A lace or satin sheath with a detachable peplum gives lots of additional wearing options after the wedding.

Mothers of the Bride and Groom

For most mothers, the wedding day is exciting, nerve-racking, tearful, and wonderfully fun. While the mothers' roles have changed over the years, with more brides planning and carrying off their own weddings, the couple's mothers still assist them with last-minute details and serve as greeters at the reception. The bride looks to her mother, in particular, as an absolute "rock" of support.

Mothers want to look and feel their very best at the ceremony and reception. Choosing a gown in the right color and style to harmonize with the entire wedding look is an important decision. The mothers' dresses need not be the same style, but the dress colors should not clash and should complement the colors chosen for the attendants. Dress lengths, however, should be the same—if one is floor length, the other should be as well.

Traditionally, the bride's mother chooses her dress first, then contacts the groom's mother to fill her in on her choice.

Styles

- Mothers needn't be dowdy! Don't be afraid of an upbeat look. Chiffon is no longer the order of the day for mothers' dresses.

- Refer to "Figure Flattering Styles" on pages 14-18 and sketch the dress using the "Traceable Bride" on pages 19-22.

Tip for a Dressmaker

Many brides start out wanting a "wear-again" dress, but change their minds as the design process goes on. Be prepared for this!

- Check out the evening wear designs in the pattern catalog and try on evening wear in your favorite shops to get ideas. Take care to avoid revealing necklines.

- Consider outfits—a blouse and skirt, a jacketed dress, a dressy suit.

- For cool-weather weddings, fabrics such as crepe, silk, velvet, brocade, knit (not too clingy), and wool are appropriate. In warm weather, sheers, linens, lightweight silks, lightweight crepes, cottons, and soft knits work well.

Color and Accessories

- There are no hard-and-fast rules but the choice for each mother should flatter her coloring.

- Keep the flower colors and attendants' gowns in mind. Mothers' dresses should blend with but not match the bridesmaids'.

- If the bridesmaids' dresses are a print, the mothers' dresses are best in solid colors to avoid a too-busy and distracting look.

- The mothers' flowers are usually a corsage worn on the dress or in the hair.

- Keep jewelry simple and elegant.

- Hats are optional. They should be small to avoid blocking the view of the ceremony. Wraps can be worn to the wedding but should be taken off during the ceremony.

NOTE: Follow the above guidelines for grandmothers.

And What About the Children?

More and more, as blended families "tie the knot," children are playing major roles in weddings. The pattern companies have responded to this trend by designing flower-girl dresses that match or coordinate with their bridal gown patterns. They are also offering wedding accessory patterns, such as ringbearer's pillow designs.

Styles

- Pick a basic style and add the desired trim—ribbon, ruffles, lace, for example.

- Add a detachable pinafore or fancy vest that can make the outfit more convertible for later use.

- For little girls, check out nightgown styles—in the right fabric they can look dressy and feminine.

- Make the ringbearer's shirt and buy the rest of the outfit. The shirt can coordinate with the flower girl's dress. If you decide to make the ringbearer's jacket, choose an easy cardigan style or make a vest instead. In addition, you can make matching cummerbunds for the groom, the groomsmen, ushers, and ringbearer.

- Both girls and boys can be miniature versions of the bridesmaids and ushers.

Color and Accessories

- Flower girls can be dressed in white, like the bride, with color accents—ribbons, trim, or the bouquet, for example. Or, they can be dressed to match or blend with the wedding party. When using a print for the attendants' gowns, choose a solid *or* a coordinating print in a smaller scale for the children in the wedding party.

- Let the ruffle or trim highlight the primary wedding color.

- For the flower girl, select a small bouquet or basket of flowers. You can have the flower girl drop rose petals in front of the bride and groom—they love to do this! Make the ringbearer's pillow from leftover scraps of your gown fabric.

- A headpiece and gloves for the flower girl are optional, depending on the formality of the wedding.

Seasonal Flowers

Spring		Summer	Autumn	Winter
Flowers		**Flowers**	**Flowers**	**Flowers**
Acacia	Green Ivy	*The same as spring flowers plus:*	*Baby's Breath	*Baby's Breath
Anemone	Iris		Bird of Paradise	*Carnations
*Baby's Breath	Narcissus	Fuji Mums	*Chrysanthemums	*Chrysanthemums
Calla Lilies	Phalaenopsis	Protea	*Carnations	*Daisies
*Carnations	Orchids	Tiger Lilies	*Daisies	Holly
Chantilly	*Roses		Dried flowers	*Mum varieties
*Chrysanthemum	Rubrum Lilies		Green Ivy	Poinsettias
Cymbidium	*Statice		*Mum varieties	*Pom Poms
Orchids	*Stephanotis		*Pom Poms	*Roses
Daffodils	Sweetheart Roses		*Roses	*Stephanotis
*Daisies	Tulips		Statice	
Gardenias	Violets		Stephanotis	

indicates seasonless flowers

Seasonal Flowers

Flowers have color, texture, and best of all—scent! They are an integral part of most weddings, even small, intimate ceremonies. Usually the bridesmaids' fabrics and the flowers are the most colorful elements in the wedding so you will want to make sure they coordinate. Most wedding flowers are available year 'round but you will pay more for out-of-season flowers. Don't disregard dried or artificial flowers; they can be less expensive and can be saved for years. Silk flowers are lovely and often look like the "real" thing.

Flowers can be as expensive as they are lovely. Mixing in-season, inexpensive flowers with your own personal preferences is one way to keep costs down. Your florist can assist you with appropriate choices for the ceremony and the reception.

Blended with real or artificial flowers, fabric rosettes (page 44) made from the wedding fabrics make a truly coordinated and very special bouquet.

Using Bridal Consultants

Bridal consulting is a growing field. A recent issue of an entrepreneurial magazine lists it as one of the top businesses for people to start. Many brides decide to work with a bridal consultant because they do not have time to attend to all of the details that are a part of planning a wedding. The consultant's job is to make sure that everything happens according to plan—no wrong flowers, missing dishes, or late cakes!

Word-of-mouth referrals from friends, caterers, and florists are one of the best guides to a good bridal consultant. Also check the local Yellow Pages or call your local Chamber of Commerce for possible referrals. Your local fabric shop may also have a list of consultants.

Interview any bridal consultant candidates before you agree to use their services. Make sure that you can communicate easily with the one you choose, that you will be comfortable working with her, and that you like the ideas she has and the services she is suggesting. It is important that you feel at ease with your consultant—after all, she's taking care of something that is very personal to you—your wedding day!

Bridal consultants offer everything from advice by the hour all the way up to a "soup-to-nuts" package in which they take care of absolutely everything. They may charge a flat rate, by the hour, or base their fee on a percentage of what you pay the individual services—caterers, florist, room rentals, for example. They should have contacts to cover all areas of the wedding and should work to get you pricing that is within your budget.

You will want to meet with your consultant to discuss your ideas and consider any alternatives she may offer based on her experience and expertise. Be very sure to agree on exactly what her role will be—what she agrees to do and what her responsibilities are versus what you will handle. Spell it all out in a contract or a letter following your discussion. In large cities in particular, a written description of the services to be provided and the cost is extremely important.

CHAPTER 5

Fitting Real Brides

In this chapter you will learn the easiest way to fit your pattern *before* you cut. If you fit *before* you buy fabric and lace, you'll be sure to buy the right amount. The most common alterations are shown on two real-life brides as they go through the fitting process step by step. For a complete guide to fitting any figure, especially the mature bride, see *Fit For Real People* by Marta Alto and Pati Palmer. It's the most complete book on fitting ever written. (See pages 37 and 158 for more information.)

NOTE: Birth control pills can cause water retention. The final fitting should be reserved for the second month after starting the pill.

Buy the Right Size

Because patterns are made for B-cup bra sizes, take only the high bust measurement—above the bust in front and below the shoulder blades in the back. Take a skin-tight measurement. This eliminates the "size-of-bust factor since your body measurement, not your bust cup size, really determines your pattern size. Use your high-bust measurement when reading the line for **BUST** on the measurement chart in the pattern catalog and on the pattern envelope.

size	6	8	10	12	14	16	18	20	22	24	26	28
bust	30½	31½	32½	34	36	38	40	42	44	46	48	50

If you are between sizes, choose the smaller size. If you have a very broad back you may need a smaller size and a broad back alteration. There *is* a little guessing but since you will be tissue-fitting the pattern on your body before cutting out your gown, you may decide to buy another pattern in a larger or smaller size—a minimum investment compared to the value of your time.

Before you begin to tissue-fit your pattern on your body, review the features of good fit, below, then read through the most common alterations for wedding gowns on the following pages.

What to Look For in a Good Fit

Wear the proper undergarments and your wedding shoes for all fitting sessions. Check the view from the side, front and back.

Front

Neckline lies close to the body and does not gape.

The sleeve cap fits smoothly across the upper arm.

There are no pull lines or wrinkles across the bustline.

Darts point to the bust point.

There are no wrinkles or drag lines across the tummy.

The skirt falls smoothly over the hips.

The hem is even and a flattering length.

Back

The armhole seam is a smooth curve and has no puckers or pulls.

There are no pull or drag lines across the back.

The center back closure is not strained.

Undergarment lines don't show through the gown bodice.

The dress fits snugly but not too tightly through the waistline.

The train hangs straight and walks easily without cupping under or restricting movement.

The Bodice

1. Measure the high bust (see previous page) to determine the pattern size needed. If the high bust measures 39", for example, the correct size is 16 since 39" is between sizes 16 and 18 (see the chart on the previous page).

2. Trim around the tissue *out-side* the black cutting line. Tape necklines and armholes as shown with short, overlapping pieces of ½"-wide Scotch brand Magic Tape.

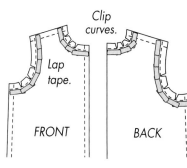

Clip curves.

Lap tape.

FRONT   BACK

3. Pin front and back tissues, wrong sides together but with seam allowances on OUTSIDE. Try on and check the back first, making sure the back is the correct width. (For accuracy and ease, you'll need someone to help you with this.)

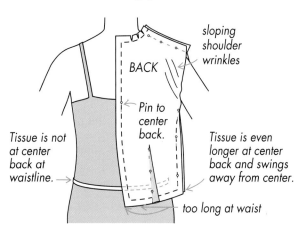

BACK

sloping shoulder wrinkles

Pin to center back.

Tissue is not at center back at waistline. →

Tissue is even longer at center back and swings away from center.

← too long at waist

4. Alter the back where needed, referring to **Fit for Real People** (page 158) for how to do each alteration required.

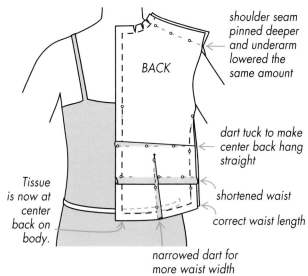

BACK

shoulder seam pinned deeper and underarm lowered the same amount

dart tuck to make center back hang straight

shortened waist

correct waist length

Tissue is now at center back on body.

narrowed dart for more waist width

5. The center front of the tissue doesn't meet the bride's center front at bust level, indicating that she needs a full bust adjustment. (See top of page 31 for how-tos.)

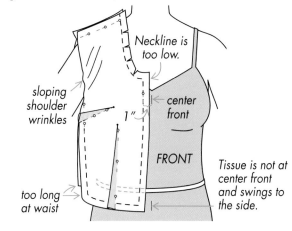

Neckline is too low.

sloping shoulder wrinkles

center front

1"

FRONT

Tissue is not at center front and swings to the side.

too long at waist

𝒯ools & 𝒯echniques 𝒯ip

- ♦ Work on a gridded cardboard surface.
- ♦ Anchor all pieces you've altered before taping the tissue.
- ♦ Insert pins vertically into the cardboard.

- ♦ Use Perfect Pattern Paper:

  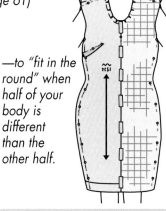

  (see page 61)

  —as an additional ruler;

  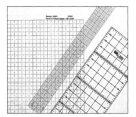

  —to make alterations easier and more accurate;

  —to "fit in the round" when half of your body is different than the other half.

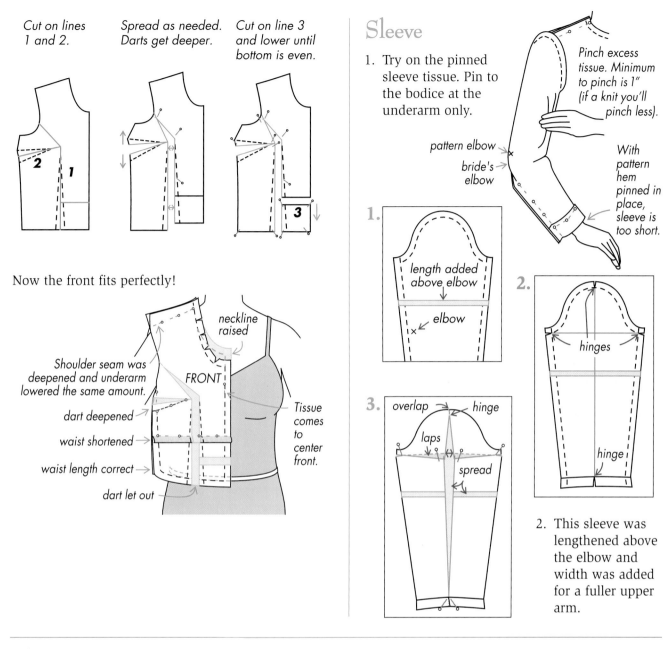

Cut on lines 1 and 2.

Spread as needed. Darts get deeper.

Cut on line 3 and lower until bottom is even.

Now the front fits perfectly!

neckline raised

Shoulder seam was deepened and underarm lowered the same amount.

FRONT

dart deepened

waist shortened

waist length correct

dart let out

Tissue comes to center front.

Sleeve

1. Try on the pinned sleeve tissue. Pin to the bodice at the underarm only.

Pinch excess tissue. Minimum to pinch is 1" (if a knit you'll pinch less).

With pattern hem pinned in place, sleeve is too short.

pattern elbow
bride's elbow

1. *length added above elbow* — *elbow*

2. *hinges* — *hinge*

3. *overlap* — *hinge* — *laps* — *spread*

2. This sleeve was lengthened above the elbow and width was added for a fuller upper arm.

Skirt

1. Pin tissue wrong sides together and try on.

2. Add width by taping tissue to sides.

3. If the skirt hangs longer in back, pull tissue up at center until the hemline is parallel to the floor.

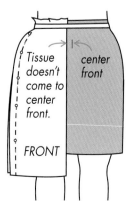

Tissue doesn't come to center front.

center front

FRONT

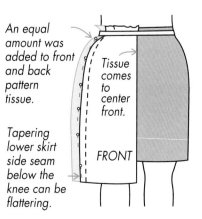

An equal amount was added to front and back pattern tissue.

Tapering lower skirt side seam below the knee can be flattering.

Tissue comes to center front.

FRONT

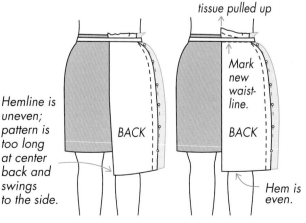

Hemline is uneven; pattern is too long at center back and swings to the side.

BACK

tissue pulled up

Mark new waistline.

BACK

Hem is even.

31

Full Bust Alterations for Princess Style

Since many bridal gowns have princess seams, the following is a review of the princess bust alteration. For more complete details, see the book **Fit for Real People** (page 158).

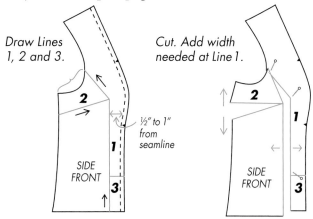

Draw Lines 1, 2 and 3.

Cut. Add width needed at Line 1.

½" to 1" from seamline

Cut on Line 3. Lower until bottom edges are even. Draw Line 4.

hinge

Cut on Line 4. Close Line 2.

Tape together.

Measure at the seamline.

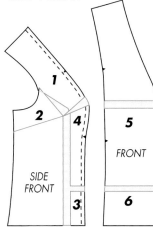

Draw Lines 5 and 6 on the Front. Cut and spread so the openings equal those at lines 4 and 3.

If the Front also needs widening in order to center the seam over the bustline...

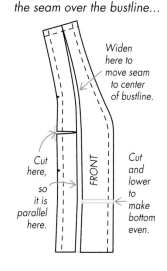

Widen here to move seam to center of bustline.

Cut here, so it is parallel here.

Cut and lower to make bottom even.

Full-Figured Bride

Measuring for Size

Cindy, who just earned her Master's degree in communications at Portland State University, measures a size 26 in the high bust.

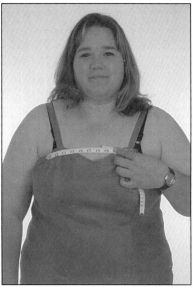

Measure the high bust.

Tip for a Dressmaker

Make sure your customer knows the importance of wearing the proper undergarments and shoes every time she comes for a fitting. Some dressmakers refuse to fit a customer who does not have the proper undergarments. Should your client arrive without the correct fitting attire, don't waste time doing an inaccurate fitting. Instead, reschedule the appointment and consider charging her for the missed appointment to lessen the possibility of forgetting again and to reinforce that your professional time is valuable.

Tip for a Dressmaker

Some customers are embarrassed or shy about being measured—this is, after all, the "bald truth!" It's your job to put your customer at ease throughout the measuring and fitting process. Tell her the numbers are just math and that they will be kept confidential. And also reassure her that the numbers are strictly for the purpose of making sure the gown fits! This usually does the trick and it shows your customer that you are truly a professional. If modesty is a concern, and your customer minds being in her underclothes, recommend that she wear a slip for the measurement process.

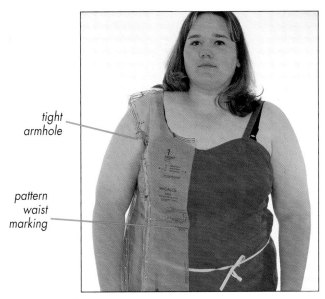

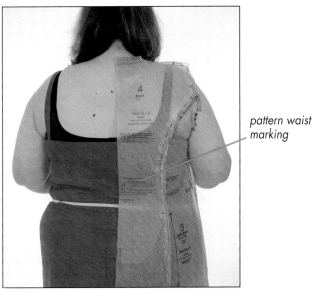

Front Before

Cindy chose a princess style that would glide over her 6'-tall, full figure. To make the size 22 pattern fit, it needs to be graded up to add the necessary width and lengthened for her height. Since the armhole is tight, length is needed in the upper chest area as well as above the waist.

tight armhole

pattern waist marking

Back Before

The waist marking is above her waist. Her waist is slanted, so the pattern will be lengthened to match Cindy's waist at her side.

NOTE: You must alter the back *before* you determine whether or not you need a full bust adjustment.

pattern waist marking

Back Altered

We lengthened the front and back chest 1/2" and waist until the pattern marking matched Cindy's waist at her side. !/2" in width was added to each panel. Another 1/2" was added to the back panel for her broad back. The center back swings toward the side. Cindy has a straight back. A dart tuck will solve the problem.

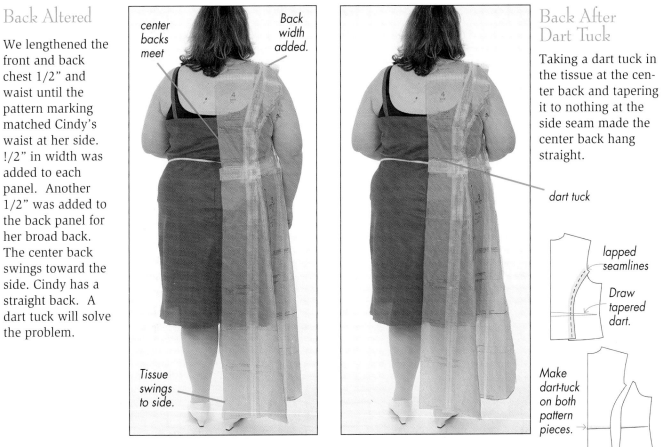

center backs meet

Back width added.

Tissue swings to side.

dart tuck

Back After Dart Tuck

Taking a dart tuck in the tissue at the center back and tapering it to nothing at the side seam made the center back hang straight.

lapped seamlines

Draw tapered dart.

Make dart-tuck on both pattern pieces.

NOTE: Cindy is wearing shoes with the heel height she plans to wear with her dress. Shoes change posture slightly, so it's necessary to do all fittings wearing the correct shoes.

Front Alterations

The Front After Grading

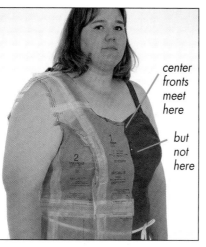

center
fronts
meet
here

but
not
here

The tissue at the upper chest meets Cindy's center front but not at the bust-line. (The tissue was anchored at the center back; with her arm raised, it was pulled *snugly* over her bust as it is important to fit the tissue snugly. DON'T ADD EASE. If you are nervous about this, cut 1"-wide princess and side seam allowances.

NOTE: If the bust curve needs to be lowered, do it before measuring. See **Fit for Real People** (page 158).

How Much to Add?

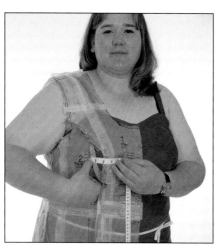

Unpinning the tissue over the bust and moving the pattern center front into the correct position on the body creates an opening. Measure from seamline to seamline to determine the necessary adjustment. Cindy needs ¾", all of which can be added to the side panel since the seamline on the front is correctly centered over her bustline.

Front Altered for Full Bust

The altered tissue (see page 32) now fits across the bust. To eliminate a little gap in the neckline, a small V-shaped tuck was taken in the tissue from the neckline; tapering to nothing at the princess seamline.

Neckline Redesign

Cindy wanted a higher neckline, so the new shape was drawn using Perfect Pattern Paper (page 61), and re-designed to create a sweetheart shape.

Sleeves

The Sleeve Before

If the sleeve is too tight, measure the distance from seam to seam and add an additional 1½" for ease. (If in doubt, also cut a 1"-wide underarm seam allowance "in-case you need it.")

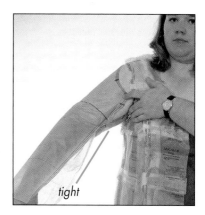

tight

The Sleeve After

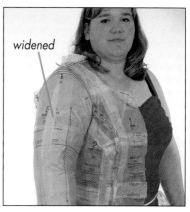

widened

The sleeve was altered by adding 1½" down the center of sleeve and ½" in the front and back halves of the underarm area of the sleeve to match the grading in the side panel (tapering to to nothing at the wrist.) The sleeve fits in width, but the seamline on the sleeve cap wasn't high enough to meet the shoulder seamline so it was necessary to add cap height; otherwise there would be diagonal drag lines in the finished upper sleeve.

Dress Length and Train

Measure the distance from the tissue edge to the floor to determine how much to lengthen a too-short pattern.

It's important to know how you will finish the hem edge. In this case, the the hem will be finished with a rolled edge, which will raise it slightly off the floor.

At right: More flare was added to the back princess seam and the back was elongated to form a short train, using Perfect Pattern Paper (pattern adjustment tissue that is the same weight as pattern tissue).

Tissue Fitting is Completed

Length was added to the front as well.

The Test Dress

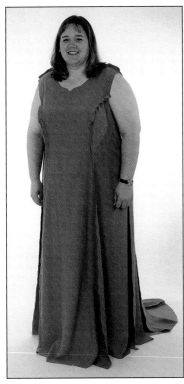

The test dress was made in rayon instead of muslin. The front fits perfectly!

The back hangs beautifully except for the pulls at the waistline.

To correct the waistline fit, shallower seams were pinned at the waistline and upper back hip area until the waistline pulls disappeared.

The adjusted sleeve fits well without drag lines or wrinkles.

Cindy will wear her "test" dress. All she has to do is shorten it to street length. What a BONUS!

Real Dress

Front in Satin
It is perfect!

Back in Satin
A perfect fit!

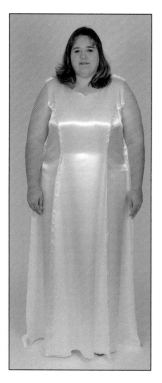

Full-Busted Bride

Measure for Size

Sheila, Cindy's sister, is a mortgage loan officer. Her high bust measures 35" which, when used as the bust on the measurement chart, is a 12. (She is between a 12 and 14 so she chose the smaller size.)

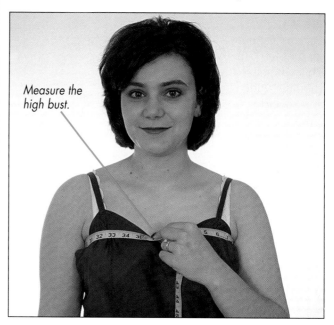

Measure the high bust.

The Finished Dress

The satin dress was joined to an embroidered overdress (page 42) of rayon georgette seamed with rolled-edge seams. The two layers were bound together at the neckline with pre-cut bias silk charmeuse binding (page 40).

NOTE: For a larger photo of the finished dress, see page 40.

Front Before

The tissue center front does not meet Sheila's center front in the bust area. (She wears a D-cup bra.)

Back Before

The cutting line of the tissue comes to Sheila's center back, but the pattern has a center back seam, indicating she needs a broad back adjustment on the side panel. This will make the shoulder wider and cover her bra strap. Her left shoulder is lower than her right and her left hip is slightly higher than her right hip.

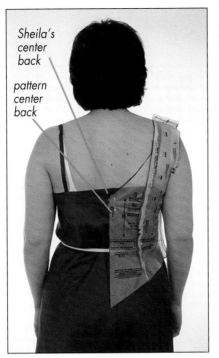

Back After

Width was added through the shoulder and down the back.

NOTE: If you would like more detailed instructions on tissue fitting and fitting while you sew, be sure to read *Fit for Real People*, acclaimed as the best, most complete and practical fit book available. Find it in fabric stores or order from Palmer/Pletsch (page 158). They also offer fit workshops in Portland, Oregon.

Bust Adjustment

Measure to Find Amount to Add

To determine how much to add, the princess seam was unpinned over the bustline and the distance measured from seamline to seamline. It measured 1". To keep the seam centered over the point of the bust, it is necessary to add width to the front *and* side panels. See page 32.

Front After Bust Adjustment

The front fits correctly. The seam placement over the bust is correct but the waistline is a little loose at the sides. That can be adjusted later in the fabric.

37

Shoulder Seams

Shoulder Seam Position

Check the side view of the shoulder seam. Here it looks like it tilts toward the back.

Shoulder Seam After

The seam was redirected toward the front by adding to the back shoulder seam allowance and marking a deeper seam on the front.

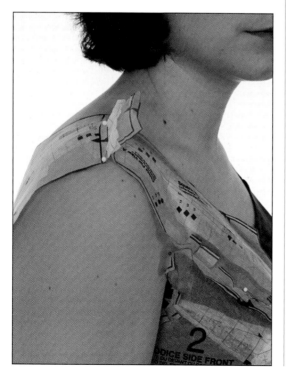

Sleeves

Sleeve Before

It is snug. There is no ease.

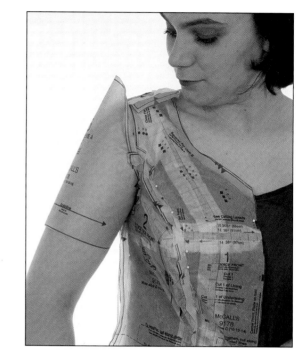

Sleeve After

The sleeve was widened for comfort.

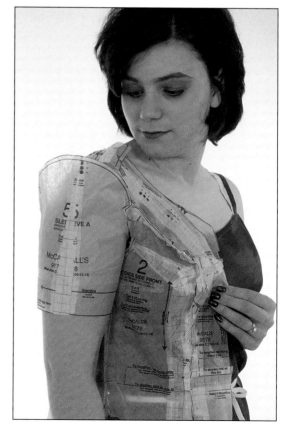

Skirt Length

The front and back skirt pieces are pinned to the bodice. Since the skirt is full, it wasn't necessary to tissue-fit the whole thing for width. It was checked in front for length and in back for train length.

Fabric Fitting

Since Sheila's pattern adjustments were minimal, making a muslin wasn't necessary. Pin-fitting the actual dress was next. Since the pattern was fit to her higher right side, it was necessary to pin a deeper shoulder seam and lower the underarm on her left side.

Front

It looks great. Satin will never look completely smooth on the body because the way it picks up light emphasizes curves. Curved seams tend to look puckered in satin, no matter how carefully you sew.

Back

A good fit!

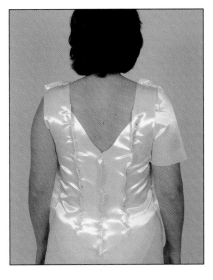

Sleeves

There appears to be enough ease and length to fit Sheila's arms comfortably.

The Finished Dress

The polyester satin was machine embroidered (page 42). Fabric roses were tossed onto the train and tacked in place (page 44). For more details on sewing this dress, see "The Exciting Possibilities," beginning on page 40.

CHAPTER 6

The Exciting Possibilities

While sewing dresses for her nieces, Cindy and Sheila, Pati Palmer, and Marta Alto tried embellishment ideas sewn with the latest equipment and notions. Marta Alto, resident researcher, spent as much time planning and testing as she did sewing. The goal in this chapter is to inspire you with the embellishment ideas that evolved.

Cindy's Dress

Cindy's underdress is a soft, drapey polyester satin-backed crepe, made with the shiny side out and an overdress of rayon georgette. Perfect Sew,® which must be washed out after use (page 42), was used too stabilize this sheer for machine embroidery.

The rayon georgette was pre-washed—it washed beautifully! (The original fabric choice, a washable polyester georgette, was a very gray-looking white, unlike the whiter rayon georgette.)

After embroidering (page 42), the georgette was seamed using a 2mm-long rolled edge, which is *very* sturdy and hardly shows.

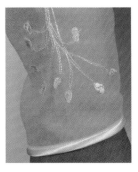

Pre-cut Bias Silk Charmeuse Binding

Using this great find (see "Resources," page 155) to bind raw edges is an easy and elegant way to finish the edges of sheers and lace. Place the *shiny* side against the right side of your garment with raw edges even; stitch in place. Turn the charmeuse to the inside, encasing the raw edge. Turn raw edge under and slipstitch in place. Since bias won't ravel, you can leave it flat and stitch in the well of the seam from the right side to secure the raw edge on the inside. Use an edgestitching foot for best results.

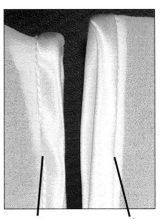

stitching without edgestitch foot   stitching with edgestitch foot

Butterflies and Veils

Machine embroidering butterflies was fun and a wonderful way to embellish Cindy's dress, headpiece, and veil. Many computer sewing machines have butterfly designs you can use (page 155).

After stiffening the polyester organza with Perfect Sew it was allowed to dry, then ironed with a dry iron to further stiffen it. After embroidering, the organza was trimmed away from the outer edges of the butterflies. Then they were shaped and stitched to the dress and pearls were added to the centers for emphasis.

The back opening edges were also bound with the pre-cut charmeuse. Button-and-loop trim (pages 61 and 113) was pinned in place, then caught when stitching in the well of the seam.

The 50 silk charmeuse covered buttons (yes 50!) were made by first fusing interfacing (page 114) to the back of the fabric circles to prevent show through and to make the charmeuse easier to handle. (Having buttons professionally covered is another option.)

The georgette was hemmed with a serged rolled edge, using a stitch length of 3.5mm and rayon thread in the upper looper. (If the rolled edge falls off of your test sample, lengthen the stitch or gather slightly with differential feed set to 1.) The underskirt edge was first finished with a 2-thread serger stitch, then turned under and edgestitched.

Cindy embellished her purchased pearl headpiece with tiny rosettes made from chiffon, plus butterflies in two sizes (some sewn with pale pink or green thread). Additional ornamentation for the headpiece was purchased in the bridal department.

The Headpiece

You can buy a veil kit with ribbon already sewn to the edges or you can buy netting or tulle and topstitch satin ribbon to the edges to finish it.

Machine Embroidery on Cindy's Dress

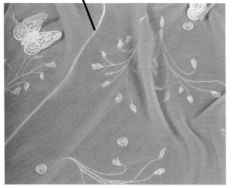

rolled edge seam

After stiffening the rayon georgette pieces with Perfect Sew, the perfect stabilizer for sheers, each panel of Cindy's dress was embroidered *before* assembling the gown. Working on a non-absorbent laminated counter made it easy to spread the Perfect Sew on the fabric by hand—just like finger painting! By the time it was applied to all the pieces, the first piece was dry and ready to stitch. Pressing it with a dry iron just before sewing made it a little stiffer and even easier to handle.

Extra-fine, 100-weight silk thread (page 155) was used for the white embroidery. For the colored areas, a standard, 40-weight embroidery thread was used. After completing the embroidery, all pieces were washed in the washing machine, then hung to dry over the bar of a plastic hanger.

Add Color To Embroidery

Customize your embroidered designs and avoid changing thread colors while embroidering by using fabric paints and dyes. (See "Resources," page 155.) Add the color *before* washing out the Perfect Sew, which helps to keep the paint from bleeding onto the unembroidered fabric.

After stabilizing fabric with Perfect Sew, embroider the fabric using extra-fine 100-weight silk thread. The shorter the stitch length, the better your dyes will follow the threads. Then, with a small amount of dye on a fine-pointed brush, touch the tip to the thread. The dye will magically follow the stitching. Press from the wrong side to set the paints, then wash out the stabilizer.

Tips for Computerized or Free-hand Embroidery

STABILIZERS: Use these to prevent puckers. Sulky has an entire line of excellent stabilizer products. If using their Solvy, use two layers. For best results, layer the two pieces with the stretch running in opposite directions and attach them to each other with spray adhesive. Attach Solvy to the fabric with the same spray and sew from the fabric side. For acetate, which shouldn't be washed, use a lightweight tear-away type stabilizer instead.

NEEDLES: Size 80 universal needles are recommended by most machine companies. Change the needle *frequently*. We used 20 needles for the embroidery on the two dresses shown in this chapter. The satin is hard on needles because it is tightly woven and there are literally thousands of stitches in a design. A needle is good for 8 hours and the designs we chose took about 15 minutes each to sew. If the thread is breaking while you embroider, change the needle. It's probably dull.

Take heed from Marta's experiences. If stitching problems and thread breakage are a continual problem, have a dealer look at your machine. Marta's new machine came with a small burr on the foot that the dealer discovered. He gave her a new foot and voila! Perfect machine embroidery! He also re-timed her machine and adjusted the tension and everything worked better.

THREADS: If you are using thread on a skinny tube (Gutermann or Sulky), place the spool on the machine so the brand is closest to the bottom of the horizontal spool pin. If you have a vertical spool pin, place so the spool rotates counterclockwise. Parallel-wound spools (Coats & Clark, and Madeira) work best on a vertical spool pin. (Some machines have both types of spool pins or an adapter.) If using a parallel-wound spool, make sure the spool turns easily.

If you have thread breakage, try Sewers' Aid. This stitch lubricant soaks into the thread. Sulky recommends squeezing three rows of it along the length of the spool.

If you are doing a lot of machine embroidery, fill ten bobbins before you begin. Use a bobbin-weight thread for machine embroidery. Rayon embroidery thread such as Sulky's Ultra Twist and Coats & Clark's new Color Twist, both 35-weight rayon, add depth to a design. Give them a try!

Sheila's Dress

Before choosing the satin for Sheila's dress, Marta tested machine embroidery on several different satins. Because the poly satin chosen for Sheila's dress is washable, it could be stiffened in the areas to be embroidered, using wash-away Perfect Sew.

To decide on the design placement around the neckline, two half-front samples were embroidered in different ways.

The waistline was piped by sewing the piping to the lower edge of the bodice, then sewing the gathered skirt to the bodice (page 128 & 131).

The neckline finish is a decorative silk trim from Things Japanese (page 155).

Trim away the base so the scallops can curve in the neckline seam between the satin and the lining. Beads were hand sewn to the embroidered flowers on the bodice and skirt. (See page 48.)

The entire bodice of Sheila's dress required underlining for enough body to support the skirt so Perfect Fuse Light fusible interfacing (page 160) was fused to the wrong side of each piece *after* embroidering.

A 12"-wide band of ivory satin finishes the lower edge of the skirt. Marta machine embroidered designs in clusters spaced 15" to 18" apart and serged the band onto the skirt using a 4-thread seam after a fitting to determine the correct finished length. (If you don't have a serger, sew a regular seam, then zigzag the seam allowances together.) Pearls were hand sewn onto the embroidery for added embellishment.

Fabric Roses

Fabric roses in various colors of satin, tulle, and chiffon embellish

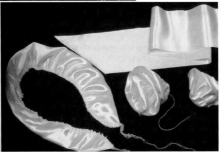

the headpiece and the back of the skirt, adding color and texture to a simple gown. There are 40 roses on Sheila's dress and each one took about 15 minutes to make.

Marta used 3½"-wide strips of bias satin for finished roses with a depth of 1¾". Each strip was cut 18" to 24" long. (You need ⅜ yard to get an 18"-long (bias) strip without piecing.) The different lengths created roses of differing fullness.

To make the edge gather automatically, Marta serged the lower edges together with a 4-thread stitch and a differential feed setting of 2. For more gathering, she pulled on the needle threads of the 4-thread stitch (a 3-thread serged seam won't gather as easily), then threaded the needle thread tails through a hand sewing needle and rolled and stitched the roses in the desired shape. Using differential feed gave the roses more character (sort of a peony look) than the sample made by just gathering. The bottom edges of the roses were covered (page 47) and then they were hand sewn to the dress.

More on Roses

You can make or purchase roses and rosettes, using one of several methods. They can be tiny or large; stiff or drapey; smooth or ruffly. Try them in chiffon, satin, tulle, or other dressy fabric. Add leaves, if you wish, like those on the bridesmaid's dress at left.

Be sure to make a sample to test the fullness, depth, and size. Consider the style of the gown, the placement of the roses, and the design statement you want to make with the embellishment. A good starting depth is about 2".

Bias Strips Folded in Half

1. Cut a bias strip of fabric about 18" long (or longer if you prefer) and twice the finished depth of your rose, plus ¾" for seam allowances.

2. Fold in half. Machine baste raw edges together. Save time by stitching from fold to fold as shown.

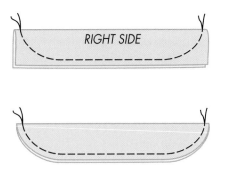

RIGHT SIDE

3. Trim, leaving even seam allowances.

Serger tip: Use differential feed set on 2 and use a 4-thread serged seam. This finishes the edges neatly, and gathers some fabrics. Pull on the needle threads to gather even more.

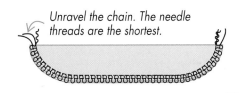

Unravel the chain. The needle threads are the shortest.

4. Gather by pulling on the bobbin thread and hand roll into a flower. Tack the bottom edges together, adjusting the gathers and fullness as you go and catching the remaining end to the bottom edge.

Bias-Cut Single Rose for Heavy Fabrics

1. Cut a bias strip the width of your finished rose depth plus seam allowance.

2. Finish one long raw edge, using a rolled edge on your serger and matching or decorative thread. Use differential feed set at 2 to prevent stretching.

3. Stitch one or two rows of basting along the curved edge. Gather and finish the rose as described above.

Bias-Cut Double Layer Rose

1. Cut a bias strip 18" long twice the depth of the finished rose plus two seam allowances.

2. Finish both long edges with a rolled edge. (Rayon thread and a 2mm-long stitch length work well.) Fold in half and machine baste on the seamline.

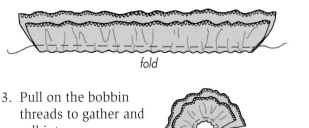

fold

3. Pull on the bobbin threads to gather and roll into a rose as described above.

NOTE: This could be a very floppy rose if your fabric is light or very drapey.

Circular Roses

1. Draw a circle with the diameter equal to the desired depth of your rose plus two ¼"-wide seam allowances.

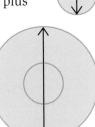

2. Draw a second circle around the first with the diameter equal to three times the rose depth plus four ¼"-wide seam allowances.

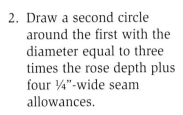

3. Draw a cutting line from the inner circle to the outer circle as shown.

4. Place the pattern on a **double layer** of fabric folded with right sides together.

5. Cut around the circle and then on the cutting line and around the inner circle. Discard the inner circle.

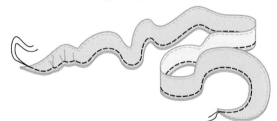
cut

6. Stitch the layers together along the outer edges as shown, using a short stitch length of 1.5mm so the seam won't ravel out.

7. Turn and press, then machine baste the raw edges together.

8. Gather to the desired fullness and finish as described above for other roses.

Fish Line Roses

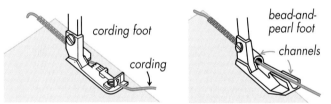

To add body and shape to the edges of a fabric rose, serge over fish line, encasing the line in the rolled edge stitch. This is particularly nice on chiffon. Start with a very long strip of bias chiffon as it takes more length to make a full rose. You can do the rolled edge with Woolly Nylon, a shiny rayon thread such as Designer 6 or Decor 6, or an iridescent metallic thread in the upper looper.

1. Cut a strand of fish line (20- to 30-pound) half again as long as the bias ruffle strip.

2. Using a short, rolled edge stitch, serge over 2" to 3" of the line by itself. Then place the fabric under the presser foot and continue serging. Leave a long tail of fish line at the end. (If the rolled edge falls off the chiffon, lengthen the stitch a little.)

3. Stretch the edge of the bias after serging to spread the fabric over the rest of the fish line.

4. Gather the lower edge and form into a rose as previously described.

Special Tips for Handling Fish Line on a Serger

If your presser foot has a hole in it for cording, insert the fish line through it and let the machine do the work.

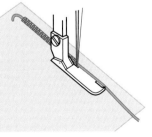

cording foot
cording
bead-and-pearl foot
channels

Or, use a cording or a bead-and-pearl foot.

If you don't have either of these feet, check your serger presser foot to see if it has a lip on the right-hand edge. If so, place the fishline to the right of the needle and along the inside of the lip as shown.

Dior Roses

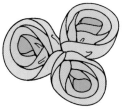

These are an elegant specialty of Bobbie Carr, author of *Couture, the Art of Fine Sewing* (see page 158 for ordering information). Complete instructions are included in her book. Roberta says, "The purist's form of a Dior Rose has three petals with each petal having three pieces."

Finishing Fabric Roses

From scrap fabric, cut a circle ½" larger in diameter than the bottom of your rose. To cover the raw edges, slipstitch the circle to the bottom of the rose, turning under ¼" all around.

More Rose Ideas

◆ For very large roses, a nice finishing touch is to glue a purchased rosebud in the center.

◆ Make leaves by folding a circle in half, then in half again. Gather or pleat the raw edge and sew the leaf to the underside of the rose.

Dyed Silk Ribbon Embellishment

Dying ribbon adds individuality and can tie the wedding party colors together. See page 155 for supplies. Gather across the dyed ribbon every 3" and tie narrower silk ribbons over the gathers. Sew the knots to the dress at 1½" to 2" intervals for a "ribbon" look. Add roses made from the same width silk ribbon.

Beads and Pearls

There was a time when a prospective bride spent hours sewing tiny beads and pearls to hand crocheted laces. Today's reality, however, is that most of us just don't have that kind of time. But, the look of lace appliqués, beads, and pearls is still as popular as ever. Now, it's easy to get the hand-beaded look—just use glue!

Tip for a Dressmaker

If your client wants hand beading done on lace and does not want to pay the price for pre-beaded yardage (or doesn't like the over-beaded look many of them have), you may be able to find a person who does hand beading as a craft to whom you could subcontract the work.

Applying Beads, Pearls, and Sequins with Glue

1. Place the fabric to be beaded on a non-porous surface; waxed paper works very well.

2. Separate all the pearls, beads, or sequins into small dishes or a muffin tin. Place a glob of bridal glue on a piece of waxed paper.

NOTE: Bridal glue dries clear and flexible. Just be careful not to use too much. It is so thick it doesn't "squirt." Squeezing a small amount on waxed paper works best.

3. Using "scissor-style" tweezers, dip the pearl or bead into the glue. Allow it to dry for a couple of seconds.

4. Place the pearl, bead or sequin on the lace or fabric. Do not move the fabric until the glue has completely dried.

NOTE: This glue application is not as sturdy as hand sewing each individual pearl, bead, or sequin, but it is much quicker. We generally reserve gluing for headpieces and accessories.

Applying Beads and Pearls by Machine

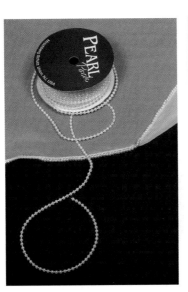

Applying these embellishments by machine, either with a serger or on a conventional sewing machine is not quite as fast as glue, but sturdier. You can purchase pre-strung beads and pearls by the yard.

♦ Thread: For these embellishments, use clear monofilament thread on top and thread to match your fabric in the bobbin. To apply to an edge with a serger, use a 3-thread stitch with monofilament thread in the upper and lower loopers and thread that matches the fabric in the needle.

♦ Feet: To apply *beads and pearls* to an edge, use a Pearls 'n Piping foot on your serger (page 53). If applying them within the body of the gown, use the darning foot on your conventional machine, drop the feed dogs, and use free-hand zigzagging with a stitch wide enough to clear the beads or pearls. Use a 3mm stitch length.

Applying Sequins By Machine

Sequins, available prestrung by the yard, are not used as often on bridal gowns as beads and pearls, but they can add a nice shine. They come stitched together with a chain stitch which, when cut, will unravel. Be sure to touch the cut ends with clear sealant to prevent all your sequins from unraveling!

Apply as you would beads and pearls with the presser foot running in the "smooth direction" of the sequins. If positioned the opposite way, the presser foot will catch the edges of the sequins and bend or break them.

Use an open-toe or a clear plastic applique foot to zigzag over the sequins. There is also a generic foot available for conventional machines that feeds sequins by the yard through a tunnel. Check mail-order notions catalogs for availability.

You can also sew through the center of sequins using thread that matches the sequins.

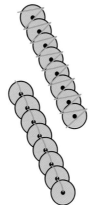

Hand-sewing Individual or Prestrung Beads, Pearls, and Sequins

When you want to decorate only a small portion of lace or when you need to replace missing beads or sequins, you can apply them by hand. Some tiny beads and sequins can only be applied by hand. While not as fast as gluing, there are some ways to streamline the process. Limit the beadwork to small areas. Pre-strung beads are the easiest to handle. Check the bridal department in your favorite fabric stores for beads or try craft stores.

♦ Plan the beadwork placement on your gown to determine whether to bead prior to assembling the bodice or after the gown is completed. If the beading is to cross seamlines, do it afterwards.

♦ Beads can enhance a lace motif or outline a design on a plain fabric. If beading your own design, draw the motif on a piece of tissue paper and pin it in place over the fabric. After completing the beading, carefully tear the tissue away. Perfect Pattern Paper (page 160) is great for this.

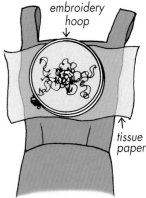

embroidery hoop

tissue paper

♦ An embroidery hoop will help keep the fabric taut while you're hand stitching. Stabilize lightweight fabrics with underlining to reinforce the design area. Don't leave an embroidery hoop on your fabric for extended periods of time—it can stretch or distort the fabric and leave a permanent mark. TEST FIRST!

♦ If your fabric is washable, use Perfect Sew, a liquid stabilizer, to stiffen the fabric. Perfect Sew eliminates the need for both an embroidery hoop and interfacing. Use a washable fabric. Bead the bodice pieces first, then rinse the fabric to remove Perfect Sew before assembling the bodice.

Perfect Sew is also used for machine embroidery. It is excellent for stabilizing chiffon for embellishment.

- Use a beading needle and a short, *double* strand of thread for strength. Wax it with beeswax or Thread Heaven so it won't tangle. Using a short length of thread prevents twisting and knotting. To avoid puckering, take care not to pull stitches too tight. Be sure your hands are clean!

- Apply single beads with a backstitch.

- For bead "swirls," string all the beads at once and then tack over the string every 2 or 3 beads to hold them in place.

- To apply single beads in outline designs, place two or three beads on the thread and use a running stitch. If you don't catch them to the dress frequently, you'll need to tack over them every 2 to 3 beads in order to create a smooth line. Avoid thread floats on the underside that are any longer than ½".

NOTE: *Prestrung beads* are faster. Position on the gown and whipstitch in place. Or, remove them directly from the string to your needle, one, two, three or more at a time.

- Sew single sequins on with a bead in the center. Bring the needle up through the fabric. Place a sequin on the needle, then a bead. Slip them down onto the fabric. Stitch back through the center of the sequin.

- For single sequins in an outline design, bring the needle to the right side of the fabric and pick up a sequin. Curved side up, hold the sequin flat and take a stitch over the edge. Bring the needle to the right side, one half the width of the sequin ahead. Each new sequin will overlap the edge of the previous one.

Pressing

When pressing a beaded or sequined garment, do not place a hot iron directly on the beadwork—it can cause scratching and melting. Avoid pressing at all if possible. If you must, place the beadwork face down on a plush towel and press lightly from the wrong side without steam.

Bows

You must make several decisions before constructing your bow:

- How large will it be? Consider your height, weight, the width of your skirt, and the length of your train when making this decision.

- Will it be single layer, double, triple, or more?

- Will it have tails?

- What type of embellishment will it have—lace, beading, roses, a combination, or none at all?

Where Do Bows Go?

You can place bows anywhere on your gown that you want to embellish. The most common placements for bows are:

- On the sleeves where lace meets fabric, or at sleeve hems

- The back where the bodice joins the skirt (see page 52)

- At the shoulder

- Around the neckline

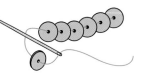

Anatomy of a Bow

bow   bow knot

tie ends

There are three parts to a bow:

1. The bow itself—a rectangle of fabric, usually lined with self-fabric.

   - For a floppy bow, no underlining is necessary.

   - For a bow with body, one layer of netting is used as an underlining.

   - For a bow with "attitude," use crinoline, two layers of net, or stiff fusible interfacing. For an extra-crisp bow, use more than one layer of stiffening.

2. The bow knot—a small rectangle of fabric that holds the bow's gathers in place.

   - In addition to the bow knot, you can use a rose (page 45) in the center of your bow for added interest.

3. The tie ends—long, shaped rectangles that extend from beneath the bow.

Tip for a Dressmaker

When discussing bows with your customer, you need to take into consideration the width of her hips and the fullness of her skirt. Bows tend to add visual weight, much like a bustle does, to a bride's "back end." Be sure you show her how the bow will look. Some brides don't want to add any more width than is necessary back there! Don't worry about bows until the dress is finished. Then you can cut fabric rectangles or paper patterns and pin them in place for size and dimension so the bride can see the full finished look of the gown.

Bow Width and Depth

For bow width, measure across your back at about 8" below your waist. This measurement is approximately your finished bow width. So that a bow placed at the center back is only a design detail and not an overwhelming focal point, plan for it to end just shy of your widest point on either side.

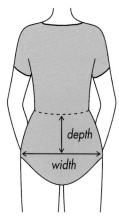

depth

width

NOTE: Your finished bow will be about 1" less than your beginning measurement due to fabric take-up from gathering.

The finished bow depth should be between one-half and two-thirds of your finished bow width.

Making the Bow

1. Cut a piece of fashion fabric twice the finished bow width plus 1" for seam allowances and twice the finished bow depth plus 1" for seam allowances.

2. Cut underlining, choosing from the following options:

   - For a *light* stiffening, cut underlining the width of the bow and one-half the depth.

   - For *heavy* stiffening, cut underlining the same size as the bow.

   - For *very heavy* stiffening, use two layers cut the same size as the bow.

3. Cut a bow knot 3¾" wide by 6" long, or any other size you prefer.

4. Sew underlining to the wrong side of bow fabric.

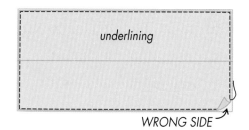

underlining

WRONG SIDE

5. Fold bow in half, lengthwise, *with right sides together*. Stitch the long edge, using a ½"-wide seam.

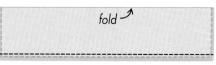

fold

6. Press seam allowance open. Turn bow right side out and press lightly along the edges.

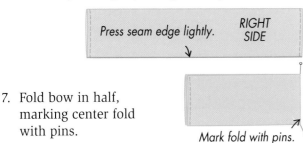

Press seam edge lightly. | RIGHT SIDE
↓

7. Fold bow in half, marking center fold with pins.

Mark fold with pins.

8. Unfold and bring the raw ends of the bow together so they overlap about ³⁄₈" in the center.

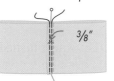

³⁄₈"

9. Do two rows of basting stitches at the center of the bow through all layers.

10. Draw up basting to gather. Secure gathers by wrapping gathering threads around the bow center.

NOTE: If the fabric is heavy, don't expect a tightly gathered bow.

11. Stitch, turn, and press the bow knot with the seam in center of the knot.

WRONG SIDE

center seam

12. Fold the knot over the basted center of the bow, lapping the ends.

13. Turn under one raw end and slipstitch to secure.

Tie Ends

If you want your bow to be a focal point, you may wish to make your tie ends large and exaggerated, with pearls, lace, and sequins. If you want to make a set of ties proportionate in size to the bow you have just created, make the ties twice the finished bow depth.

Create a Pattern

1. Draw a line the finished length of your tie ends (line AB).

2. The top width of the tie equals one quarter of the finished bow width. Mark point C to the right of point A and connect with a line.

3. The bottom width of the tie equals one half of the finished bow width. Mark point D to the right of point B and connect with a line.

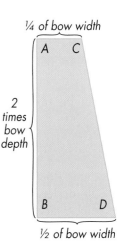

¼ of bow width

A   C

2 times bow depth

B   D

½ of bow width

NOTE: If you want, you may angle the bottom of the tie ends up to a maximum of 45 degrees.

4. Connect lines C and D to complete your tie. Add seam allowances.

angle if desired

5. Cut 4 pieces of fashion fabric using your pattern. If you used underlining for your bow, cut the same type for your ties.

6. Stitch ties with right sides together, leaving an opening across the top.

NOTE: It is easier to stitch the ties with the underlining on the top. It helps prevent the one bias edge of the ties from stretching.

underlining

7. Trim and grade seams and press open before turning. Turn and press lightly.

8. To give your tie some depth, pleat the top.

pleat top

9. Baste ties to the back of the bow knot.

Attaching the Bow

The placement of your bow is also subjective. The normal placement is at the back of the gown where the bodice meets the skirt.

◆ Attach the bow last, after the gown is completed.

◆ Place the knot at center back and stitch in place just on the left side of the gown, next to the zipper.

◆ Stitch the upper left end of the bow to the bodice of the gown, allowing the bottom of the bow to float freely.

◆ Attach one-half of a clear plastic snap to the upper right end of the bow; sew the other half to the bodice. This allows you to get into and out of your gown! The snap on the right side should be at the exact same level as the tacking on the left side or the bow won't hang properly.

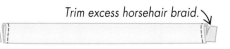

Sew bow in place. *plastic snaps*

NOTE: If your bow is large and very heavy, you may want to use more than one snap. Place another just to the right of the zipper and another halfway between the center and the end of the right side of the bow.

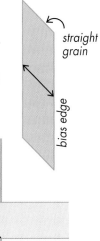

◆ Ask your bridesmaid to arrange the ties just before you walk down the aisle.

If the bow is at the neckline, on the sleeves, or elsewhere on the skirt, it can be permanently attached at both ends.

More Bow Ideas

◆ Small bows may be filled with horsehair braid. Use braid the same width as the finished bow and thread through with a safety pin.

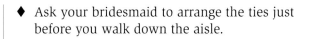

Trim excess horsehair braid.

◆ Appliqué lace to the bow and/or its ties. (Do this before sewing, while the pieces are flat.)

◆ Make two bows and connect them with one knot. The top one should be slightly smaller than the one beneath it.

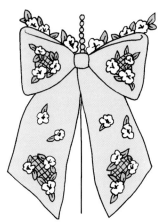

◆ Add a rose or two to the center of the bow over the knot.

Piping

Piping is a very effective finish for a neckline or a waistline. It helps gathers lie more smoothly.

Create Self-Fabric Piping

1. Cut bias strips the length you'll need and twice as wide as the piping cord diameter plus 1¼" for seams. For example, if your piping cord is ⅛" diameter, the strips should be 1½" wide.

straight grain

bias edge

NOTE: If you need to piece the bias, sew the strips together as shown, stitching along the straight grain. Trim the seams to ¼" and press open.

2. Wrap the bias around the piping cord with *right sides out* and raw edges even.

3. Using a zipper or cording foot, stitch close to the cord.

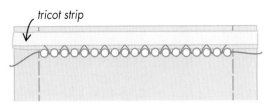

Attach Piping in a Seam

1. Place piping along the edge of the garment piece, matching raw edges. Pin. Stitch in place, using the zipper foot or a special piping foot to get as close as possible. To avoid puckering, *do not stretch the piping.*

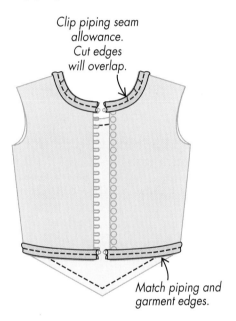

Clip piping seam allowance. Cut edges will overlap.

Match piping and garment edges.

2. Clip the piping seam allowance where necessary to allow the piping to lie flat.

♦ For an outside corner (right angle), stop stitching about 3" from the corner. Leave the needle inserted in the fabric. Pin the piping up to the corner and clip at the point where the piping turns the corner. Stitch to the turning point. Leaving your needle inserted in the fabric, raise the presser foot and turn the work. Continue stitching.

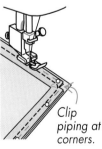

Clip piping at corners.

♦ For an inside corner, follow the same steps as above but cut a small triangle out of the piping seam allowance at the turning point instead of simply clipping the fabric.

Pearl Piping

Purchase pearl strands attached to a tricot strip. Remove pearls that cross over into seam allowances.

tricot strip

NOTE: You can attach a string of pearls to tricot to make your own piping by sewing or serging it to an edge using the pearls and piping foot.

Pearl Edge Finish on the Serger

If you want an easy neckline or other edge finish, serge pearls to the fabric edge. If using a lining, baste the lining to the fabric with fabric wrong sides together first.

1. Thread the serger with monofilament nylon in the right needle and both loopers. Adjust for a balanced 2- or 3-thread stitch, making it about 2.5-3.5mm long.

2. Serge, using the pearl foot. The seam allowance will be trimmed away as you serge over the pearls.

♦ To prevent puckers when applying pearls, adjust to a "minus" (.5 to .7) differential feed setting. If differential feed is unavailable, hold the fabric taut with one hand in front of the foot and one hand behind it.

♦ When serging pucker-prone, lightweight silkies, adjust for a slightly shorter and narrower-than-normal stitch and a "minus" .5 or .7 differential feed setting. Try a new needle, as well, to help prevent snagging the fabric.

♦ Cover the monofilament nylon thread with a thread net to keep it from slumping off the spool or cone into a tangled mess.

♦ To join pearls along a circular edge, serge to within a few inches of the beginning serging. Then cut the pearls to fit, nudge the beginning and ending pearls together, and serge for several stitches over the beginning of the pearls. Work the threads off the stitch finger, tie them off, and secure them with seam sealant.

Pintucks

You can make pintucks in most types of fabric using one of three methods. Remember to test the desired technique on your fabric. Some heavy satins do not respond well to pintucking and velvet doesn't pintuck at all!

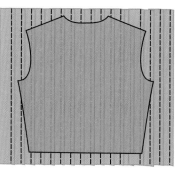

NOTE: Always pintuck the fabric first, then lay your pattern piece on the fabric and cut it out.

Test First

To estimate the fabric width you'll need, make a test sample.

1. Cut a piece of fabric at least 8" long and wide enough for half a dozen finished pintucks. This will give you a large enough sample to check the effect the pintucks will have.

2. Create pintucks in the test swatch by basting several different widths of tucks until you find the width you want to use.

3. When you are satisfied with the finished width of your tuck, remove the basting and measure how much fabric the tuck took up. Measure the pattern piece you plan to tuck and multiply the width of that piece by the width needed for each tuck. Tuck *at least* that width of fabric.

measure

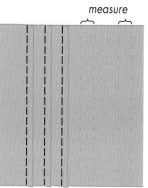

Conventional Pintucking Method

1. On the fabric right side, lightly mark a beginning point for the pintucks. Fold the fabric along the marked line and press.

2. Using an edgestitching foot and a straight, balanced stitch, sew the desired width of your pintuck (usually ⅛" to ¼" wide) using a straight, balanced stitch.

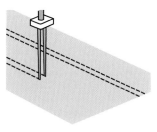

3. Press the pintuck to one side. Measure from the first pintuck stitching line the width of one pintuck, plus the desired space between pintucks, plus the second pintuck width and mark. Fold again, press, and stitch as before.

4. Continue marking, folding, pressing, stitching, and pressing until the piece is pintucked with the desired number of tucks.

5. Cut your pattern piece from the pintucked fabric.

Double-Needle Pintucks

For a faster and simpler pintucking method, use a double needle. These needles come in sizes ranging from 1.6cm apart to 6.0cm apart.

NOTE: Check your sewing machine's throat plate opening to be sure it can accommodate the double-needle width you plan to use to make pintucks!

1. Draw a straight line on the right side of the fabric to be tucked.

2. Begin stitching, centering the marked line between the needles. Use a balanced stitch, set for about 8 to 10 stitches to the inch. The twin needles will draw the fabric up into a pintuck and the bobbin thread will form a zigzag stitch on the wrong side.

3. To "fill" the pintuck, use pearl cotton or button-hole twist under the fabric as you stitch so the bobbin thread captures it under the zigzag stitches that form.

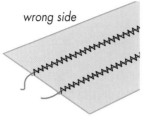

wrong side

4. Cut the pattern pieces from the pintucked fabric.

NOTE: Twin needle pintucking works on satin but it will have an unavoidable "puckered" look. You can use this as part of the overall design look—or choose a different pintucking method if you don't like the look.

Serger Rolled-Edge Pintucks

Perhaps the fastest and easiest pintucking method is to set your serger for a narrow rolled edge or a narrow balanced stitch. Try Woolly Nylon in the loopers and clear, monofilament thread in the needle. Or try rayon or metallic threads in the needle for a more decorative look.

1. Press mark the tuck fold lines.

2. Plan the serging direction so that the top side of the stitch will always show on the right side. Pintucks along the lengthwise grain are smoother than those serged on the crosswise grain.

3. Disengage the knife, if possible, to avoid cutting the fabric, or, don't disengage the knife. It will make you sew straighter!

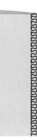

4. Serge along the fold line slowly, *without cutting the folded edge with serger knife.* Press the tucks to one side.

Heirloom Sewing

"Heirloom sewing" is generally used on a Victorian-style gown. You can incorporate insertion lace, pintucks, and gathered lace trim to create the beautiful effects associated with heirloom sewing. For how to create serger heirloom sewing, see *Creative Serging* (page 156). If you want to do this by hand, consult books by Martha Pullen, well-known expert on the subject.

Recycling Your Gown

Garrett John from Dunbarton, New Hampshire, wears his Mom's wedding dress. The bride wanted her wedding gown recycled into a christening gown for her first born. So, if you don't want to pass the dress on as a bridal gown, this is an option that can be treasured by future generations.

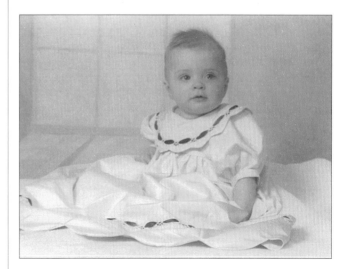

CHAPTER 7

Bridal Fabric

Choosing Your Fabric

You have your pattern and you've sewn and fitted it in muslin so you know how it will look on you. The fitting shell has given you a good idea of the flow and drape you want and now you're ready to buy the fabric for your gown. You probably know, for example, that you want your full skirt to stand out from your hips and have its own body, or that you want your gown to float around you.

A good starting point for fabric selection is to look at "Suggested Fabrics" on the back of the pattern envelope. Generally, the first fabric listed is the one the designer had in mind when the garment was designed. However, since you are the "designer" of your gown, do not limit yourself to only those fabrics listed. The fabric you've fallen in love with may be the perfect choice even if it's not listed on the pattern envelope.

Quality

Buy the best quality fabric you can afford. Don't waste your time and energy on cheap fabric. It will look cheap in the final product, you will have difficulty working with it, and if it looks inexpensive on the bolt, no amount of beautiful work can change that. If you are a dressmaker, strive to educate your customer about fabric. She may or may not know anything about fabric and how to judge its quality. It is up to you as a professional to show her; keep samples of both *good* and *bad* fabric to demonstrate fabric quality.

♦ **Wrinkle Test.** Hold a portion of the fabric in your hand and crush it, then let go. If wrinkles form in the fabric, you'll have a wrinkled skirt as soon as you sit down the first time—and they'll only get worse as the day progresses.

♦ **Flaws, Fade Lines, Runs.** As the clerk unfolds your fabric, watch carefully. Fabric that has been folded on the bolt for a long time often has a crease that is now permanent, or at best, very difficult to remove. Finer fabrics, especially satins and silks, are usually rolled on a tube instead of being folded around a flat bolt. Ask the clerk to roll your fabric, if possible, to avoid unnecessary creases after it's cut from the bolt.

♦ **If the fabric is a print, make sure it's printed on grain.** If it isn't, you'll either have to cut the pieces to follow the grain so that the skirt will hang correctly but the print will not hang straight— or cut the fabric off grain using the print as a guide. Neither solution is very good.

♦ **Is there enough fabric on one bolt?** Buy fabric for your gown in one length only. Dye lots vary from bolt to bolt, even within the same numbered dye lot. The typical gown requires 10 to 14 yards of fabric, so be sure there's enough on the bolt. If you absolutely love the fabric but cannot buy it in one piece, make sure that there is enough to cut the bodice and the skirt front from one piece and the back and the skirt back from the second piece. As the eye travels around the body to the back of the gown any change in color will be less obvious.

NOTE: For bridesmaids' dresses, you need only make sure you can cut each dress from one length of fabric. Slight color changes from one dress to another won't be noticeable.

ℐip for a Dressmaker

You will have customers call and say, "I have fabric and a pattern, can you make me a dress?" Be aware that you may need to say no if you feel the fabric and pattern won't work together or if the fabric is such poor quality that it won't look good no matter what you do to it. This is a judgment call on your part. But, you and your customer will be happier in the end if you are honest and up front. You may be able to steer the customer toward either (a) a more appropriate pattern for her fabric, or (b) upgrading the fabric to one that is more appropriate for the pattern she has chosen.

◆ **Fabric Width.** Some specialty fabrics come in a narrower-than-normal width, making it difficult to cut or piece a large, full skirt. For example, some silks are only 36" wide. If you fall in love with a narrow fabric, you may be able to alter the skirt to accommodate this. If not, you will need to choose a different style skirt or choose a different fabric. Skirts with too many seams can look busy. For more ways to deal with cutting your gown from narrow fabrics, see page 126.

fabric width

Trace top and bottom of skirt.

Fold pattern until it fits fabric width.

◆ **Purchase all fabrics, trims, linings, and lace at the same time so that you're sure of a color match.** Generally, match everything to the gown fabric. If you have particular flowers for your bouquet in mind, take one with you for color-matching purposes. If you want to use a piece of antique lace from your grandmother, take it to the store when shopping for the other components. Look at fabric in the daylight, if possible. It often looks quite different under the fluorescent lighting used in most shops.

◆ **Fabric Care.** While not as critical for a wedding gown as it is for a suit or everyday dress, the general rule of thumb is to make sure all components of the garment can take the same kind of care. Make sure the fabrics you combine in your gown are compatible so that you do not ruin your dress. When one layer in a multi-layer skirt or bodice shrinks during pressing and the others don't, the results can be disastrous and difficult to salvage.

Tip for a Dressmaker

It is a good idea to have samples of bridal fabric in your studio. Be sure that the ones you have on hand are still available before you show them to your customer—she's bound to choose the one that's out of stock (Murphy's Law). Be knowledgeable about the fabric you have, which laces and trims match or are compatible, etc. The customer will rely on your expertise to guide her, and often does not know which fabrics would be appropriate for her gown style. Point out trims that match or coordinate with the fabric types and help your customer visualize the final result. Having samples of fabric also makes it possible to demonstrate the drape and gathering properties of different fabrics. Your customer may not realize that a heavy bridal satin is much bulkier when gathered than a drapey silk satin, for instance, or that a soft silk will reveal figure contours that she might prefer to hide.

Seasonal Fabrics

Fabrics can very well "say a season" through their color, texture, and weight. Choosing the right fabric for the season of your wedding will not only enhance the look and style of the ceremony, but will prove practical as well. For example, velvet definitely doesn't look like a summer wedding and it would be hot and uncomfortable as well.

Spring	Summer	Autumn	Winter
cottons: polished, eyelets, prints	cottons: polished, eyelets, prints	brocade	brocade
crepe de chine	*crepe: lightweight	*crepe: medium to heavy-weight	*crepe: medium to heavy-weight
*crepe: light to medium weight	crepe de chine	**lace: all types	**lace: especially the heavy, re-embroidered types
**lace: lightweights, all-over types such as Chantilly	**lace: lightweights, all-over types such as Chantilly	peau de soie	
peau de soie	polyester silkies	satin	peau de soie
polyester silkies	shantung	shantung	satin
shantung (silk or silk-like)	sheers: all types	silk worsted	shantung
sheers: chiffon, georgette, organza, gauze, voile		taffeta, moiré	silk worsted
		velvet, velveteen, velour (late autumn only)	taffeta, moiré
			velvet, velveteen, velour chiffon

*indicates seasonless fabrics   **lace appliqués can be cut from all lace types

Common Fabrics and Their Characteristics

Below are listed some of the most common fabrics used in wedding gowns and their characteristics.

Fabric Type	Sewing/Handling	Characteristics	Uses/Notes
Delicate Surfaces			
Brocade Peau de soie Polyester silkies Satin all weights (can be silk or polyester) *Bridal satin* *Charmeuse* *Crepe-back satin* *Satin-back crepe* Silks *China silk* *Crepe de chine* *Faille* *Habutai* *Lamé* *Shantung*	• Moderate sewing ease • Slips during cutting • Snag-sensitive surface • Use one-way nap and yardage layouts. • Stitching lines show if ripped out. • Sensitive to overhandling and overpressing; test first. • Heavy fabrics are difficult to gather and may not ease well into sleeve caps. • Check the care code; some, such as silk charmeuse and some satins may show water spots. • Steam may cause puckers. • Fit should not be tight. • Many ravel badly.	• Most have a smooth, lustrous surface. • Good for figure camouflage • Combine nicely with all over laces • Brocade may have a raised or flat pattern. • Some silks and silkies have a soft, dull glow. • Some satins have a high-gloss surface. Peau de soie is a medium-weight satin with a dull finish. • Lighter weights drape well. • Heavyweight satins have lots of body. • Crepe-back satin is nubby on one side, smooth and shiny on the other. Use either side.	• Traditional wedding gown fabrics • Softer fabrics are perfect for draped styles. • China silk is great for an overskirt as well as for underlining other fabrics. • Heavier types are best used for sculptured shapes like the princess silhouette. • Heavy bridal satin can be enhanced with appliqués and lace cutouts. • Satin has a soft drape and is good for full skirts. • Brocade "walks" well down the aisle and is an excellent choice for an extended train.
Taffeta, Brocade, Metallics, Sequined, and Beaded Fabrics			
Brocade Lamé *Stretch* *Tissue* *Lace* Matelassé Taffeta *Iridescent* *Moiré*	• Moderate to difficult to sew • Fit should not be tight. • Use a "with nap" layout. • Ravel badly—finish seams immediately after cutting out the pieces. • Use very fine, universal or ball-point needles. • Can slip when sewing; baste carefully with soft thread. • Seams may pucker. Taut sew. • Can be difficult to ease sleeve caps into armholes • Needle holes often show if you must rip out seams. • Easily damaged by heat; set iron on **low** temperature. • Check care code; usually dry clean only.	• Dulls shears and needles • Frays, ravels, and snags • Weight of beaded/sequined fabrics may cause the fabric to sag. • Rustles or "talks" when you move. • Moiré has a watermark pattern on it. • Iridescent fabrics have a sheen that changes color with changes in light. • Taffeta creases easily. Press carefully to avoid unwanted creases and press marks.	• Very dramatic fabrics • Choose designs with few seams and/or darts. • Plan to underline/line the garment. • Perfect the fit **before** cutting. • Moiré needs special care when pressing to avoid destroying the watermark design with steam. • Very prone to perspiration stains and water spots • If made of acetate, finger-nail polish remover will dissolve fabric.
Lace Yardage			
Yardage *9", 18", 36", 45",* *54", 60", 72" wide* Trim *⅛"-8" wide* NOTE: For more on lace and lace trims see pages 82-86.	• Usually have no "grain" so you can cut lengthwise or crosswise; some have a direction that requires a "with nap" pattern layout. • Do not fray or ravel • Plan motif placement before cutting. • To protect texture, press carefully.	• Re-embroidered lace has a raised look. • All over laces have no defined pattern. • Galloon lace can be cut apart into two pieces so you can buy half the amount for twice the yardage.	• Suitable for a wide range of gown styles • Lightweight lace needs an underlayer of net or other sheer fabric for support. • Embellish lace with beads or pearls. • Available in a wide range of fiber types

Fabric Type	Sewing/Handling	Characteristics	Uses/Notes
Sheers			

Crisp
  Nylon sparkle
  Organza (polyester and silk)
  Voile
Filmy
  Chiffon
  Crepe chiffon
  Gauze
  Georgette
  Lightweight tricot
  Silks
Soft semi-sheer
  Dimity
  Handkerchief linen
  Organdy (cotton)
  Linen
	• Sewing ease ranges from easy to very difficult.
	• Can be slippery to handle; use a rotary cutter for greater control.
	• Layer sheers in paper or on old bed sheets to prevent slippage while cutting.
	• Use self fabric for bindings, facings, and interfacings.
	• Inner construction must be neat because it shows through. Use French seams if possible.
	• Avoid overhandling.
	• Check care codes; press carefully.
		• Georgette and chiffon are very effective for overskirts.
		• Georgette and chiffon are also available in lovely printed designs.
		
		NOTE: See page 149 for information on veil fabrics such as nettings.
			• Use organza (especially silk organza) as underlining/interfacing in specialty garments.
			• Pattern styles should allow plenty of ease (minimum 8" at hip).
			• Effective used in layers
			• Use for underdress, slip, or lining in any season.
			• Popular for spring and summer weddings
			• Available in both natural and synthetic fibers

Napped Surfaces			

Velour
Velvet
  Cotton
  Rayon
  Silk
Velveteen
	• Great for winter weddings
	• Use *with nap* layout.
	• Not difficult to sew if you use correct techniques, special pressing methods, and take your time
	• Stitching lines show if ripped out, especially in silk and rayon velvets.
	• Before cutting, baste selvages together to prevent slippage.
	• Hand baste darts and seams to prevent slippage.
	• Always hand pick zippers.
		• Color is softer when garment is cut so nap is smooth when stroked from top to bottom. Color is richer when nap is rough when stroked from top to bottom. Hold fabric up to yourself in both directions to decide which "color" you prefer.
		• Fabrics are easily flattened with incorrect pressing.
		• Silk velvet drapes beautifully, is very luxurious, and molds to body curves. It's also pricey!
			• Select simple styles with few seams.
			• Fabrics add visual weight to the body.
			• Satin and heavy, re-embroidered laces work best as accents.
			• Velveteen is not as plush as velvet but is often more affordable.
			• Bias-cut interfacing and lining will be drapier.
			• For crisper, shaped styles, use silk organza for interfacing.

Informal Fabrics			

Cottons and cotton blends
  Eyelet
  Home dec fabrics
  Polished cotton
	• Easy to sew
	• Easy care but may need more pressing if 100% cotton
	• Extra yardage is required for cutting border prints to best design advantage.
	• Check the care code—most are washable.
		• Polished cottons can lose their sheen with washing and overpressing; test first. Take care when pressing to avoid water spots.
		• Fabrics may wrinkle badly.
		• Home dec fabrics have a wide range of coordinating prints.
		• Home dec fabrics may not be washable due to Scotchguard™ treatment.
			• Comfortable in hot, humid weather
			• Recommended for informal weddings
			• Popular for both bride and attendants
			• Most easily converted to daywear for added wear after the wedding

Knits			

Stretch
  Jersey
  Lycra
  Tricot
Moderately stretchy
  Interlock knit
Stable
  Doubleknit
	• Easy and quick to sew or serge; easy to fit
	• Interlocks can run. Place pattern pieces so when cut the fabric would run from the cut edge *up* the body.
	• Use one-way layout and special needles.
		• Sequined fabrics require special sewing, pressing, and care techniques.
		• Lightweight knits drape well.
		• Fabrics are available in many fiber contents. Check care codes for washability.
			• More casual than traditional bridal fabrics
			• Can look more tailored if worn with a jacket or vest
			• Lycra fabrics now available in lamé and sequined versions

CHAPTER 8

Bridal Sewing Basics

You've selected the wedding fabrics so now you just proceed to sew as usual, right? *Wrong.* Most traditional bridal fabrics are relatively delicate and can look worn if handled too much. In general, less pressing and handling results in a more beautiful gown. Less is better.

Bridal wear should be sewn to achieve the loveliest appearance and fit for your special day. Using the right supplies and the best sewing techniques for your fabric will ensure that the dress of your dreams is durable enough to become an heirloom for your children or grandchildren. After one wedding dress I know of was worn by a grandmother, mother, aunts, and daughters, the dry cleaner told the family that they couldn't pass it down again because it wouldn't survive the cleaning process one more time!

Basic Bridal Sewing Supplies

Below is a list of "must haves" for bridal sewing, along with some that "it would be nice to have."

♦ **Thread.** The most important guideline is to buy good quality thread. Bad thread can cause puckered seams and it may break continually while you sew with it. Polyester or cotton-wrapped polyester threads work well on most fabrics. Use an extra-fine thread for lightweight fabrics.

♦ **Silk Thread.** This is one of the best threads for bridal sewing. It is strong and fine and a good choice for basting because it won't leave a mark behind when you remove it. It has natural elasticity, preventing popped seams. The most common size available is 50 weight, but extra-fine silk 100+ weight is available through Things Japanese (page 155). If your seams pucker it may be because the thread is too heavy. Filament (long-fiber) silk thread performs better than spun (short-fiber) silk. Filament is more expensive, as only 20% of a silk cocoon can be used.

Sharp Sewing Machine Needles. As with all sewing, start with a new needle sized for your fabric (smaller numbers are finer needles and are best for fine fabrics).

♦ **Lightweight silkies and sheers:** Fine ball point needles, sizes 8/60, 9/65, or 10/70. If skipped stitches are a problem in your test sample, try a needle for microfibers in sizes 8/60, 10/70, or 12/80.
♦ **Medium-weight satins:** Size 12/80
♦ **Heavy satins and brocades:** Size 12/80
♦ **Velvet and velveteen:** Size 12/80
♦ **Lace:** Size 10/70 or 12/80
♦ **Knits (including Lycra stretch knits):** Stretch needles in size 11/75 or 14/90

Sew a test seam to see if the needle you have chosen is the right size, stitches well, or leaves holes in your fabric when the seam is ripped out. Since many hours of sewing can dull a needle, have a new package of the selected needle type available. If pull lines develop alongside the stitching line, it usually indicates a dull or damaged needle. DON'T SEW OVER PINS! This is the fastest way to dull a needle.

♦ **Fine Hand Needles.** Choose Sharps in size 9 or 10.

♦ **Perfect Sew™ Needle Threader.** Pulls thread through the eye of a needle quickly and easily.

♦ **Extra-Fine Pins.** Buy a new box of 1⅜" (.5mm) steel pins with glass (won't melt) heads. They are a must for delicate fabrics. If pin holes are a problem, use fabric weights when cutting.

♦ **Flower-head Pins.** These 1⅞"-long pins are useful for lace and loosely woven fabrics since they are easy to grasp and won't get lost in the fabric.

♦ **Thimble.** To avoid getting blood on your gown!

NOTE: For "pin prick" blood stains, try this trick. Thread a needle with a double strand of thread. Run the thread through your mouth putting a little saliva on the strands. Then push the needle through the spot on the fabric. Repeat until the blood spot disappears. This works because it contains an enzyme that dissolves blood. *Do not attempt to remove blood with hot water.* It will set the stain instead. A cleaning product called *Z'Out*® works on most fabrics, but TEST FIRST.

♦ **Beeswax** or **Thread Heaven** to run thread through to prevent tangling when hand sewing and to strengthen thread for sewing hooks and buttons. Iron the thread after waxing so the beeswax will soak in.

♦ **Sharp Shears and Embroidery Scissors.** Dull ones snag fine fabrics, can cause pulls, and can result in inaccurate cutting.

♦ **Sta-Tape.**™ Use this lightweight nylon tape to stabilize bias edges such as a V neckline (page 97).

♦ **Small Seam Ripper.** Buy a new one. Ripping is easier with a sharp one.

♦ **Shot-of-Steam Iron.** An old iron that spits water may ruin your gown! Pressing is faster and easier when you have the option of a shot of heavy steam. A **steam generator iron** holds a lot of water, produces lots of steam, and can be used vertically or horizontally.

♦ **Seam Roll and Tailor's Ham for Pressing.** If you don't use these regularly in your sewing room, get them now. They will make all your pressing more professional. Use the sausage-shaped roll when pressing seams open. The garment drops away from the seam edges, preventing seam-edge indentations on the right side of the garment. The ham, shaped as its name implies, duplicates many body curves. Use it for pressing darts and curved seams to perfection.

♦ **Transparent Cotton Organdy Press Cloth.** Use to prevent scorching and overpressing.

♦ **Perfect Sew.** This patented stabilizer used to stiffen fabric for machine embroidery was developed in Australia. For uses see pages 40, 42, and 48.

♦ **Glue.** Use when underlining a dress for instant basting or for gluing on pearls and beads. Recommended types include *Sobo*, *Fabri Tac* (a bridal glue), and Aileen's *Tacky Glue*. They withstand washing and some will withstand dry cleaning. Bridal glue, which dries clear, is best for gluing sequins and pearls to veils.

♦ **Glue Stick.** This handy glue in a tube can be used to position lace before stitching. TEST first!

♦ **Perfect Pattern Paper.** This gridded paper, designed for McCall's by Pati Palmer (page 160), is made for pattern alterations and designing. If your body shape requires tissue-fitting both halves due to obvious differences in size, shape, and contour, trace your pattern pieces onto this tissue.

♦ **Horsehair Braid.** This sheer, bias, synthetic braid is used to add body to edges (see pages 93, 114, 122 and 133). It is available in several widths.

♦ **Organza.** Used primarily for underlining, this sheer fabric can be used for interfacing and binding, too.

♦ **Button Looping.** These crocheted or elastic loops attached to a braid trim are easy to stitch in place. Button looping is available with different loop spacing. If this is your only closure, use non-stretchy loops so your underwear won't be exposed.

♦ **Satin-covered Buttons.** Available in white or ivory, those with fabric shanks are the nicest. Sturdier, satin-covered bustle buttons are also available and can hold the weight of a bustled train.

♦ **Boning.** Strips of plastic or metal encased in fabric sleeves are used for support in strapless or off-the-shoulder styles. Rigalone is a plastic sew-through boning without its own sleeve. The advantage of a sleeve is that the boning can be removed for easier handling while further construction is being done. Metal spiral boning has lateral flexibility as well as vertical.

♦ **Bridal Bra Cups.** These are necessary for backless and strapless styles when extra shaping is needed or underwear might show.

♦ **Lace Trimming Scissors.** Double-nubbed scissors trim away threads and fabric whiskers precisely and easily. Rounded tips protect the fabric.

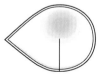

The Nice Extras

♦ **Pattern Weights.** Use instead of pins, especially on metallics and other fabrics that mar easily.

♦ **Sharp Pinking Shears.** Use these for a neat seam finish that won't show through to the outside after pressing.

♦ **Cardboard Cutting Board.** You can pin into this large surface for easier altering and cutting.

♦ **Rotary Cutter and Mat.** Position these so you can cut at a height that gives you leverage yet is easy on your back.

♦ **Cut and Press Board.** Steam or press your fabric, cut, and fuse your interfacings all on one large surface. See *Dream Sewing Spaces* (page 158) for directions for making one, using wood padded with wool or cotton and covered with muslin.

♦ **Needleboard.** Use for pressing velvet and other napped fabrics. It's expensive, but worth it.

♦ **Clean White Terry Cloth Towel.** Place on the ironing board to prevent flattening when pressing beaded fabrics, lace, and other textured fabrics.

♦ **Emergency Spot Remover.** Try vinegar, soda water, *Z'Out*, or dry cleaning solution. TEST!

♦ **French Curve.** Use to true up curved design lines—especially important when you're combining patterns.

♦ **Gathering Foot.** Gathers ruffles quickly and easily. Some can gather and attach the ruffle to the gown in one pass. Practice on scraps first.

♦ **Roller Foot or "Even-Feed" Foot.** This specialty presser foot prevents fabric layers from slipping.

♦ **Rolled Hem Foot.** This is a handy foot for doing rolled hems on full skirts. Practice first!

Tip for a Dressmaker

Invest in some of the specialty feet offered for your sewing machine and learn how to use them correctly. They are available through mail-order sources or from your sewing machine dealer. They can cut down on your labor and will pay for themselves once you have mastered their use.

♦ **Beading or Pearl/Sequin Foot (available for serger and sewing machine).** This foot makes easy work of applying bead strands. The strand is fed through channels under the back and over the front of the foot. It also works for applying heavy wire, cording, fishing line, or strings of sequins to an edge.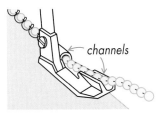

channels

♦ **Pre-cut Bias Silk Charmeuse.** This wonderful new product from Things Japanese (page 155) could save you hours of sewing time. It's available in white in 1¼" and 1¾" widths. Use either the shiny or dull side.

♦ **Double-Stick Basting Tape.** Use this ⅛"-wide basting tape to keep zippers from slipping during sewing. It replaces pin and needle basting—important on fine fabrics that needle mark.

♦ **Drafting Tape.** When both sides of the fabric look the same, mark the wrong side with small pieces of this tape.

♦ **Seam Sealant (*Fray Check®* and *Fray Stop®*).** Use this clear liquid to prevent raveling. It's great for metallics and beaded fabrics that are difficult to finish with more conventional methods.

♦ *Seams Great™* or *Seams Saver.™* Use these precut tricot strips to encase seam edges and narrow seams on fabrics that may irritate the skin.

Getting Ready to Cut and Sew

♦ Oil and clean your sewing machine. Sew test seams on scraps to remove excess oil. Make sure the machine bed and sewing table are smooth and snag free. Clean the bobbin area often.

♦ Wash your hands and clean the work area. Keep the pets away to avoid damaged fabric and take a kitchen break when you need a snack.

♦ Make sure your pressing surface and iron soleplate are clean. Test-press a scrap of your fabric to gauge temperature.

♦ Lay out lace on colored sheets so you can see the designs easier.

♦ Fill several bobbins of your thread color at once.

♦ If possible, organize your sewing and pressing equipment in one area.

Fabric Preparation

Roll the Fabric Onto Tubes

After selecting your fabric and having it cut, have the store roll it, single layer, on a long tube to prevent wrinkles and creases. Napped fabrics such as velvets can be folded, then safety pinned by the selvage to a dress hanger, for a short time.

Cover the fabric with a dry cleaning bag, tissue paper, or a clean sheet to store until you're ready to sew. Keep it away from coffee, food, kids and pets!!

Tip for a Dressmaker

Keep the tubes on which client's fabric is shipped to you to use for fabric that arrives folded from the client. Ask stores to save their empty tubes for you, too.

Preshrink Fabric?

Yes, but only if you and your attendants plan to wash your gowns after the ceremony. If you decide to preshrink the fabric, be sure to do the same with the lining and trim. Make sure that if one attendant pre-washes her fabric, they all do, since it can affect the drapability and color of the fabric. Some fabrics lose their body or sheen when washed.

To preshrink fabrics that are dry-clean-only, arrange them wrong side up in a single layer on a large, flat surface and steam generously. If all of the fabric doesn't fit on the surface at once, steam one section and wait until it is cool and dry before rearranging and steaming the next section.

If your gown has a very full silhouette requiring a lot of fabric, ask the dry cleaner to steam it for you—even if the fabric is washable. There is just too much yardage to handle comfortably and carefully yourself.

Getting Fabric on Grain

To make sure that the fabric's grain is straight, tear or cut along the crosswise grain. If the fabric does not tear easily, cut along the 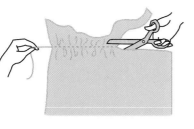 thread line created by snipping into the selvage and pulling a crosswise thread.

Pin the straightened fabric to the cutting board, making sure the crosswise grain and lengthwise grain (parallel to the selvage) are at *perfect* right angles to each other; follow the lines printed on the cutting board.

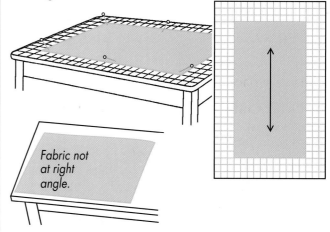

Fabric not at right angle.

If the fabric will not lie with edges at perfect right angles, straighten or "square" the grain by pulling on the short ends until it does.

Another method is to square the fabric by steaming it. Pin the fabric to a pressing table (some people use their beds) and steam. After cooling and drying, the fabric should remain square.

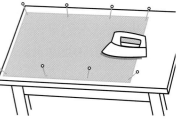

To find the *true bias* in wovens, fold the fabric until the lengthwise grain is parallel to the crosswise grain. The fold line is the true bias.

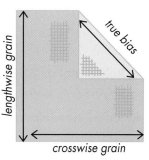

lengthwise grain

true bias

crosswise grain

Layout and Cutting

♦ Find the largest cutting surface possible at a height that won't ruin your back. You've got a lot of cutting to do. Put all the leaves in your dining room table and cover with a gridded cardboard cutting surface if necessary. Raise to the right height by placing a large soup or fruit can under each leg.

For a portable, easy-to-use cutting surface, the Sew Fit cardboard cutting tables are a great investment. They are sturdy and come in two heights.

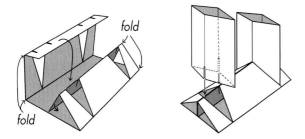

- Don't let your fabric hang off the cutting surface while cutting. If your surface isn't large enough, fold the excess fabric at the end of a table or put it over an ironing board set at table height.

- If your fabric came from a bolt instead of being rolled, make sure the foldline is not permanent. If the foldline is visible, position the pattern pieces to avoid it.

- Pin only within the seam allowances.

- Angle pins toward the center of each piece to eliminate slipping.

- A rotary cutter can be helpful with delicate-surfaced fabrics—it cuts down on the problem of slippage because you are not raising the fabric off the cutting surface as you do when cutting with shears. Remember to use the appropriate cutting mat under your fabric and begin with a new blade. (Sew Fit makes large mats to fit their tables.)

- Cut in long, even strokes when using shears, while holding the pattern flat with one hand, close to the edges. This will minimize the number of pins required to control the fabric.

- Cut nubby, heavier weight silkies single layer if they have a tendency to stick together. Or, put a layer of tissue between the two layers to keep them from sticking.

- For cutting techniques on special bridal fabrics, see "Sewing Special Fabrics," beginning on page 69. For lace cutting techniques, see pages 80-81.

Marking

Test tracing paper and washable or air-erasable ink markers to make sure they won't show or that will disappear if erasable. Other marking methods include:

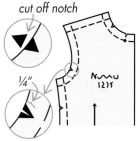

cut off notch

- **Snip marking.** Cut off the protruding notch point, then snip the center of notch ¼" into the seam allowance. On lighter weight silks that ravel badly, test first to be sure that the fabric won't ravel around the snip mark, creating a problem in the seam allowance later. Also, snip center fronts and backs, fold lines, and circles.

- **Pin marking.** The quickest way to mark darts is to put pins straight down through the dart markings. Snip mark the stitching and fold lines at the raw edge. Then lift the pattern carefully, pulling the pin heads through tissue.

snips

Turn the fabric over and put pins in where the first pins are poking through.

Pull apart the fabrics and pin darts in place.

Alternate direction of pins.

- **Thread trace seams and darts.** Use silk thread (page 60), which will prevent permanent indentations when the garment is pressed during construction. It is also easy to remove. You'll be able to see your marks from both sides of the fabric.

With the pattern still pinned to the pattern piece, fold the tissue back along the stitching lines. Using an uneven basting stitch, sew next to the tissue fold through a single layer of fabric. Use one small stitch where seams cross and at dart points.

small stitch where seams cross

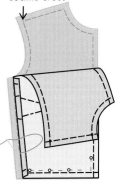

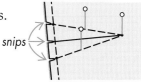

Knots keep thread from pulling through.

dart point

- **Thread Trace Circles and Notches.** Begin in the seam allowance and cross the stitching line. Knot the thread ends to prevent the marks from slipping out of your fabric.

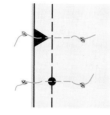

- **Points.** Lay a ⅝"-wide tape measure on the pattern with one edge along the garment raw edge, then lightly mark along the inner edge of the tape with a #2 or #3 pencil. Repeat on the remaining seamline. The pivot point is exactly where the lines cross.

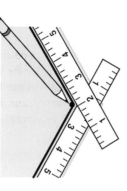

Sewing Seams

- **Princess Seams.** Pin the seams together at each end, then distribute ease in the curve, clipping the inside curve as needed to fit.

- **Taut Sewing.** Hold the fabric taut while stitching, as shown, to prevent puckered seams. *Allow the fabric to feed normally. Don't stretch or pull it.* Loosen the tension on your machine slightly if taut sewing doesn't solve the problem.

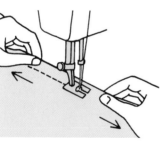

- **Ease.** To make a longer seam fit a shorter one—in a princess seam, for example—machine baste on the seamline to the longer seam and pull up the bobbin thread.

- **Ease Plus.** Ease while you stitch by putting your index finger behind the

---

---

presser foot, then hold the fabric as you stitch. It will bunch up behind the presser foot. When the fabric has bunched to the point of not being able to feed, release some of it, then hold again, repeating as necessary. If you find that it has eased the fabric too much, clip the bobbin thread in a few places to release some of the ease.

Enclosed Seams

- **Trim and Grade Enclosed Seams.** Make sure the widest layer is next to the outside of the garment.

- **Bevel Seams.** Trim, then grade two (or more) enclosed seam allowances to different widths to reduce bulk. With the seam that will be widest (the one that faces the outside of the garment) on the bottom if you are right-handed, or on the top if you are left-handed, turn your scissors to the side (almost flat against the table) and trim the seam so that the widest seam allowance is ⅜" wide. As you cut, the remaining layers will each be slightly narrower due to the angle of the scissors. The heavier the fabric, the more visible the beveled layers will be in the trimmed seam.

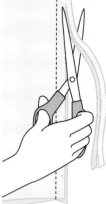

- **Notching Outside Curves.** When sewing outside curves, use small stitches so you can notch almost up to the seamline. Use pinking shears to cut evenly spaced notches. Notching makes room for the seam when it is turned to the inside.

bottom of jacket

- **Clipping Inside Curves.** This helps seams lie flat. *Clip most inward-curving seams such as necklines and princess seams.* Clip ¼" into the seam allowance, alternating clips from one seam allowance to the other to prevent V dents. Clipping at an angle (on the bias) prevents raveling (from **Couture, The Art of Fine Sewing**—see page 158).

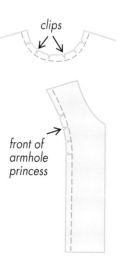

clips

front of armhole princess

For a better edge along an enclosed seam (neckline, armhole, etc.), press the seam open *before* turning the facing or lining to the inside, or use understitching instead.

♦ **Understitching.** First trim, grade, and clip the seam as needed. Then stitch through all seam allowance layers on the facing (or lining) side of a seam, close to the seamline. Smoothing the seam allowances so they are under the facing side, hold the work taut in both hands, pulling to the sides as you stitch from the right side of the facing. Press the facing to the inside from the wrong side first. *Never* press before you understitch. After the edge is turned, press the finished edge.

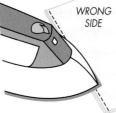

Seam Types

♦ **Hairline Seam.** This seam is even narrower than a French seam and is used on sheer fabrics to create a seam that is barely visible. Use when a French seam is difficult to do—a curved seam for example.

With right sides together, stitch a ⅝"-wide seam. Stitch the seam again with a narrow zigzag next to the original stitching. Trim the seam allowance close to the zigzagging. With the tip of iron, press on the right side to avoid imprinting the seam edge on the right side.

♦ **Rolled Edge Seams.** These decorative seams look gorgeous showing through sheers and laces. Use a texturized thread such as Woolly Nylon for softness and better thread coverage and remember to loosen the tension.

To stabilize loosely woven or stretchy fabrics while doing a rolled edge seam, add a strip of sheer tricot (such as Seams Great) on top of the seam layers. Stitch through all three layers and trim the excess tricot close to the stitching.

♦ **French Seams.** Use on lightweight silks and on sheers. This seam completely encases the raw edge of a fabric and prevents raveling. It is best on straight and slightly curved seams only.

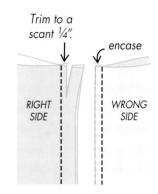

Use standard ⅝"-wide seam allowances. With *wrong sides together*, stitch a ⅜"-wide seam. Press the seam flat to set the stitches. Trim seam allowances to a scant ¼" and press the seam open. Turn so the fabric is right sides together and the stitching line is positioned exactly at the fold. Press flat again. Stitch ¼" from the edge. (*On very ravelly fabrics, trim only a small portion of the seam at a time, while you are stitching the second seam.*) Press the seam flat and then press it to one side.

♦ **Serged Roll Edge.** Serge a rolled edge seam, using a stitch length of 2mm to 2.5mm. Test for strength on fabric scraps first to decide if it's appropriate for your fabric and if you like the appearance. For more information on serged seams, refer to ***Creative Serging*** (page 158). Plain serged seams in sheers can give the illusion of a French seam because the distance between the serger knife and the needle is always the same.

Tip for a Dressmaker

French seams are difficult to alter! Be very sure of the fit before stitching the final seam in a French seam. It is best to baste the seams you plan to finish in this manner prior to your fitting with the client.

Seam Finishes

♦ No seam finish is necessary if the garment will be lined.

♦ For straight seams, try a turned-and-stitched (clean finished) seam. After finishing your seam with this method, do not re-press as it will cause the seam edges to imprint and show on the right side.

Allow 1"-wide seam allowances. Stitch. Stitch ¼" from each seam allowance edge. Turn under along the stitching and edgestitch. Stitch from the right side of the seam allowance for better control of slippery raw edges.

♦ Pink the edges (after the seam is sewn, please). Stitch ¼" away from the seam allowance raw edge first and then pink, or just pink if the second row of stitching will show through to the right side. Pinking both edges together saves time.

Pinked (with or without machine stitching)

♦ For an easy, non-bulky seam finish, apply a seam sealant (such as Fray Check™). Use it sparingly!

Fray-Check™

♦ For a narrow seam finish, stitch through the seam allowances ¼" from the seamline. Or, use a medium-width zigzag or a blind hemstitch for the second line of stitching. Trim close to the second stitching. Press side seam allowances toward the back of the garment and others toward center front or center back.

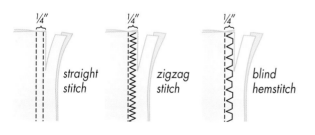

| ¼" | ¼" | ¼" |
| straight stitch | zigzag stitch | blind hemstitch |

♦ For a couture finish, try hand overcasting the seam allowance edges.

hand overcast

♦ Serging seam allowances can add bulk and leave thread indentations when pressing.

Gathering

Gathering is an integral part of most wedding gowns and veils. Don't cheat on gathers—it will show! All gathers should be even and straight. Gathering is done the same way on all but the heaviest fabrics. For most fabrics:

1. Loosen the needle tension one number.

2. Adjust for a longer-than average stitch length. On lightweight fabrics use a shorter stitch length; on heavy bridal satin use a longer stitch. TEST on a fabric scrap.

3. For the first row of gathering, stitch ⅝" from the raw edge.

4. Do a second row of gathering stitches ½" from the raw edge. Begin with the needle inserted *exactly* in line with the beginning of the first stitch in the first row of stitching. This gives you better control of the gathers after you draw up the stitches.

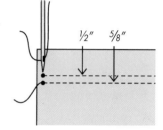

NOTE: If your fabric is heavy or if you think it will be difficult to gather, do a third row of stitching ⅜" from the raw edge.

5. Pull on the bobbin threads only, pulling all of them at the same time. Pull evenly and slowly with the same tension on all threads. Breaking a gathering stitch is frustrating!

6. Adjust the gathers to fit the edge to which they will be sewn. Make sure the gathers are even and exactly where you want them. Straighten them so they look like little pleats.

7. Press the gathers flat *in the seam allowance only.* This will reduce bulk in the seam allowance but will leave the gathers soft below the seam, as they are meant to be.

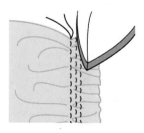

8. Pin the gathered section in place. Stitch from the gathered side on the seamline. Try to keep your needle one thread to the left of the gathering stitches on the seamline. Use your fingers to feed the gathers evenly under the presser foot and to keep them perpendicular to the seamline.

Gathering Very Heavy-Weight Fabrics. Gather by zigzagging over buttonhole twist or pearl cotton in the seam allowance, close to the stitching line. Be careful not to catch the gathering cord in the zigzag stitches. To gather, pull up on the cord. Pin and sew the gathered piece to its mate on the stitching line next to the cord. Remove the gathering cord to avoid a bulky seam.

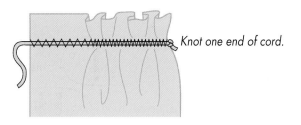
Knot one end of cord.

Pressing

Pressing is absolutely one of the most important steps in any sewing project and pressing delicate-surfaced fabrics demands the most care to avoid damaging the fabric. Now that you're completely panicked, read on!

♦ Use a cotton ironing board cover. Coated covers can add heat and cause shine.

♦ Use the lowest possible setting on your iron. On a 12" square of your fabric, TEST the iron temperature to determine if steam will dull the surface. I usually stitch a curved seam, similar to one that will be in the garment, and test press it thoroughly before proceeding. It's too easy to overpress and, with rare exceptions, you cannot undo it.

♦ Press from the wrong side whenever possible. Always use a see-through cotton organdy press cloth when you must press on the right side of the fabric.

♦ Press seams flat first to remove puckers.

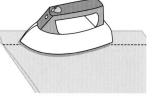

♦ Use a seam roll for pressing seams open. It prevents the railroad track look of seam edge imprints on the outside. The roll allows the iron to touch only the seam.

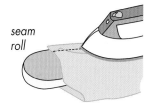
seam roll

♦ To set the press in fabrics made of synthetic fibers such as polyester, press seams open on a seam roll. Hold the iron on the seam with the tip, and open the seam allowance with the fingers of your other hand. After heating the fabric with the iron, press the seam with a wooden clapper to cool the stitches and set the press. The pressed seam should look flat but soft—not hard.

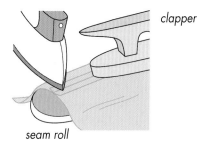
clapper

seam roll

♦ Press darts and curved seams on a ham. Position the dart or curved seam against the curve on the ham most similar to the curve on the body.

♦ To prevent dart ridges, slip paper under the dart edge before pressing.

clean paper strip

♦ You'll get a better edge if you press open all enclosed seams before turning. Use the pointed end of the point presser on the clapper to press open the corners.

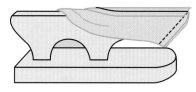

♦ Press princess seams toward the center for less puckering. If the bride is full busted, this is particularly important—the outwardly curving side panel seam would bunch up if pressed open.

CHAPTER 9

Sewing Special Fabrics

Tips for Special Fabrics

By their nature, most bridal fabrics require special handling. Many of them are slippery, making it important to observe some special guidelines to ensure accuracy and make your cutting job easier.

♦ To eliminate slippage while cutting, lay the fabric on top of a sheet placed on your cutting surface, then position the pattern pieces. The sheet will help hold the slippery fabrics. (Obviously, this is not appropriate when using a rotary cutter.) Working on a sheet-covered cutting surface also eliminates snags and ensures cleanliness.

♦ Use extra-fine pins to hold the pattern pieces in place on the fabric. Pin into the seam allowances only. Pins can leave marks on shiny surfaces, particularly noticeable on whites.

♦ Use pattern weights to eliminate the danger of leaving pin marks in delicate fabrics.

♦ Sew on a large surface. Put your sewing machine on a dining room table. Use quilters' gloves, which will help you grab those slippery fabrics and guide them through the machine.

Slippery Silks and Silkies

Seams

♦ To prevent puckers, try taut sewing, (page 65). Use a shorter stitch length (10 to 15 stitches per inch) as well. Also, try an even-feed foot, straight stitch roller foot, or a jeans foot to help prevent the layers from shifting while sewing.

TIP: Seams sewn on the straight of grain are more susceptible to puckering than those on the bias. For very full skirts this is generally not an issue. If your style is a slim skirt, however, you may want to add just a bit at the bottom hem to gradually bring the edge of the seam out to a slight angle. This puts a little bias in the seam for pucker-free stitching. The additional width at the bottom will not be noticeable.

add

♦ Use a new needle in the proper size for your fabric (page 60). TEST on scraps.

♦ If your machine is "eating" your lighter weight fabrics, change to a throat plate with a small round hole plate for all straight stitching. If you do not own such a plate, cover the zigzag hole with Scotch® Brand Magic Transparent® tape, being careful not to cover the feed dogs with it. When the needle goes through the tape it will form a small hole.

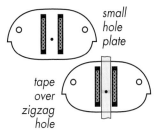

small hole plate

tape over zigzag hole

CAUTION: To avoid bothersome needle breakage, remember to change back to a larger hole plate when zigzagging.

♦ Start stitching right at the edge of the fabric by holding onto the thread tails and pulling it taut as you begin to stitch.

"thread tails"

♦ If puckered seams continue to be a problem, change to a smaller machine needle size. Also, try a finer thread.

♦ If very lightweight and delicate fabrics are too slippery, place tissue paper under the seams next to the feed dog—on top of the seams, too, if needed. Carefully tear away the paper when you are finished sewing.

Tip for a Dressmaker

To start and end a seam the couture way, use a very short (.5mm) stitch. This eliminates the need to backstitch, as stitches this small won't come out by themselves! Seam beginnings and endings will be smoother because there is no thread buildup in one area (as there is when you backstitch). Be aware, however, that these stitches are also very difficult to remove if you need to adjust a seam width!

Pressing

♦ Silk loves steam—a real plus when pressing. Just be careful so you don't get water on it. It will water spot.

Tip for a Dressmaker

For a handy, timesaving reference, make a notebook of test samples of the fabrics you sew on. Once you have determined the appropriate pressing method, use a laundry pen to note the fabric name and fiber content as well as the iron setting, whether you used steam, etc. on the fabric. Saves re-testing similar fabrics later.

Satins and Other Shiny Fabrics

Layout and Cutting

♦ For safety, cut all pieces in the same direction using the "with nap" layout. The surface luster on many satins has an obvious shading, depending on the direction in which you hold it.

To test for shading variation, stand before a mirror in good light and wrap a length of the fabric around your shoulders. Compare the halves. One may have more shine than the other. It will be obvious and you will need to decide which you like best. Mark your favorite direction with an arrow pointing down in the selvage.

If you need to cut your skirt pieces across the entire width of the fabric, you will need to cut the length of satin in half and turn the pieces so that they are both facing in the same direction. First, mark arrows along the selvage for nap direction and mark the right and wrong sides. Cut a length longer than the pattern piece and turn it around.

Seam Finishes

If you fully line your gown, the only seams you'll need to finish will be at the waist, center back, and armhole. The waistline seam can be bound and caught to the lining.

For faille, Habutai, lamé, shantung, most weights of satin, charmeuse, peau de soie, and brocade, try:

♦ **Pinking the edges.** Test to see if it will control raveling satisfactorily.

♦ **Zigzagging.** Set your machine for a three-step zigzag stitch and test on scraps first.

♦ **Serge finishing.** Use a 3-thread overlock or, for less bulk, a 2-thread overedge. If the serging shows as an imprint on the right side of the fabric after pressing, try pressing over a seam roll or use woolly nylon in the loopers for a softer edge finish.

NOTE: If you've made an imprint with pressing by mistake, you can sometimes remove the imprint by lifting up the seam allowance and gently pressing again on the wrong side of the fabric next to the seamline. Then, of course, re-press over a seam roll.

♦ **Binding *with Seams Great™ or Seams Saver.*™** After stitching, trim the seam allowances to ¼". Encase the seam allowances in ⅝"-wide nylon Seams Great™ or Seams Saver.™ Pull the tricot strip slightly taut so it wraps around the seam while stitching, making this a one-step application. (Pull on it before stitching to see in which direction it curls.) Set your iron temperature for nylon before pressing the seams!

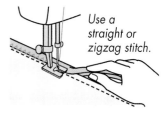

Use a straight or zigzag stitch.

♦ **Hong Kong seam finish.** Cut 1"-wide bias strips of lightweight fabric (lining or silk organza). Sew the bias strip to the seam edge, right sides together, using a ¼"-wide seam allowance. Try not to stretch the bias as you stitch—it can prevent the seam from lying flat. Wrap the seam raw edge with the bias strip. From the right side, stitch in the ditch.

Stitch ¼" in from edge. *Wrap, then stitch in the ditch.*

Pressing

♦ Always test on a scrap before doing any pressing. Start at the lowest steam setting first. Sew a seam and press it with and without steam to see if there are any problems. A too-hot iron can cause over-pressing and dull the surface. If pressing causes puckers, try pinning the pressed seam taut to the ironing board until it is cool.

Metallics, Sequined and Beaded Fabrics

Make a muslin test garment for these fabrics to perfect the fit—even for bridesmaids' dresses. These fabrics tend to be costly and do not stand up well to seam ripping and extensive alterations. (For beaded or sequined lace, see page 88).

Layout/Cutting/Marking

♦ Use a "with nap" layout. It's best to cut the pieces from a single layer of fabric. To be sure you don't miss cutting any part of the dress, make full pattern pieces for those that must be cut on the fold and make duplicate pieces for the left half of the body (pattern pieces are generally printed for the right side of the body). Perfect Pattern Paper (page 61) comes in handy here!

♦ Since metallic fabrics ravel badly and sequins and beads do fall off, cut the fabrics only when you are ready to begin sewing. *Do not over- handle these fabrics.*

♦ For sequined fabrics, arrange the pattern pieces in a with nap layout so the sequins feel smooth as you run your hand from neckline to hemline.

♦ On sequined or beaded fabrics, bind the cut edges with masking tape to prevent the sequins and beads from coming off where their securing threads have been cut.

♦ Don't use your best scissors! Sequins and beads will dull them. Don't use your paper scissors either as they may snag the underlying fabric.

♦ It is *not* a good idea to use snip marks on these more delicate fabrics!

Seams

♦ Ball point or stretch needles are best since the tip will slide between the threads of the fabric and is less likely to break metallic threads.

♦ For sequined fabrics, mark the seamlines with thread tracing (see page 64). *Carefully* remove the sequins from the seam allowances only and set aside. Knot the threads to prevent the sequins from further unraveling.

♦ Plain seams using a longer stitch length work on heavily-sequined or beaded fabrics. Use French seams (page 66) on lightweight metallic fabrics.

♦ Stitch seams using a zipper foot so you can sew next to the beads or sequins.

♦ After pressing the seams open (see "Pressing" below), hand stitch spare sequins over the seamline to cover any "holes."

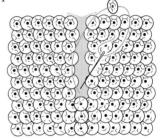

Seam Finishes and Closures

♦ For metallic fabrics, use seam binding, *Seams Great™* or *Seams Saver™* to finish the seams if the garment will not be lined.

Tip for a Dressmaker

Insist that the client have their garment lined! Metallic and sequined fabrics are very scratchy and can easily irritate skin, something the client will not be happy about when the garment is finished.

♦ Turned-and-stitched (clean finished) seams (page 67) are another good choice if the fabric is ravely.

♦ Insert zippers by hand to be sure the metallic threads won't distort.

♦ On sequined fabrics, use loops, hooks and eyes, zippers, or snaps instead of buttons/buttonholes.

Pressing

♦ Do not use steam; it will remove surface shine. Sequins can also melt. Experiment by sewing and pressing a test sample.

♦ Always use a press cloth and press from the wrong side. Pressing on a terry cloth towel prevents flattening the surface.

♦ Try pressing with the handles of your shears, or with the wooden pressing tools used by quilters.

Taffeta

Layout/Cutting

♦ Use a "with nap" layout. Single-layer layouts are best for iridescent or moiré taffeta.

♦ Pin in the seam allowances only or use pattern weights to avoid pin marks.

♦ Use the same cutting techniques as you would for satins, lifting the fabric as little as possible while cutting with good sharp dressmaker's shears. Rotary cutters can also be used on taffeta.

Marking

Test markings on scrap fabrics first. As with most delicate bridal fabrics, mark as little and as lightly as possible.

♦ Thread tracing is the marking method of choice for taffeta.

♦ Snip markings will work unless the taffeta is very loosely woven.

♦ Some taffeta mars easily from a tracing wheel and the carbon may show through. Test and choose an alternate method if necessary.

Seams

♦ Use taut sewing (page 65) with a stitch length of 1.75 to 2mm (10 to 18 stitches per inch). Since puckered seams tend to be a problem, loosen the tension a little. The jeans foot, with its small hole, also prevents puckers.

♦ Try a roller or even-feed foot to help prevent seam slippage while you stitch on taffeta.

♦ Plain seams work well with taffeta. French seams are not recommended as they add too much bulk.

Seam Finishes

Choose from hand overcast, pinked, pinked and stitched, zigzagged, multi-stitch zigzagged, or serged seam finishes. TEST the one(s) you have chosen and press to see if it creates an imprint on the right side.

Pressing

Taffeta glazes (shines and shrinks) with improper pressing so it is especially important to test on a scrap first.

♦ Begin with the lowest setting and do not use steam as it can cause water spotting and will remove the watermark pattern on moiré taffeta.

♦ Light pressing gives the best results.

♦ Press from the wrong side as much as possible.

♦ Use a press cloth when pressing on the right side.

✒ Tip for a Dressmaker

Do not press seams that may need to be altered until after the fitting! It is very difficult to remove press lines from taffeta; if the seam needs to be let out, the press line will show! And stitch marks, too!

Sheers

Crisp-surfaced sheers are the easiest sheers to sew. The soft sheers are the most difficult.

Layout/Cutting

♦ To prevent slippage and make layout easier, secure filmy and soft sheers to tissue paper.

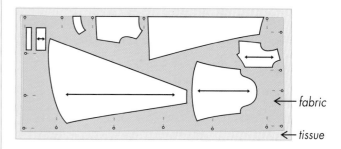

← fabric

← tissue

♦ Use pattern weights instead of pins to help control slippage.

♦ Eliminate facing pieces. Either line to the edge (page 96) or bind (page 73) to finish.

♦ A rotary cutter definitely makes cutting easier, since the cutter holds the fabric down. (When cutting with shears, you lift fabric off the cutting surface, which causes cutting inaccuracies.

- Cut lightweight, soft sheers from a single layer of fabric. Place the fabric on a flannel-backed tablecloth to help control movement when cutting. DO NOT use a rotary cutter!

Marking

Sheers will show everything, so choose your marking method carefully.

- Thread trace (page 60), using silk thread.

- If your fabric does not ravel badly, use snip marks (page 64).

- *Never* use dressmaker's carbon or tailor's chalk. It will show if not completely removed.

Seams

- Do not backstitch. Instead, use a short stitch length at the ends to avoid bulky thread buildup.

- French seams (page 66) are usually the best choice for sheers. Not only are the raw edges completely encased, but the resulting seam is also stronger. Instead of a French seam, you may want to seam the pieces together with a 3-thread narrow-rolled-edge stitch done on the serger. For best results, elongate the stitch.

- Serged seams can look like French seams.

- Since puckered seams are a common problem in sheer fabrics, use taut sewing (page 65).

- Even when using plain seams, the finished seams should be narrow—no wider than ¼".

- Make sample seams to test the various methods and determine which one matches your fabric, fiber content, and overall garment feeling.

- The same seam methods used for slippery silks and silkies apply to sheers (see page 69).

Tip for a Dressmaker

When making French seams, wait until after the final fitting to trim side seams to ¼" and do the final stitching. You may find the bride's weight changes as her wedding day approaches and you may need to make some last-minute adjustments to the fit.

Seam Finishes

- **Use French seams.** See page 66.

- **Pink the edges** (after the seam is sewn, please). You can either just pink, or stitch ¼" away from the seam edge and then pink, but only if the stitching will not show to the right side.

- **Double-stitch and trim.** Straight stitch a ⅝"-wide seam. Stitch again through both seam allowances ¼" from the first stitching. Trim close to the second stitching. Press seam allowances toward the back. On chiffon, apply seam sealant (page 62) sparingly next to the second row of stitching.

- If your sheer fabric is crisp or is not extremely lightweight, serge to finish the seam. TEST on a scrap to make sure the finished seam won't show on the outside.

- Consider leaving the seam unfinished if the sheer is being used as a bodice overlay. If, however, the fabric is going to be a skirt overlay, finishing the seams is a must.

- When hemming full sheer skirts, allow the gown to hang at least 3 days before marking. Use a machine, hand, or serged narrow rolled hem or lettuce leaf rolled hem (pages 134-136).

- A double hem (page 134) works well on sheers, but can only be used on a straight skirt.

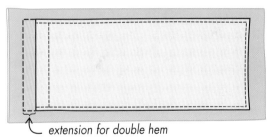

extension for double hem

- Bind the seam to finish the armhole of a garment with a sheer sleeve. Cut 2 bias strips, each 1" wide and a little longer than the armhole seam length. Trim the armhole seam to ¼". Stitch bias to the seam allowance just outside the seamline and turn the binding over the seam edge. Fold under ¼" and slipstitch the fold to the seamline.

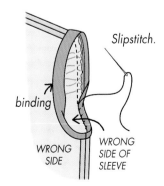

Slipstitch.

binding

WRONG SIDE

WRONG SIDE OF SLEEVE

Pressing

Test the iron heat and steam on fabric scraps. Pressing temperature will vary with fiber content.

♦ Make sure the soleplate of the iron is snag-free and really clean.

♦ Use a cool iron to prevent scorching the fabric.

♦ Depending on fiber content, steam can be used.

♦ Press embroidered sheers face down on a terry cloth towel to protect the texture.

♦ Chiffon has a tendency to shrink when steam pressed so minimize pressing and use a dry iron at a low temperature.

Napped Fabrics

Some of the most elegant gowns are fashioned from velvet or velveteen. Especially wonderful for winter weddings, velvet is surprisingly easy to work with. Most of us have an unnatural fear of velvet, probably from some dress in the past that we've "flattened" with improper pressing and handling.

Velvet is actually woven as a double cloth—that is, two layers of fabric are woven simultaneously, then cut apart to form the napped surface. Velvet is made in weights ranging from very light, such as chiffon to very heavy such as upholstery. You can choose from crushed velvet to panné to velvet with some Lycra in it! The new "burn-out" velvets can be treated like sheers. Fiber content also varies and includes silk, cotton, rayon, acetate, polyester, nylon, and blends of the above.

Layout/Cutting

Most velvets, whatever their fiber content, will shrink at least a little during construction pressing so it's wise to steam shrink yours before cutting. Set your iron on a wool setting and with the *wrong side of the fabric facing up*, steam the fabric generously, holding the iron above the fabric. *Don't touch the fabric or press the iron to it*; you'll crush the pile.

♦ Determine the direction of the nap by brushing your hand lightly over the surface of the pile. If it feels very smooth, you are brushing *with* the pile. If you feel some resistance, you are brushing *against* the pile. See page "Layout and Cutting" on page 70 for a way to see and decide on the pile direction you prefer.

Tip for a Dressmaker

Once you have decided which direction you want to cut your fabric, chalk arrows pointing in that direction on the wrong side of the fabric. This will help you remember to put all your pattern pieces in the same direction and save you from an expensive error.

♦ For the deepest color, cut the fabric with the pile running up. For a lighter look, cut it with the pile running down. Be consistent when cutting out the pattern pieces so the pile runs in the same direction on all pieces. Shading differences on velvet are *very* noticeable—to your guests and to the camera lens!

♦ Line to the edge to minimize bulk. Satin or lace is often used for binding and piping on napped-fabric gowns. You can cut collars, lapels, and cuffs out of them as well for added contrast in the completed gown.

♦ Since velvet and velveteen have deep pile, it's best to cut them single layer, wrong side up, to avoid slippage and inaccurate cutting. Take heed from those who have made mistakes—be sure to flip pattern pieces to get a right and left side for each garment section. Or, make duplicate right and left pattern pieces, using Perfect Pattern Paper (page 61).

♦ Pin pattern pieces to the fabric in the seam allowances only to avoid unnecessary pin marks. Long pins make pinning easier through thick pile.

♦ Cutting with a rotary cutter is *not recommended* for velvet, since you can shear off the nap too much with the sharp blade, resulting in uneven or ragged edges.

Marking

♦ When you must mark the right side of the fabric, use silk thread to avoid making imprints that won't come out.

♦ Use soap slivers or chalk on the wrong side of velvet and mark sparingly.

♦ Snip marks also work.

♦ DO NOT use a tracing wheel—you'll crush the pile of these luxurious fabrics.

Stitching

- Make fitting alterations in the pattern tissue *before* cutting out the garment pieces. Hand baste darts and seams with silk thread to keep fabric layers from slipping while you stitch.

- Set the machine for a straight stitch with 2.5-3mm or 10 stitches per inch.

- Sew in the direction of the pile. Practice stitching on a test swatch before stitching on the garment.

- Loosen the tension slightly and use a roller or even-feed foot, or a zipper foot.

- Slash, trim, and press darts open to reduce bulk. *Slash and trim darts.*

- Use taut sewing (page 65) for pucker-free seams.

- If you are stitching velvet to a smooth fabric such as satin, put the velvet on top to help keep the underlayer from creeping while you sew. Pin generously or hand baste the layers together first!

Pressing

As always, test press on a large scrap. Most velvets like steam; all of them are allergic to having the iron placed directly on their surface.

Tip for a Dressmaker

If you work with a lot of velvet/velveteen fabrics or think you will, invest in a good velvet needle board. They are quite expensive but will cut your pressing worries to almost nothing. To use, put the napped side of the fabric against the needles of the board and press as you would any other fabric.

- Place the RIGHT SIDE of the fabric on a large scrap of the napped fabric. Hold the iron above the fabric and steam the seam or dart. Finger press the seam open with your fingers and allow the fabric to cool completely before moving it.

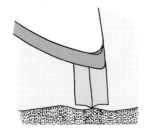

NOTE: On extra-heavy fabric, loosely catchstitch the seam edges to the inside of the garment.

TIP: If you are working with silk, rayon, or acetate velvet, it is possible to complete the entire garment without ever using an iron. Finger pressing does the trick! This does not work on velveteen, however. (Thanks to Diane Hoik for this tip!)

Seam Finishes

Choose from: unfinished (especially if the gown is to be completely lined), pinked, pinked-and-stitched, multi-stitch zigzag, serged, tricot-bound, and Hong Kong finishes. Test for your particular fabric weight and drape.

Informal Fabrics

These fabrics are a delight to handle and you are probably familiar with most of the techniques required. Some of the cottons you may use for bridal sewing, however, do require a little extra thought.

Always preshrink cotton fabrics by laundering them following the care instructions provided on the fabric bolt.

Layout/Cutting

- If you have chosen a border print, you'll need to lay the pieces out on the crosswise grain instead of the usual lengthwise straight of grain. Triple check hemlines before cutting to be sure they will match when stitched and be sure to flip pattern pieces to cut right and left halves.

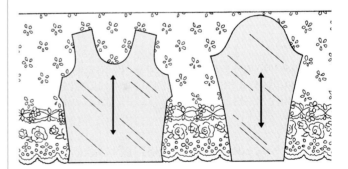

- Use a "with nap" layout for fabrics with one-way printed designs.

Marking

All marking methods work well, but test first to be sure that show-through (especially on white) is not a problem.

Seams

Generally, no special sewing techniques are required for these fabrics. However, if you are sewing on an open-textured or eyelet fabric, tape the toes of the presser foot to avoid catching them in the fabric.

Scotch Brand Magic Tape® closes the presser foot toes.

Pressing

The high cotton content of these fabrics makes them easy to press. However, if they are synthetic blends, be more careful. Always test press on a scrap first.

Seam Finishes

Choose from: serged, pinked, stitched-and-pinked, zigzagged, or unfinished edges. If left unfinished, be sure to line the garment for a neat appearance.

Knits

Do not pre-treat knits following the fabric care instructions; laundering knits relaxes the fabric and removes finishes, both of which can cause skipped stitches. Steam press knits that will require dry cleaning to "preshrink" them.

Layout/Cutting

Some knits have a more pronounced rib that can affect the color so it's important to use a "with nap" layout to ensure a uniform color shading.

♦ Check for a permanent crease line and plan to cut around it if one is present.

♦ To avoid stretching, do not allow the fabric to hang off the end of your cutting table.

♦ The majority of knit fabrics stretch the most across the width of the fabric. Since the stretch should go around the body for the most comfortable fit, be sure to lay out patterns with the grainline arrow on the *lengthwise grain*.

♦ If the selvage is uneven, use a rib as a guide for the straight of grain.

Marking

Use your favorite marking method—pins, marking pens, clipping (only on knits that don't run), chalk, thread tracing, tracing wheel and carbon, or a soap sliver.

Seams/Seam Finishes/Hems

Try to fill your bobbin with your machine set on a slow speed to cut down on stretching the thread. When the seam is stitched, overstretched thread has a tendency to relax, causing puckered seams. Use a new stretch needle, size 11/75, for most knits.

♦ Use taut sewing (see page 65) to further prevent puckered seams.

♦ Seams can be serge finished, pinked, or left unfinished since most knits do not fray. Serging is often the best and fastest method for seams in knits because it is a flexible stitch, appropriate for stretchy fabric. Remember, though, that you will need to make sure the gown fits *before* serging since the seam will be trimmed, leaving no room for letting out the seams later.

♦ Stabilize shoulder seams with seam tape or clear elastic to eliminate stretching during wearing.

♦ The best hems for knits are: stretch hems, serged-and-topstitched, machine blindstitched, zigzag blindstitched, and double-needle topstitched. One of the decorative stitches on your machine may also be appropriate. Experiment!

♦ Always let a knit garment hang for at least 24 hours before marking the hem.

♦ For a really fine finish, hem the garment by hand. Use a crewel needle and blindstitch or catchstitch, keeping the stitches loose to avoid unsightly pulling on the right side of the garment.

Pressing

♦ Test press first. Do not move the garment until it has cooled completely to avoid stretching.

♦ For very ribbed knits, use a velvet board or thick terry cloth towel on the ironing board to avoid flattening the surface.

♦ Synthetic knits are easily damaged by too much heat—especially tricot, which can melt. Use just enough heat to do the job.

Alicyn Exclusives© courtesy of The McCall Pattern Company

CHAPTER 10

All About Lace

Lace Selection

Elegant and intricately beautiful, lace has long been synonymous with weddings. It has been in existence for thousands of years and has been used to decorate garments since the Renaissance.

If you fall in love with a certain lace even before you've chosen your pattern or the other fabrics for your gown it will dictate all remaining choices.

Choosing the Right Lace for Your Gown

Lace comes in a variety of textures, designs and weights; it ranges in price from inexpensive to more than $350 per yard. Beaded lace, scalloped border lace, re-embroidered lace, all-over lace, and lace trim are widely available. Laces are sheer or semi-sheer, with a floral or geometric motif on a mesh background. They are constructed with knotted and twisted threads, so either the crosswise or lengthwise grain can be used. The right side of the lace has a more pronounced thread outline around the motifs.

If you find a lace you love, but it is too expensive for your budget, take heart! With some careful planning, you can adorn your gown with as little as one yard of lace by cutting out motifs and using them on the bodice, the skirt, or on the sleeves. This can be even more effective than an inexpensive lace used in large quantities. If you cannot afford a beaded lace, you can bead it yourself (page 47).

Check out current bridal magazines for ideas for using lace in your gown and take your favorite design ideas to the fabric store with you. Study the laces available to determine how you might be able to use them to create the look you want.

When combining lace with another fashion fabric in your gown, select similar textures and weights. For lightweight fabrics such as crepe or crepe-back satin, choose Chantilly or Peau d'Ange. For heavier weight fabrics such as bridal satin, velveteen or peau de soie, choose Venice, Alençon

or Cluny. Compare the lace and gown fabric under bright natural lighting to check the color match.

Look at lace against a dark contrasting background to see the design, then on a white or natural background to see which best shows off the lace.

Lace Categories

Lace is either *imported* (made in Europe, primarily France) or *domestic* (made in the U.S.A.).

Imported laces are relatively narrow—2" to 6", 9" to 18", and 36" wide—so can only be used for bodices or sleeves, or you can use portions of them for appliqués or trim. They are generally silk or cotton and re-embroidered with a cord or ribbon outlining the design. Exquisitely designed with many floral motifs widely spaced on a fine net ground, imported laces have a soft, supple hand. Because the re-embroidering is hand clipped between each motif, they are more expensive than domestic laces.

Domestic laces are lovely but more affordable copies of their re-embroidered counterparts. The designs are more closely spaced, less sheer, and not as intricate or as three-dimensional as the imported laces. Because they are less expensive and come in wider (up to 102"), all-over patterns, domestic laces can be used extensively in your gown styling.

Tip

When ordering by mail, try to order the lace and fashion fabric from the same company to help ensure a better color match.

Tip for a Dressmaker

Have lace samples and photos of how other brides have combined fabric and lace available in a notebook. Show it to your customer so she can visualize possibilities for her own gown design.

How Lace is Sold

All-over Lace. A wide lace with two finished edges and the same motif repeated throughout; usually made of synthetic fibers such as polyester and nylon.

Appliqué.
A single lace motif purchased individually or separated from lace yardage.

Sets. (*above and to left*) The same lace pattern available in several widths, or a combination, one plain (flat) and one re-embroidered.

Beading. Lace strip with finished button-hole openings through which ribbon is laced *prior* to attaching to gown.

Clipped. Individual lace motifs are separated at regular intervals from one another on a net background.

Flounce. Lace with one straight and one scalloped edge; usually 18" to 36" wide.

Galloon. Any lace with two decorative edges. It is versatile and economical because you can cut it apart to create two or more design strips or motifs to use as lace appliqués.

cut apart to create two design strips.

Strip. The entire yardage length available in quality lace, 4½ to 6 yards long. (Usually Alençon.)

Trim. Narrow laces (up to 6" wide) available as *edging* (one straight and one decorative finished edge); *insertion* (two finished straight edges used to insert in a seam or on top); *ruffling* (pre-gathered or pleated); *galloon* (two scalloped edges—see below left); and *finishing lace* (two finished edges).

Types of Laces

Alençon (A-LON-SON). Free-form pattern outlined with a satin cord. Available in trim or yardage. Cut apart for individual motifs.

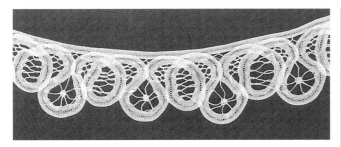

Battenberg. A heavy lace made with patterns of linen braid and tape connected with thread bridges.

Chantilly.
A delicate overall floral pattern outlined with a fine thread.

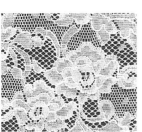

Cluny (CLOO-NEE).
A heavy, cotton-like lace with the look of hand crochet.

Eyelet. Fabric with open embroidery designs; usually cotton or cotton blend.

Peau d'Ange (PO DONJ).
The French word for angel skin. This type of Chantilly lace has heavier floral patterns and is made with flossier yarn, giving it a soft, supple hand. It is most often used for appliqués.

Schiffli.
A fine net embellished with machine embroidery that looks like hand embroidery. The same embroidery can also be done on organza.

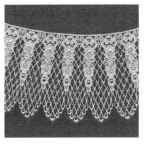

Venise (VE NEEC) or **Guipure** (GEE PYURR). Lace without a net background. Made from heavy yarns with motifs joined with thread bridges. Widths range from ½" to 45". The two photos here give an example of the broad range of designs that are available.

Ideas for Using Laces

Look through magazines, books, and pattern catalogs for ideas and inspiration. Clip clip out examples for your files or bulletin board.

Sewing with Lace

Sewing with lace is not difficult, just different. Its looks are deceiving—lace is anything but delicate. It is made to be cut apart, shaped, stitched, and manipulated—and it does not ravel.

Fabric and Pattern Preparation

Do you need to pre-shrink your lace fabric? NEVER (unless it is dirty, such as an antique lace you want to incorporate into your gown). If lace must be washed, do it very carefully by hand, or dryclean if necessary. TEST a scrap.

After fitting your pattern, make a duplicate pattern of all pieces that will be cut from the lace so you can cut them from a single layer of fabric. Use white tissue or the gridded tissue Perfect Pattern Paper (page 61). You can see through them so lace pattern placement is easier.

TIP: Tape the tissue paper to the fold line of a half pattern piece. Fold the pattern over and trace around the seam edges to outline the other half. For pattern pieces that don't have fold lines, simply cut another pattern out of tissue. Mark the right and left on the right side of each tissue so you won't cut two left sides.

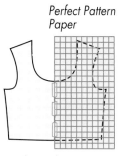

Perfect Pattern Paper

Flip and trace.

Layout and Pinning

When working with lace, layout is the most important step—you don't need an engineering degree, but careful planning is a must. Always place lace on a dark surface so the motifs are easy to see. Try doing the pattern layout with the lace on top of a dark-colored sheet.

Play with the tissue-paper pattern pieces until you're satisfied with the motif placement. The larger the motif, the more crucial this placement is. If the lace has a large floral motif, place the pattern carefully to avoid a "bulls-eye" effect at the bustline.

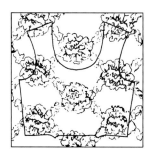

Decide whether you prefer your lace motifs running horizontally or vertically. Cut all lace pieces in the same direction. Since laces are textured, regular short pins will get lost. Pin instead with 1" to 1½"-long pins with large colored heads. They're easier to see.

Tip for a Dressmaker

Lace has no true grain and can therefore be cut in any direction. It is easiest to draw a portion of the lace design at pattern edges that need to be matched (similar to the technique for matching plaids). Then you can manipulate the pattern pieces all over the lace yardage to maximize usage. See directions on page 81 for lapped seams.

Cutting Lace

Cutting for Conventional Seams

For all over lace patterns and those in which the motif pattern is not pronounced, *conventional seams* as indicated on the pattern are fine, but increase the seam allowances to 1" wide.

TIP: Be careful with tips of scissors, as they can snag or tear the net backing on lace. See page 61 for special lace cutting scissors.

Cutting Lace Motifs

Whether you want to create appliqués or sew lapped seams in your lace, you need to know how to cut around lace motifs. You will also need to decide on your seam finish before you cut.

You'll need a pair of very sharp embroidery scissors. Trim around the lace motif pattern, leaving a short "whisker" of thread around the lace. Don't worry. This is not a homemade look. Whiskers are actually a sign of an expensive, imported lace. And, the lace won't ravel like other fabrics.

Expensive, re-embroidered laces are the easiest to clip because their motifs are clearly outlined in cord. Inexpensive lace and all-over patterns require closer inspection to determine where to cut.

Tip for a Dressmaker

Since lace is expensive, you will want to have your client purchase the least amount she needs—not even an extra ¼ yard for "insurance." To help, lay out the pattern pieces at the store right on the fabric, paying attention to motif placement and matching challenges. Then just have the salesperson cut the amount you've measured.

Cutting for Lapped Seams

The other type of seam treatment for lace is called the "lapped" or "invisible" seam. Use this technique when sewing on heavier, re-embroidered laces, especially for conspicuous seams such as yokes, shaped bodices, center backs and fronts, and skirt side seams. With this technique the seams are disguised by lace motifs.

Pattern layout takes longer for this technique but the professional look is worth it! (Don't take the time to match all seams—it will be impossible to do this anyway. Use conventional seams in less conspicuous areas such as at the shoulders, bodice, and sleeve underarm seams.

1. Work on a dark background. After positioning the pattern on the lace as desired, trace the lace pattern along the pattern tissue edge. Use this as a guide for the layout of the corresponding seam. When lapped, the two seams should match.

trace

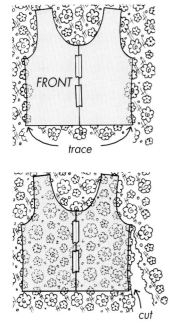

cut

Position back to match side seam motifs on front.

2. Cut around the motifs *outside* the traced seamline.

3. Cut the back to match and continue the motif.

4. Lap the front over the back. Stitch together with a short, narrow zigzag stitch.

Match designs when lapping front over back.

NOTE: Use this motif overlap method along the center back to cover the zipper and on all seams and darts.

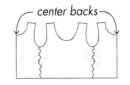

center backs

Marking Lace

Transfer markings with tailor tacks and basting thread in a contrasting color. Don't bother with snips and notches—they are impossible to see in the intricate patterns of most lace. (For more on marking darts, see page 86.)

Stitching on Lace

Set your machine at 12 stitches per inch (2mm). (The more open the lace, the closer the stitches should be.) To eliminate puckering, stitch slowly and use taut sewing (page 65). Sew by hand on all heavier laces.

If the lace pattern is quite open, you may have problems with the presser foot catching in the mesh. To prevent this, wrap tape around the front of the foot as shown on page 76. You can also try using a small-hole needle plate, except, of course, when zigzag stitching.

If the lace continues to get caught on the foot or in the feed dogs, place tissue paper on both sides of the seam before stitching. Carefully tear away the tissue after stitching. Use this as a last resort—it's very time consuming and it may be difficult to remove all the tissue. Tweezers help!

photo courtesy of The McCall Pattern Company

Lace Appliqués

Attach lace motifs to the bodice and sleeves while the dress is still unassembled. Thread trace the seamlines to ensure motifs don't extend into the seam allowances. If underlining, do that first. Then catchstitch the embroidered motif in place.

NOTE: When cutting beaded lace or appliqués apart, glue threads to the back with bridal glue so the beads or sequins do not fall off.

Unless you decide to fuse lace motifs in place (see below), hand baste them to the fashion fabric only, then attach them, using one of the following methods:

♦ Use a narrow zigzag stitch.

♦ Use your machine's built-in *blind-hem stitch*, experimenting on a scrap first to determine the proper width of the left-swing stitch and the length of the straight stitches in between. Lightly glue-baste the motif to temporarily hold it to the bodice. Position the presser foot at the outside edge of the motif so that the hook portion of the hem stitch just catches the edge of the lace motif.

♦ Fuse lace appliqués in place. Before choosing this method, *test the fabric and lace for heat sensitivity.* Use a press cloth to prevent the fusible web from bleeding through the open areas of the lace onto the soleplate of the iron.

1. Use paper-backed fusible web. Cut it about ¼" smaller than the motif size.

2. Iron the paper-backed web to the wrong side of the motif. Peel away the paper.

3. Place the motif on the garment piece and press lightly.

TIP: To create larger motifs, sew several smaller ones to English netting. Trim excess netting away from the outside edges.

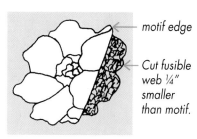

motif edge

Cut fusible web ¼" smaller than motif.

For a trapunto effect, tuck a small amount of fiberfill between the appliqué and the garment layer before stitching the appliqué in place.

Insert fiber fill or cotton ball.

Lace Cut-Aways

Another nice effect is to cut away the fashion fabric behind the lace for a see-through look. This is exceptionally nice on sleeves and the back of a train, for example.

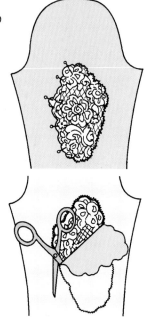

1. Pin the motif in place. Do not glue-baste in this case, since you'll be removing the fabric behind it!

2. Zigzag around the edges of the motif, using a wide, medium-length stitch on the machine.

3. Using small, sharp embroidery scissors and working on the wrong side, cut away the fashion fabric behind the motif. Be very careful not to cut the lace.

Attaching Trims and Edgings

In-the-Seam Application

1. Gather the trim, if necessary. Some lace trims have gathering threads woven in along the upper straight edge, especially imported French lace trims, making it easy to gather the lace evenly. (Also see "Applying Gathered Lace and Trim" on page 84).

2. Sew the trim to the right side of one garment piece along the seamline.

5⁄8"

3. With the piece with the lace attached on top, place seam edges right sides together; pin. Stitch the seam, sewing along the bobbin stitching line from the previous step.

Edge Application

1. With right sides together, stitch lace or trim to the seamline of the garment section.

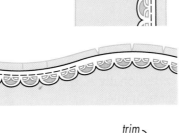

seamline

2. Turn and press.

NOTE: Clip inward curves and notch outward curves before turning. Topstitch to hold the trim in place.

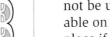

3. Edgestitch.

trim

4. Trim seam or hem to within ¼" or closer to the edgestitching.

NOTE: If the edge is already finished, lap the finished edge over the trim and stitch close to the edge.

Flatlock Lace Trim to an Edge

1. Set your serger for a 2- or 3-thread stitch. With lace and fabric right sides together and with trim on top, flatlock, trimming away seam allowances or hem.

NOTE: If fabric is ravelly, press under the seam allowance and flatlock without cutting the fold.

press under

2. Pull on the trim until the edge is flat. You'll see a ladder of stitches on the right side.

TIP: If the serger stitches hang off the edge, the seam will pull flatter. Make a test sample.

Special Tips for Skirt Hems

Apply lace edging after the dress is completed and the hem length has been determined

♦ Once the hem is complete, pin the lace to the bottom of the gown with the scalloped edge extending slightly beyond the finished edge. Work with the gown over an ironing board—a flat work surface that you can adjust to a height that suits you and allows the skirt to hang free.

♦ If the lace is very delicate or has a lot of curved edges, it may be easier to catchstitch the lace by hand. If the lace is heavy or wide, it may be easier to machine baste it in place. A long basting stitch is usually sufficient because the lace will not be under stress. Use the longest stitch available on your machine. You can zigzag the lace in place if you prefer.

♦ Apply lace to the finished edge of the skirt before lining. If necessary, baste the skirt to the bodice to mark the hem first.

Apply Straight Lace to a Curved Edge

To make straight lace curve, you will need to cut around the motifs and overlap as shown for lapped seams on page 81. To camouflage curves, choose a lace trim with lots of pattern detail.

Using your steam iron, shape the trim to the curve, stretching the outside edge and easing the inside edge. On more severe curves, the lace will need to be positioned and slashed in the following manner prior to stitching.

1. Pin the trim to the edge, clipping into the design *around motifs* at regular intervals where there is excess fabric.

2. Overlap slightly and pin in place, using your steam iron to curve the lace as much as possible to match the garment curve. Stitch to the gown by hand or machine, being careful not to pull the inside edge as you stitch.

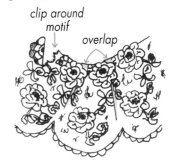

clip around motif

overlap

Applying Straight Lace to Corners

Practice this goof-proof mitering technique for turning perfect outside corners.

1. Fold the lace at the point of the miter as shown.

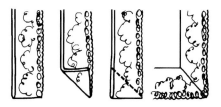

2. Bring the folded edge over to the outside edge of the trim, forming a 45-degree angle. Crease to form a guide for stitching. Unfold and stitch along the crease, backstitching at both ends of the seam.

3. Trim away the excess lace ⅛" from the stitching; press seam open.

Applying Gathered Lace and Trim

If lace is not pre-gathered, buy 2½ to 3 times the required length. If there is no gathering thread in the lace heading, place a heavy thread such as buttonhole twist on the heading and stitch over it with a long, wide zigzag stitch (page 68). *Do not catch the thread in the stitches.* Secure one end of the heavy thread and draw up the other to gather.

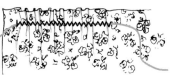

gathering lace

Divide and mark the lace and the edge to which it will be sewn into equal sections. Match marks and adjust gathers to fit, placing more gathers at corners. Enclose the gathered trim in a seam or place the edge under a turned seam allowance. Hand or machine stitch in place.

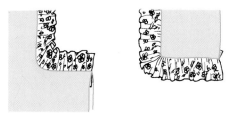

Make Heirloom Yardage from Lace Trim

Making your own heirloom yardage using lace insertion is a beautiful alternative to purchased lace yardage, particularly for a Victorian style gown. It is appropriate for the bodice, sleeves, and as trim in other areas of the gown—and you can even make a complete gown from it. Heirloom yardage is usually made using cotton batiste or organdy, or other lightweight wovens. Some fabrics, such as satin, may be too heavy for the look you are trying to achieve. Make a test sample first.

If you plan to use heirloom lace for your gown, make the lace yardage first by sewing rows of insertion together (and adding other trims as desired). Then position and cut the desired garment pieces from the new yardage. (You may want to read more about making heirloom lace in one of the many books available on French Hand Sewing, such as those by Martha Pullen. Creating heirloom lace is also discussed in **The Serger Idea Book** and **Creative Serging** (page 158).

Attach Flat Insertion to Your Fabric

1. Position lace on the right side of the fabric and pin in place. Topstitch over the edge with a narrow zigzag stitch.

2. Cut away the fabric underneath close to the stitching lines. You can also serge the lace into place, as described on the previous page. Press the serged seam toward the garment fabric and topstitch along the lace to hold the seam in place.

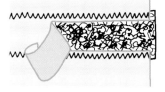

Overlap Rows of Lace or Lace and Fabric

Another way to use trim is to create new lace yardage with overlapping rows of lace trim or alternating rows of lace and fabric. Use for the sleeves or bodice of your gown. As with heirloom lace, you make the lace first, then cut the garment pieces from the new lace fabric.

Overlap the depth of the scallop and straight stitch along the straight trim edge, or follow the scallop.

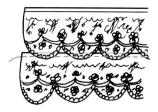

Or, for an open airy look, overlap just slightly; straight stitch in place.

Using Scalloped Lace

Lace yardage often has a lovely scalloped edge that you can use to enhance your design. For example, you can cut it from the yardage in the desired width and apply it as you would other lace trim. This is one way to guarantee that your trim matches your lace.

Scalloped Lace On V Necklines

1. Finish the neckline edge of the bodice to the point of attaching the bodice to the skirt.

Tip for a Dressmaker

Treat the skirt and bodice sections separately for as long as possible. Attach them when you can't proceed any further with the pieces apart. This helps eliminate the problem of overhandling the fabric.

2. Put the bodice on yourself or a dress form, then pin the scallop trim in place. (It's easier to work "in the round" than flat.) Begin positioning the lace by placing scallops so that they meet at the center of the V as shown and work from the center out to the shoulders. Keep the inner points of the scallops just past the edge of the neckline and clip where needed to spread or overlap. Smooth and flatten the trim so that it lies flat against the body and pin securely.

3. After pinning the lace in front, bring it around to the back and leave a short length at each end. (You may or may not end with a complete scallop at center back. You'll need to judge, as the designer of the dress, how you want to complete the back.) Consider the following:

   ♦ If a scallop design is very close to being complete at the center back opening, you can "fudge" by slightly squeezing the scallops around the neckline until a complete scallop ends at center back. If it's a small amount, it won't be noticed.

   ♦ If the scallop pattern is way off, try to adjust the lace so that you have one-half of a complete scallop on each side of the center back.

   ♦ If there's just no way that you can even out the scallops at the meeting point and you aren't satisfied with the way the scallops will look, examine the trim to see if you can tuck it or spread it by cutting the scallops apart and overlapping them as needed to make them fit.

4. Stitch the trim in place, making sure that you catch each scallop point to the bodice edge.

Scalloped Lace Along a Scoop or Round Neckline

1. Complete step 1 as described for the V neckline and put the bodice on yourself or a dress form.

2. Position the trim at the center front with the motif centered or with two motifs meeting at center front. Try both to see which one looks best.

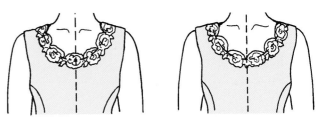

3. Once you've determined where the first scallop will lie, pin and shape the trim around the neckline, following the directions above for "Scalloped Lace On V Necklines."

NOTE: The only time you may be able to attach lace to a neckline without clipping or shaping in some way is when working with an off-the-shoulder style.

Scalloped Lace at the Waist

For a unified design, you might want to use scalloped lace at the waistline in addition to the neckline. The scalloped edge should point toward the floor, not toward the bodice. If the scallops on the neckline meet at the center of the neckline V, then they should do the same at the point of a waistline V.

If the scallops are centered on a round neckline, then they should be centered at the waistline. In other words, scallops should line up visually

from neckline to waistline. Stitch the bodice to the skirt, complete the closure and *then* add the scalloped lace to the finished waistline seam in the following manner:

1. Pin the trim to the gown, beginning at center front and working around to the back. Because the waistline is larger than the neck, you'll have more scallops.

2. Try to match the lace ends to the positioning of the neckline scallops—if you have half scallops at the center back at the neckline edge, you should have half scallops at the back waistline too. If it's not possible, do the best you can—the neckline will be more noticeable than the waistline.

3. Hand stitch the trim to the gown.

Special Lace Techniques

Included in this section are additional sewing techniques for handling lace in bodices and skirts, as well as tips for working with beaded or sequined fabrics.

Sculpting Lace

One of the beautiful aspects of working with the heavier laces like re-embroidered Alençon is that they can be shaped and darted—almost invisibly—for a form-fitting shape.

Sculpted Darts

1. Thread trace the legs of the dart onto the lace garment piece. Clip up to the point of the dart, following the lace motif outline.

2. Overlap the thread traced legs of the dart and pin in place.

3. Using a long, narrow zigzag stitch and working on the right side of the garment, stitch along the outline of the lace motifs (as for an overlapped seam as shown on page 81).

4. Press the area over a ham to shape, then trim away the excess lace on the underside.

Sculpting a Lace Bodice

Lace can be sculpted right on the body by clipping the lace where needed, overlapping to shape, and pinning in place. If you are making the gown for yourself, have a friend help you shape it to you (or use a dress form). If you are underlining the bodice, pin the lace directly to the underlining; if not, wear a close-fitting T-shirt and have your friend pin the lace to it as she shapes it to your figure.

NOTE: Do the front and back in two separate steps or you won't be able to take off the shirt!

Clip and lap the lace motifs so that the clipping is invisible. Pin and baste to secure.

On heavier laces, hand whipstitch the shaped lace in place. On lighter weight laces, remove bodice and machine stitch the lace in place. Trim away the underlayer.

For back closure information see "Closures," beginning on page 111.

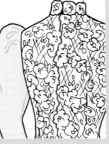
Sculpting Lace to a Bodice Neckline

1. Cut the scalloped edge from lace yardage in the desired width along the desired lace motifs.

2. *With right sides up*, pin lace along the finished neck edge and back opening, with the inner point of the scallops extending slightly past the finished edge onto the garment. Miter corners as needed (page 84). Hand baste lace in place, clipping, lapping, and/or easing as needed.

3. Arrange lace on the front and back (and yoke if your pattern has one, having lace cover the yoke seam). Place scallops over the neckline and extend below the bustline as desired. Hand baste in place, clipping, easing and overlapping as necessary to fit curves. Mirror the lace placement on right and left sides for a balanced and professional design.

4. If necessary, cut and separate appliqués and motifs from lace and fill in open sections. Hand sew in place.

A Bodice of All-Over Lace

1. Loosely position the pattern pieces on the lace. Be careful not to place large motifs at the point of the bust—to avoid the "bulls-eye" look. On the main sections of the bodice such as center front, center back, or sleeve, the largest lace motif should be carefully centered.

2. Underline the lace, using organza or fine netting to preserve its sheerness. Use lining fabric in a color to match the lace or use a flesh-tone lining.

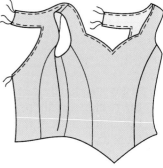

TIP: If the neckline or back keyhole need a little extra help to hug the body and prevent gapping, machine-baste close to the edge and pull up basting threads to ease the neckline to fit. Tie off threads. Then apply the lace. The lace stitching will hold the easing in place.

A Skirt of All Over Lace With a Scalloped Border

A scalloped lace hem works best with a gown that has a straight or only slightly curved hemline.

1. Determine the exact finished hem length and mark it across all skirt pattern pieces, marking parallel to the original hemline.

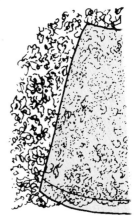

2. Center pattern pieces over the major motifs. Align the center front and back seams perpendicular to the lower scalloped edge.

3. Align the hemline with the scalloped edge, starting from the center front and back seams and working toward the side seams.

4. If the hemline is slightly curved, clip the lace between motifs from the side seams to the point on the hem where it begins to curve.

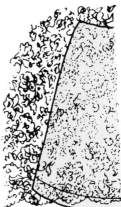

5. Overlap the motifs until the scalloped edge follows the curved hemline. It may be necessary to take tiny snips along the cut edge of the lace so the section will lie flat.

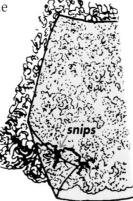

6. Baste the repositioned lace in place and check the hem length and curve. Secure with hand or machine stitching. On heavier textured laces it's easier to sew laces with a hand whipstitch than by machine.

7. Cut away excess lace below the scallop curve. The lace will not match perfectly, but the seam will be well hidden in the lace texture.

Handling Beaded or Sequined Lace

1. Arrange the beaded or sequined lace in a single layer with the beads or sequins facing up. When cutting pieces to be placed on the fold, cut the pinned piece first, stopping at the fold line, then flip the pattern, pin, and cut the second half.

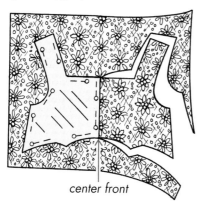

center front

For pieces marked "Cut 2," be sure to cut one piece with the printed side of the tissue facing up and one with the print facing down. Whenever possible, cut around rather than through the beads and sequins, as they can easily damage or dull your shears.

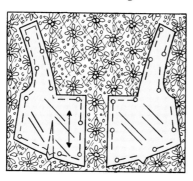

2. After cutting, pull off any beads within 1" of the cut edge. Glue the threads to the back of the lace with bridal glue or pull thread ends to the wrong side and tie off so the rest of the beads and sequins don't fall off.

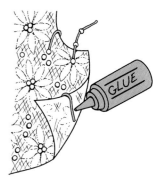

3. Transfer all construction marks to the wrong side of the fabric. Staystitch ½" from all raw edges to prevent the loss of beads or sequins.

4. When stitching seams, use a zipper foot positioned so that the needle is in the left-hand position. By shifting all the presser foot pressure to the seam allowance, you cut down on bead or sequin breakage within the garment. Test stitch on fabric scraps first. Use a size 11 (75) needle.

Replace the needle frequently as stitching through sequins dulls the needle faster.

5. Finger press seams whenever possible as sequins and some beads are heat sensitive. Do not use steam as it removes the shine from sequins.

Appliqués from Beaded or Sequined Lace

If cutting appliqués from beaded lace, use bridal glue on the back of the lace, as shown in step 2 above, to secure thread ends so beads or sequins won't fall off.

CHAPTER 11

A Bridal Gown from Start to Finish

The goal is to minimize handling and crushing the fabrics with which you will be working. Gowns with waistline seams are constructed in three stages: bodice; skirt; and back closure/finishing details. Dresses without waistline seams allow you to insert the zipper before sewing the back to the front. The following order will serve as a guide, but will change depending on gown style. Use it as a checklist.

Design

- ❏ Look at bridal magazines to begin designing dress.
- ❏ Sketch gown.
- ❏ Determine pattern(s) to use.

Tissue-Fitting & Muslin

- ❏ Cut out pattern and tissue-fit. Alter pattern.
- ❏ Cut out and stitch a muslin test dress.
- ❏ **First Fitting**: Readjust test dress as needed.
- ❏ **Second Fitting**, if needed
- ❏ Transfer changes to tissue pattern.

Buy Fabric & Trims

- ❏ Select fabric and trims; purchase or order. (Purchasing after fitting results in better yardage accuracy.)

Cut

- ❏ Cut out gown.

Assemble Bodice

- ❏ Attach boning to underlining or interlining, if applicable.
- ❏ Baste underlining to wrong side of bodice pieces.
- ❏ Stitch and press seams and/or darts (if not done before boning):
  - • bodice
  - • interlining
  - • lining
- ❏ Attach horsehair braid to princess seams if needed.
- ❏ Insert zipper if gown has no waistline seam.
- ❏ Stitch and press shoulder seams in all sections.

Bodice Assembly, continued...

- ❏ Pin or baste side seams. With all layers pinned together, try on gown for a fitting.
- ❏ **Bodice Fitting and Alterations**
- ❏ Cut and apply lace, as applicable.
- ❏ Assemble the layers.
- ❏ Prepare neckline treatment.
- ❏ Complete garment neckline.
- ❏ Baste layers together at armholes.

Sleeve Assembly

- ❏ Apply lace, if applicable.
- ❏ Underline, if applicable.
- ❏ Complete wrist closure, if needed.
- ❏ Apply facing, if needed.
- ❏ Stitch sleeve seams.
- ❏ Ease or gather sleeves.
- ❏ Prepare lining, if applicable.
- ❏ Insert lining into sleeve.
- ❏ Baste sleeves into armholes.
- ❏ **Sleeve Fitting**
- ❏ Set in sleeves permanently.
- ❏ Apply sleeve heads, if needed.

Skirt Assembly

- ❏ Apply underlining if needed.
- ❏ Stitch skirt seams.
- ❏ Stitch lining.

Skirt Assembly, continued...

- ❏ Stitch skirt overlay seams and hem (if applicable).
- ❏ Apply lace motifs, if applicable.

Attach Skirt to Bodice

- ❏ Gather skirt, if needed, and baste to bodice.
- ❏ **Fitting**
- ❏ Remove skirt basting.
- ❏ Attach skirt overlay to skirt.
- ❏ Baste lining to skirt.
- ❏ Permanently attach skirt unit to bodice unit.

Final Touches

- ❏ For gowns with waistline seam, insert zipper or finish it if you partially inserted it into bodice earlier (page 112).
- ❏ Sew on buttons, as applicable.
- ❏ Hem gown after hanging for 3 days.
- ❏ Add waistline stay if needed.
- ❏ Add any lace appliqués or trims not already attached.
- ❏ Bustle the gown, if needed.
- ❏ Attach hanging loops.

Tip for a Dressmaker

Use this checklist to establish a price for gowns based on a unit pricing method.

Tip for a Dressmaker

You may need numerous fittings with your client depending on (1) the style of the gown, (2) the client, and (3) the time frame between ordering and delivery of the gown (she may lose/gain weight). These fittings can be interspersed anywhere in the checklist.

CHAPTER 12

Shaping the Bodice

Alicyn Exclusives© courtesy of The McCall Pattern Company

Most bodices are fitted in some areas: around the bust (empire waist styles), at the waist (princess and basque waist styles), at the hip (dropped waist styles), or even all the way to the hem (sheath styles). Good fit is crucial to the success of your gown. Be sure to follow the fitting steps in Chapter 5 (page 29) and don't cut corners!

There are many more layers in the bodice of a wedding gown than in everyday garments. Most bridal gowns have at least three and sometimes four layers: the fashion-fabric outer layer; an underlining layer; a lining layer; and an interlining layer. A shaped gown will look half-finished without them.

Underlining

An underlining is cut from the same main pattern pieces as the gown and is sewn to the wrong side of the fashion fabric. It must be firm enough to shape and support the fabric or sheer enough to serve as a background to support lace. Underlining should never overpower the fashion fabric but it should help conceal seam allowances and boning. An underlining is necessary when you want a good fit and a smooth bodice and when:

♦ The fashion fabric is lace, a sheer, or other fabric that you want to be less transparent. Underlining also adds body to those fabrics that need it.

♦ The bodice will be boned.

♦ You want to create a special effect with underlining and lace.

Some of the most commonly used fabrics for underlining bridal gowns include, cotton organdy, silk organza, netting, lightweight fusible interfacing, cotton batiste, sew-in interfacing, and crinoline.

Netting. Netting is used to underline lace bodices. It stabilizes lace without interfering with its sheerness. Be sure it is a net that has some give, such as English net, not tulle or petticoat net.

Organza. Silk organza is a good, all-around underlining. It provides stability without adding bulk. It can be shaped better than polyester although it may be difficult to find. It is lighter than crinoline and is used as a lightweight underlining. It is also used as a sheer background on which to apply lace motifs. I recommend it for any silk gown.

Crinoline. This is a stiff fabric used for styles that need extra body, such as a large, off-the-shoulder collar. It's also great for shaping bows and scallops. One form is similar to a heavily starched woven cotton fabric. It gets softer with lots of handling. Crinoline is also available in a plastic version like the large mesh for craft projects. Use crinoline where you need stiffening under heavy fabrics. Be sure to test your fabric/underlining/stiffening compatibility.

Ambiance Bemberg rayon lining fabric also works well for underlining. Any natural fiber such as silk or cotton will hold the shape of the bodice. For more structured princess silhouettes and A-line silhouettes, use light- to medium weight, nonwoven fabrics (not fusible) or woven permanent press underlinings. Alicyn Wright, bridal expert and designer for McCall's, strongly suggests avoiding acetate fabrics for underlining in bride gowns.

The use of underlining is highly subjective. If you are copying a dress from a book or magazine, it may be difficult to determine just what the designer used for the shaping in the dress you see in the photograph. It may be necessary to test several samples in order to get just the right combination of fabric, lining, and support material to achieve the look you want. Remember that there are no hard-and-fast "rules" about what to use. You, as the designer, are in charge—and isn't that part of the fun?

How to Underline

1. Cut the underlining and fashion fabric separately. Mark construction symbols on the underlining.

2. Place the underlining on the *wrong side* of the fashion fabric. Press the layers together.

3. Baste the layers together ½" from the edge, using a long stitch on your sewing machine and loosened tension. Do not baste the hem edges.

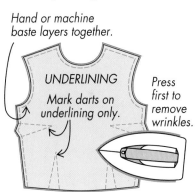

Hand or machine baste layers together.

UNDERLINING

Mark darts on underlining only.

Press first to remove wrinkles.

TIP: To glue-baste, lift the underlining and dab tiny drops of fabric glue every few inches very close to each cut edge (except hem). Finger press and allow to dry at least five minutes before handling.

Tip for a Dressmaker

I strongly recommend lining all of your garments as lined garments hang and feel better. They wear better too— linings take the stress off outer seams.

Lining

A lining is sewn separately, then attached inside the gown at the garment edges—waistline, armholes, neckline. The neckline is usually finished with only the lining. The armhole is finished with lining, binding, facing or sleeve. Lining hides all inner construction, helps shape the bodice, and minimizes wrinkles and clinging. My personal preference is to line all garments; fabrics you should definitely line include sheers, all-over lace, metallics, and napped fabrics.

Choose a lining that is lighter in weight than your fashion fabric to avoid changing the hand as much as possible. Lining fabrics are available in a variety of fiber contents including polyester, rayon, and silk. Taffeta is a good choice for lining if you like its rustling sound. Crepe-back satin is another lovely alternative for some gowns. Ambience rayon is soft next to your skin.

How to Line

1. Cut the basic dress pattern pieces out of the lining fabric. Sew together, making a duplicate of your gown. Press seams open. It's not necessary to use any special seam finishes on lining seams as they need to be as flat as possible inside the gown to avoid adding unnecessary bulk.

2. Place the lining inside the bodice as shown, aligning the raw edges of seams as shown, unless your gown is sheer (see below).

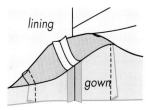

lining

gown

NOTE: If your gown is sheer and not underlined, place the *right side of the lining to the wrong side of the gown*, so the seam allowances won't show through.

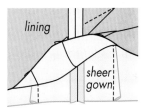

lining

sheer gown

3. Stitch the lining to the gown bodice, finishing edges where desired.

4. Leave the lower edge of the bodice lining free until after attaching the skirt (page 132). Then hand sew it in place over the waistline seam allowance. Or, finish the waistline seam with lace and hand sew the seam allowance to the bodice lining.

Eliminating Facings

This technique is particularly effective on velvet, lace, and metallic fabrics. You can sew the lining and fashion fabric together at the neck and/or armholes. When turned to the right side, these edges are finished.

The "Corset" with Boning

Boning is used when you need a "corset-like" fit in the bodice. The amount and type depends on how much support is needed. A full-busted figure requires more support than a small-busted one. If the gown is made of a heavy satin and has a long train, more boning will be required to keep the bodice from sagging. This is also true for heavily beaded fabrics.

Besides providing a smooth fit, boning is essential in off-the-shoulder or strapless gowns for the necessary support. Plastic boning in a fabric "sleeve" is available at fabric stores. For extra support, use steel-coil boning, usually available from bridal and tailoring supply businesses.

Boning can be sewn to an underlining, but it is best to position the boning as far away from the outside of the dress as possible so it won't show through. It is also more comfortable to wear if it is positioned between two fabric layers. Therefore, when sewn to an interlining and then to the wrong side of the lining, you get the best of all worlds.

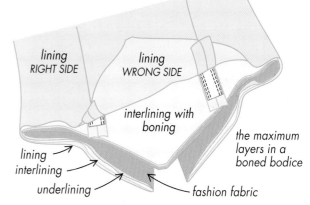

lining RIGHT SIDE

lining WRONG SIDE

interlining with boning

the maximum layers in a boned bodice

lining
interlining

underlining

fashion fabric

For the interlining, consider the following choices: organza (it doesn't add bulk); an additional layer of the lining fabric; lightweight taffeta; or batiste. A heavy nonwoven interfacing called "interlining" is available through bridal mail-order sources. It is used under heavy fabrics—such as heavy bridal satin and velvets.

Fit the "corset" of interlining snugly to the body. Then fit the lining and the bodice. The interlining is sewn to the lining after fitting. Pin the bodice to the skirt to see if extra boning is necessary due to the weight of the skirt.

How to Make a Boned "Corset"

1. Cut the main bodice pieces of the gown from the chosen interlining fabric.

2. Stitch darts and/or princess seams, as applicable; press open.

3. Attach the boning (see "Positioning Boning," page 93).

4. Stitch the shoulder seams of the interlining and press open.

5. Check the fit. This layer will be very close to the skin and should fit snugly like a corset.

6. After perfecting the fit of the corset, baste the shaping layer to the lining. Then complete the bodice. It is usually easier to remove the boning during construction and re-insert it just before finishing the dress.

Positioning Boning

At a minimum, boning is placed halfway between the center front and back and side seams.

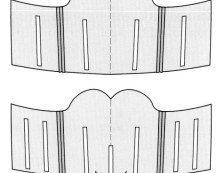

Additional boning can be added anywhere more support is needed—center front, side seams etc. Extra boning may be required for a V-waistline to keep it smooth. Boning will extend to the waistline seam even if the seam is below the waistline. When marking the positions for boning channels, be sure that they stop at the seamlines and do not extend into seam allowances.

1. Lightly mark boning positions on the interlining with a soft lead pencil. The boning should not extend past the waist, armhole, or shoulder seamlines.

2. Remove the boning from its fabric sleeve and cut the fabric sleeve the length of the area to be boned plus 1".

3. Stitch fabric sleeves in place along both long sides and across the top, rounding the corners as shown.

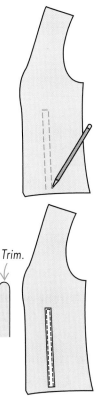

Trim.

4. Trim the ends of the plastic boning in a curve. For an extra smooth finish, use an emery board to round off sharp edges.

5. Insert the boning into the sleeve so its natural curve will curve into the body; slipstitch closed when you are ready to finish the bodice.

Boning a Strapless Bodice With a Heart-Shaped Neckline

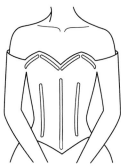

Boning will prevent a strapless bodice from slowly working its way down the body all day so you won't have to keep yanking it up!

For a bodice with a heart-shaped neckline, you'll add boning all along the top edge of the bodice front. For added "hug," try adding some elastic across the top of the back—just enough to hug, not to pucker the fabric.

Shaping with Horsehair Braid

Sew horsehair braid (a nylon mesh) to the wrong side of the front princess seams of the bodice to add subtle shaping to princes seams.

1. Use ½"-wide horsehair braid. Stretch a length of the braid and steam press. The braid will become narrower as you stretch it.

2. Center the stretched and narrowed piece on a second strip of ½"-wide braid. Stitch the two together through the center.

3. Starting at the waistline or shoulder seamline, center the braid over the seamline, curving it to the contour of the seam. Pin in the center, parallel to the braid edges.

4. After trimming braid to fit, cover the ends with tricot, lining fabric, or a piece of soft interfacing. (A quick way to do this is to cut a small piece of fusible interfacing and fuse it over the ends.)

tricot-covered end

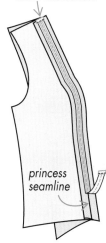

Center and stitch to seam allowance.

princess seamline

5. Stitch the braid to the *seam allowances only* of the princess seam, one seam allowance at a time.

Interfacings

In bridal sewing, the places you usually interface—collars, cuffs and necklines—are stabilized in other ways, such as with boning, stay tape, or binding or by lining to the edges. Facings are not common, since most gowns are lined and underlined. If you decide you need an interfacing in your gown, consider the following guidelines.

Fusible Interfacing

♦ When using fusible interfacing, fuse it to the lining or underlining, not to the fashion fabric.

♦ For lightweight silky fabrics, use polyester or nylon knit interfacing or a polyester weft interfacing to avoid puckered interfacings after fusing and laundering. Preshrink first by positioning the interfacing on the wrong side of the garment piece and holding the steam iron just above the interfacing to steam it before you fuse. If it is going to shrink, you will see it happen as it draws up from the heat of the iron and steam.

♦ Make a test sample and wash it if you are planning to wash the garment. Follow the manufacturer's directions for fusing and use a 6" to 9" square of fabric. If the fusible bubbles, does not adhere, or changes the character of your fabric, use a sew-in interfacing.

NOTE: Perfect Fuse, a new line of fusible interfacings is available from Palmer/Pletsch (page 160).

♦ If the interfacing shows through to the right side, through all layers of the gown, try a different color (beige instead of white or black).

Sew-In Interfacing

♦ Choose silk organza, fashion fabric, or lining fabric to interface most bridal fabrics. Glue-baste to the fashion fabric as shown on page 91. *Never fuse to acetate fabrics, velvets, or beaded or sequined fabrics.*

Tip for a Dressmaker

Save time by fusing 6" to 9" squares of a variety of interfacings to large pieces of different fabrics. Label with a permanent marker. Wash and/or dryclean as appropriate for a permanent record of how each interacts.

A Word About Seams

To achieve the fitted bodice so common to wedding gowns, the design generally calls for princess seams that start from the shoulder or the armhole.

To stitch pucker-free princess seams (especially in fabrics such as taffeta and heavy satin that are more difficult to ease), try the following technique:

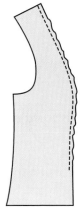

1. Using "ease plus" (page 65), stitch ½" from the raw edge on the curved edge of the side front. Staystitch ½" from the edge on the inside curve of the front and clip to staystitching as necessary when pinning front to side front.

2. With right sides facing and notches matching, pin the front and the side front panels together. Stitch with the eased piece *on the bottom* so the feed dogs can help ease the fabric. Stitch slowly.

3. To meld the stitches, with the eased seam on top, press the two layers together *along the stitching line* and within the seam allowances. Use steam only if appropriate for your fabric.

4. Press shoulder princess seams open unless very curved for a full bust. Press very curved princess seams toward the center front to avoid excessive puckering. Press over a tailor's ham from the wrong side. Pressed seams should have a soft appearance, not a hard, flat look. If you overpress, try "unpressing"—press the seams together again as if you had just stitched them. Then press them open carefully. Sometimes this works, sometimes not. It's worth a try!

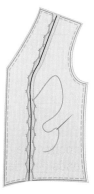

If the seam refuses to lie flat over the curve and your bodice is underlined, you can catchstitch the seam allowances to the underlining to keep them in place. Catch underlining only!

Tip for a Dressmaker

If you sewed a test garment to check the fit, clipping the inward princess seam won't cause a problem.

CHAPTER 13
Bodice Construction Basics

Bodice Assembly

Most bodices are assembled in the following general order:

1. Baste the under-lining to the fashion fabric.

   NOTE: If adding a boned *underlining* (see pages 92 and 96), sew darts (step 2, below) or princess seams in the underlining *and* the fashion fabric prior to basting.

2. If there are darts or princess seams, sew them now. Press. (See **Fit for Real People**, page 158, for how to alter darts to fit your body.)

   TIP: To ensure the underlining is caught in the dart all the way to the point, machine stitch on center lines through the fashion fabric and underlining *before* stitching darts. It is best to baste past the point if your fabric won't needle-mark.

   TIP: For a pucker-free dart point, change to a 1mm stitch length when you are 1" from the point. The last four stitches should be on the very edge of the fabric. Once off the fab-ric, raise the presser foot and pull the dart toward you. Pull a little slack in the thread, then lower the needle into the dart seam allowance. Lower the presser foot. Stitch in the seam allowance to anchor the dart threads. Or, leave long thread ends and tie off with an overhand knot using both threads.

3. Press darts and curved princess seams over a ham (page 68).

4. If you have lace appliqués, apply them now (page 82), leaving edges loose that will cover seams later.

5. Stitch the shoulder seams of the fashion fabric/ underlining unit and press open.

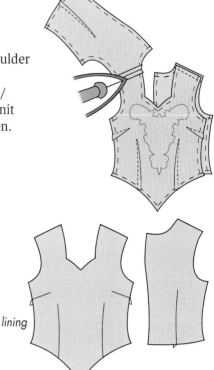

6. Stitch and press the lining darts or princess seams.

   lining

NOTE: If adding a boned *interlining*, see pages 92 and 96.

7. Stitch the lining shoulder seams. Trim seam allowances to ¼". Press open.

8. Sew the lining unit to the fashion fabric unit around the neckline.

   NOTE: If adding a collar, or if you want a neckline finish other than lined-to-the-edge, see "Necklines & Collars" beginning on page 97.

   Trim seams, grading and clipping as necessary.

stitch

9. Turn right side out and press carefully. Understitch (page 68) for a cleaner, flatter turned edge.

10. Apply the button closure before attaching the skirt. Apply the zipper after attaching the skirt (See "Closures," beginning on page 111.)

11. Pin side seams and try on to check fit.

12. Sew lining side seams *with right sides together*. Press open, clipping as necessary so they will lie flat.

13. Sew fashion fabric side seams *with right sides together*. Press open, clipping as necessary so they will lie flat.

14. Set in sleeves and complete the dress. If the gown is sleeveless and lining to the edge as shown below would cause distortion when you pull the bodice through the shoulders, finish the armholes with bias fabric (page 73).

Sleeveless Bodice

1. Complete the bodice through step 8. See step 14 above before proceeding with this method.

2. Sew the lining to the bodice around the armholes. Trim and grade the seam and clip the curves.

3. Turn right side out through the shoulders. Press.

NOTE:
If using a zipper, insert before sewing side seams.

5. Check fit, then sew side seams together, lining to lining, and fashion fabric to fashion fabric.

armhole seam

fashion fabric

Integrating Boning

Boning can be sewn to either the underlining or the interlining. Ideally, the boning is placed as far away as possible from the fashion fabric, which is best accomplished by boning the interlining.

Boned Underlining

If you are applying boning to the underlining, apply it *before* sewing the underlining to the fashion fabric. Machine baste the underlining to the fashion fabric with the boned side up. If bones go over darts or princess seams, sew darts in the underlining and fashion fabric separately, *before* adding boning.

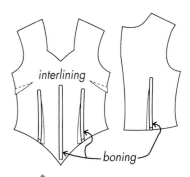

Boned Interlining

If you are using an interlining as a shaping layer, apply the boning to the wrong side. If boning will cover a dart or a seam, sew those first.

interlining

boning

Stitch the interlining shoulder seams. Press open.

Baste interlining to lining, wrong sides together, around the neckline, armholes, and the back opening edges.

Boning will now be as far from the right side of the gown as possible.

For more information, see "Shaping the Bodice," beginning on page 90.

CHAPTER 14
Necklines & Collars

Traditional Necklines

V Neckline

Because V necklines are cut on the bias, they can easily stretch out of shape during handling. To prevent this, *stay* the seamline with Sta-Tape™ or the selvage of a lining fabric.

1. Place the pattern on the wrong side of the fabric and adjust the fabric as needed until the fabric matches the tissue.

2. Mark the point of the V through the pattern onto the fabric. Remove pattern.

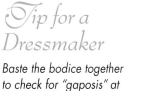

Mark point of V.

Tip for a Dressmaker

Baste the bodice together to check for "gaposis" at this point. Try the bodice on your customer. If her chest is more concave than the bodice, it will gap. Pin tiny tucks into the V—as many as needed—to remove the gap and make the V lie close to the chest. Adjust the stay to account for the tucks, then ease the neckline to the stay. Note that this alteration should have become apparent during the tissue and the muslin fitting, and corrected, but it can still be corrected even at this stage of construction.

3. Working on the wrong side of the fabric, place a strip of Sta-Tape™ on the seam allowance next to the neck seamline on each side of the stay. To keep bulk to a minimum, do not extend the stay into any seamlines.

4. Stitch through the edge of the tape ½" from the cut edge of the neckline, easing the fabric to the tape. Stitch each side with the fabric on the bottom so the feed dogs assist with the easing.

5. Construct the remainder of the bodice (page 95).

6. To finish the V neck, work flat leaving the side seams open for a final fitting. Pin the lining to the bodice, right sides together, matching the points of the neckline and the shoulder seams. Pin generously, easing the lining to the outer shell as needed.

7. To stitch the V neckline seam, set the machine for 20 stitches per inch. Since you have stayed the neckline, directional stitching is not important. Stitch to the point of the V. Take two stitches *across the point* to prevent puckers at the point. (Always pivot with the needle down in the fabric.) Pivot and continue stitching around the remainder of the neckline.

two small stitches

8. Clip, trim, grade, and understitch the seam. Clip the seam allowance as close as possible to the point of the V. Press first from the wrong side, allowing the fabric to turn naturally. Press *lightly* from the right side.

Scoop Neckline

This neckline style requires no special techniques for bridal sewing. Just make sure you clip the seam, trim, grade, and understitch for a smooth, non-bulky finish.

♦ To prevent the scoop neckline from stretching, staystitch it directionally as the arrows show.

♦ If your dress has a very scooped neck and you have a full bust, the neckline may pull away from the body and expose a bit more than you want. You may want to stay the neckline, using the technique described for V necklines (page 97). You can actually tighten the stay to ease the neckline in against your chest if necessary. To do so, try one of the following:

♦ Stitch a piece of clear elastic to the inside of the neckline, beginning just below the shoulder seams. Cut the elastic about ½" shorter than the length of the area to which you will be stitching it.

clear elastic

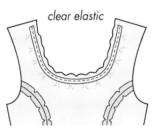

♦ If the gown is finished and the neckline gapes, use clear nylon thread to do a row of short hand stitches along the neckline seamline, drawing them up slightly to gather the neck edge a little so it will scoop in toward the chest.

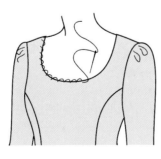

Illusion Neckline

This style has a strapless bodice with a sheer fabric upper bodice usually made of organza, illusion, or lace. You can easily create this style with your existing pattern.

Start with a jewel neckline front and back. (The example below shows a princess style.) Make the following changes to the pattern:

1. Pin the pattern pieces together and try on the tissue. On the front, draw a line over the bust to below the underarm, curving it as you desire.

front

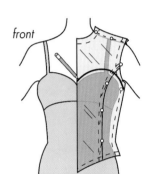

2. Draw a line across the back, curving it as you desire.

back

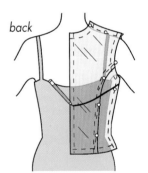

3. Cut the pattern pieces apart where you have drawn the lines. Add seam allowances to each new piece.

add seam allowances

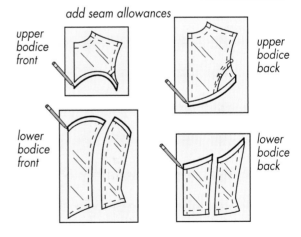

upper bodice front

upper bodice back

lower bodice front

lower bodice back

4. Cut the new lower bodice pieces from fashion fabric, underlining, and lining.

5. Cut two layers of sheer fabric for the upper bodice. If using lace, cut one layer of lace and one of a sheer or netting.

To assemble the bodice:

1. Construct the lower bodice front and back. Construct the lower bodice lining. Apply interlining, underlining, boning, or whatever shaping is necessary. Do not sew the side seams yet.

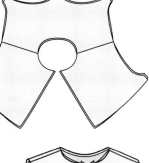

2. Place the upper bodice and upper bodice lining pieces *wrong sides together*. Treating both layers as one, sew the shoulder seams, using a French seam (page 66).

3. Finish the center back. Apply button loops to the left side and buttons to the right side. (Refer to "Buttons/Loops," beginning on page 113.)

   NOTE: The sandwiched button and loop application technique on page 114 must be done prior to sewing the shoulder seams.

4. Finish the neck edge with bias binding (page 101), lace trim (pages 85-87), or a Victorian collar (page 107).

5. Staystitch the lower edges of the upper bodice.

6. If you created a V at the center front of the lower bodice, staystitch along the seamline on both sides of the point using a short (2mm) stitch length. Clip to the staystitching at the point.

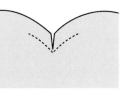

7. If the back is curved down toward the waist, staystitch and clip to stitching so you can easily attach it to the upper back. (Inward curves need to be clipped in order to sew them to outward curves.)

8. Sew side seams in upper and lower bodice pieces. French seams (page 66) are recommended for sheer illusion upper bodice.

9. Pin the upper bodice to the lower bodice pieces, front to front and back to back with right sides together. Clip inward curves in the upper bodice as necessary, clipping to but not through the stitches.

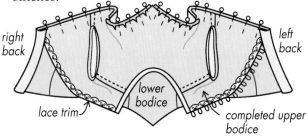

right back

left back

lace trim

lower bodice

completed upper bodice

10. With the upper bodice on top, machine baste together, front to front and back to back. On the front begin at one side seam, stitching to the point of the front V, stopping *exactly* at the point. With the needle down in the fabric, lift the presser foot and turn the work so that the bulk of the bodice fabric is behind the needle. Lower the presser foot and continue stitching.

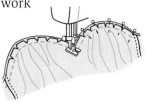

11. Place the lower bodice lining right sides together with the lower bodice pieces, sandwiching the upper bodice between them as shown. Clip the lower bodice as necessary. Stitch the layers together, using the previous stitching as a guide. Trim the seam and press it toward the lower bodice.

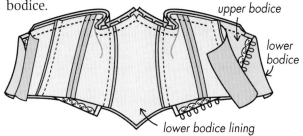

upper bodice

lower bodice

lower bodice lining

12. Grade the seam allowances. Clip as necessary. Press the seam toward the lower bodice lining.

13. Understitch close to the seam through the lining and seam allowances, starting and stopping 1" from the center front and keeping the yoke free from the stitching.

Turn right side out. Insert the zipper into the lower bodice (pages 111-112). Insert sleeves. Fit bodice once more, then stitch the side seams. Complete the gown.

Scalloped Neckline

Scallops are a lovely and effective treatment around necklines and sleeves and are not difficult to make. To create them from lace, see page 85. For fabric scallops, you can use any circle for a template —the bottom of a glass, for example. Scallop size and placement is up to you.

To create a scalloped edge:

1. Trace the bodice pattern pieces onto Perfect Pattern Paper, a gridded tissue (see page 61).

2. To determine the area to be scalloped measure the neckline edge, *excluding seam allowances.*

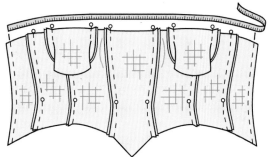

3. Divide the neckline length by the desired diameter of the scallops to find out if they will fit evenly. For example, if the neckline measures 24" and you want 3" scallops, you can have 8 scallops around the neck. However, if the neckline measures 26", you will need to increase the scallop diameter slightly in order to fill the neckline with scallops. Alternatively, you can divide the neckline length by the number of scallops you want to determine the scallop diameter that will fit.

Play with a sample layout to determine pleasing scallop size and placement on your gown. Also consider repeating scallops somewhere else in the gown—along the hem or the edge of the sleeve, for example.

4. After deciding on the size and location of the scallops, draw them onto the traced bodice pattern pieces using a glass, compass, or other round object of the appropriate size. Add seam allowance.

NOTE: Keep the weight of your fabric in mind when planning scallops. Remember that the deeper your scallops are, the more difficult they will be to stitch and turn, particularly on heavier fabrics.

5. Cut the bodice, lining, and underlining (if needed) from the revised pattern. For support and to help the scallops retain their shape, cut a 3"-wide piece of crinoline or other support material appropriate for your fabric. Use the top part of the pattern as a guide.

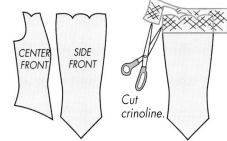

6. Construct the bodice to the point of finishing the neckline.

7. Stitch the seamlines of the crinoline or other stiffening fabric together by overlapping along the seamline and stitching through both layers. Trim close to the stitching to eliminate unnecessary bulk.

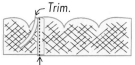

8. With seamlines matching, baste the stiffening to the lining along the neckline on the stitching line. Trim the stiffening above the stitching as close to the seamline as possible without cutting the seamline stitches.

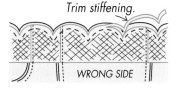

9. Staystitch the upper edge of the bodice and the lining to prevent stretching while handling.

10. Pin the fashion fabric and the lining *right sides together*, matching centers and seamlines.

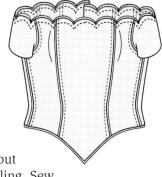

11. Stitch, using a short stitch length so you can trim closely without fear of the fabric raveling. Sew two short (.1mm) stitches at the inner point of each scallop so they won't pucker (as described for V necklines on page 97).

12. Clip the seam allowance to the inner point of each scallop.

13. Trim and grade the scalloped seam allowance, notching the outward curves. Stagger the notches to avoid weakening the seam or creating a lumpy look when pressed.

14. Turn the lining to the inside and press from the wrong side.

Straps for a Camisole Neckline

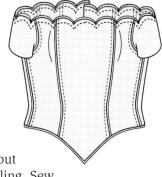

For a camisole bodice, you will need spaghetti straps. For most bridal wear, corded tubings are too stiff and tailored looking. Self-fabric straps are recommended.

To make sturdy, easy-to-turn straps, use this self-filling technique. The seam allowance inside gives the tube soft body.

1. Cut bias strips 4½ times the desired finished width; the seam allowance will be the filler. For sheers, cut the strips 5 to 6 times the finished width as more filler is needed. Trim one end of the bias strip to a point.

2. Cut a length of string a few inches longer than the strip and stitch the string to the *right side* of the pointed end of the bias strip.

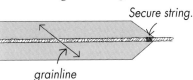

Secure string.

grainline

3. Fold the bias strip in half, right sides together, positioning the string inside along the fold. Some string will extend beyond the strip end.

4. For easier turning later, start stitching a bit wider than the desired finished width, then taper into the desired finished width as shown. Stretch the bias strip slightly as you stitch (so the stitches won't break later). *Do not catch the string in the stitching.*

5. Carefully pull the string and turn the tube to the right side. If it won't pull through, trim a little of the seam allowance away.

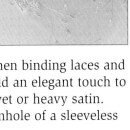

6. Pin one end of the tube to your ironing board and steam and stretch it to make a smooth thin tube. Pin the other end to the ironing board until it is cool.

TIP: The *Fasturn*™ is a great tool for making tubes of any size.

Neckline Binding

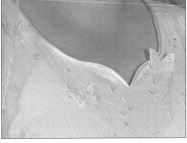

French binding is an elegant neckline finish to use in place of a faced edge. It's especially effective when binding laces and sheers, or when you want to add an elegant touch to heavy bridal fabric such as velvet or heavy satin. It's also a nice finish for the armhole of a sleeveless gown.

1. Cut bias strips of contrasting or self fabric 2" longer than the neckline edge, and six times the desired finished depth. (A strip 3" wide makes ½"-wide finished binding.)

TIP: Cut the strips with a ruler and a rotary cutter so they will be a perfectly even width.

2. Fold the strip in half lengthwise with *wrong sides together*; press.

3. Trim away the garment neckline seam allowance.

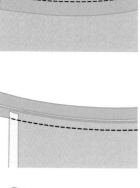

4. Pin the folded binding to the neckline, with all edges even, and with the binding extending over the center back opening at least ¼". Stitch, using a seam allowance width equal to the desired finished binding width.

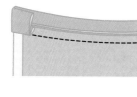

5. Press the binding toward the seam allowance.

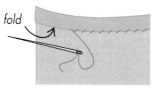

6. Fold the binding around the seam allowance at each end and press. Trim excess, leaving no more than than ¼" of wrapped binding.

7. Turn binding over the seam allowance to the inside. Slipstitch the folded edge in place just inside the seamline.

fold

Collars

Collars can be very beautiful on wedding gowns, although more often they are the focal point on bridesmaids' dresses. Keep the collar size in proportion to your overall body size—one that is too large can easily overwhelm a small frame, for example.

off-the-shoulder collar

You may want a lace collar on a satin gown or a lace overlay on a fabric collar. Lace trimming is another possibility. The fashion fabric collar can be the backdrop for a piece of antique lace, or you could decide to make the collar from the only portion of your grandmother's dress that was salvageable. As you select and plan a collar treatment, consider the following:

♦ Large, ornate collars are most successful when made of heavy bridal fabrics or fabrics with lots of body (such as brocade).

♦ Lighter weight polyester and silk fabrics may not have enough body to make the collar stand or lie correctly. You can try underlining with one to two layers of net or crinoline. Experiment with a small sample collar until you get the look you are seeking. Use fusible interfacing to change the drape of a lighter weight fabric. Test to be sure the fabric reacts well with the fusible. Perfect Fuse Sheer™ and Perfect Fuse Light™ are fusible polyester weft interfacings that work well (page 160).

♦ Cut the collar on the bias so it will lie better and the outer edge will curve nicely.

♦ Use organza or lining fabric for the undercollar to eliminate bulk and weight, especially if you are using heavy bridal satin for the upper collar.

♦ Underline with net if you want your collar to have more body.

♦ Thread trace (hand baste) along the seamlines of the collar to avoid placing lace where you'll later stitch a seam.

straight-grain ruffled collar

Ruffled Collars

If you have designed a dress with a ruffled collar and have purchased a pattern that does not include one, you can make one. Be sure to test your ruffle in scrap fabric first to avoid costly mistakes!

The ruffle techniques featured here are also appropriate for other areas of your gown. Choose from three basic types of ruffles: bias, straight-grain, or flared. All but the flared ruffle can be made single or double layer.

A gathered ruffle should be two to three times the measurement of the edge to which it will be attached. Making a test ruffle first (preferably in your actual fashion fabric) allows you to adjust it for the desired fullness before you cut the necessary pieces from the fashion fabric.

Begin with a 3 to 1 ratio (the ruffle is three times as long as the neckline or other edge to which it will be sewn). Decrease the fullness if necessary after making a test ruffle.

The weight of your fabric or lace and your own personal preference dictate the ruffle fullness. Ruffles cut from soft or lightweight fabrics should be fuller than those cut from stiffer fabrics or they will look skimpy. The ruffle width depends on the style of the dress, the design, your personal preference, and the desired hemming method. You must decide on the hem treatment for the ruffle *before* cutting it out. (See page 104 for ruffle hemming techniques.)

Gathered Bias Ruffle

Bias fabric is used to make ruffles such as the style illustrated on page 106.

1. Decide how wide you want the finished ruffle to be. Add width for the desired hem treatment and for seam allowances as needed.

2. Cut the ruffle on the true bias, piecing where necessary. Press the seams open and trim.

3. Hem the lower edges as desired. Finish the short ends of the ruffle at the back of the neckline opening with a rolled hem (hand, machine, or serged).

4. Gather the long, unfinished edge of the ruffle (see "Tip for a Dressmaker" below left). Attach to the garment.

Straight-grain Ruffle

To create a straight-grain ruffle like the one illustrated on the previous page, follow the steps for a bias ruffle, cutting strips on the straight grain and joining them as needed. Trim and press the seams open. Hem the ruffle (page 104) and attach as described above.

Straight-grain Ruffle with a Header

If you want a tiny ruffle at the top of a wider ruffled collar, create a header on a straight-grain ruffle.

1. Decide how deep you want the header (typically 1") and add that depth to the ruffle. Allow for a rolled-hem edge finish at the upper edge of the header and the lower edge of the ruffle.

2. Finish both edges of the ruffle strip with a rolled edge (see page 104) and do two rows of gathering stitches at the bottom of the header.

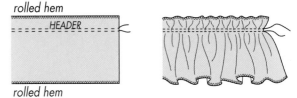

rolled hem
HEADER
rolled hem

3. Complete the bodice and the bodice lining and attach the two at the neckline seam. Complete the back closure.

4. *With right side up*, pin the gathered ruffle to the finished neckline; place the top row of gathering stitches just at the neckline edge.

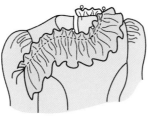

5. Draw up the gathering threads to fit, adjusting gathers evenly around the neckline.

6. Stitch the ruffle to the neckline edge between the two rows of stitching. Carefully remove the gathering threads.

Folded Bias Ruffle

1. Cut the ruffle twice the desired finished width, plus 1¼" for seam allowances.

2. Fold in half lengthwise with *right sides together*. Stitch the short ends. Trim the seams and clip the corners. Press the seams open over a point turner, then turn the ruffle right side out and press.

3. Gently press the fold to create a *soft* edge, not a hard one. Baste the raw edges together.

4. Gather the long, unfinished edge of the ruffle.

5. Attach to the garment.

Circular Ruffle

double circular ruffle collar

A circular ruffle has a flounced effect and is made by joining a series of circles to make one long ruffle strip. A double circular ruffle is two ruffles sewn together along the inside curved edge.

1. To make a pattern, determine the finished depth of the ruffle. Add 1¼" for the seam and hem allowances. Multiply x 2. Add the diameter of the inner circle. (The smaller the inside circle, the more flare the ruffle will have and the more circles you will need to make a ruffle long enough to fit the neckline or garment edge.) Draw the larger circle with a diameter equal to the combined numbers. Draw the inner circle.

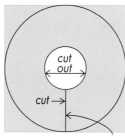

cut out

cut →

finished width plus 1¼"

2. Cut the circle on the line indicated in the illustration and use as a pattern to cut the required number of circles. (The inside edge, minus seam allowances, should equal the neckline edge. This ruffle is not gathered along the top edge.)

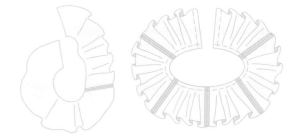

3. Sew the circles together, using ¼"-wide seams. Press seams open and pink or serge seam edges.

4. Finish the hem edge of the ruffle—serge with a rolled edge hem (see below) or line it to the edge (page 105). Clip inside edge at even intervals. (A fold will form at each clip. The more clips, the more folds.) Sew the ruffle to the neckline of the garment, *right side of the ruffle against the wrong side of the garment*. Trim and turn ruffle to outside.

NOTE: For a double, sew two ruffle strips together along the inside edge. Repeat with self-fabric lining. Place right sides together and sew along three sides. Trim and turn. Hand sew to garment.

Edge Finish Options for Ruffles

Use any of the following techniques to finish the raw edges of ruffles.

Hand Rolled Hem

Use the easy hand method shown on page 134 to create a finely rolled and stitched edge on a ruffle.

Serger Rolled Hem

You can also create wonderful rolled hems using your serger. For this hem finish, add ⅝" to the finished ruffle width and follow the directions for the rolled edge in your serger instruction manual.

Use Woolly Nylon in the loopers to fill in the rolled hem. If you are making a satin ruffle, you may want to try rayon or another specialty thread in the loopers for an interesting edge finish.

TEST serge on a scrap first to set tensions correctly and to be sure that your fabric will roll nicely. A longer stitch length works better on some fabrics. Some bridal satins are too heavy to roll and you'll end up with lumpy edges. Try a different finish.

Blindstitched Scalloped Rolled Edge

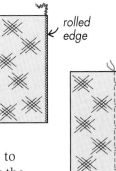

After you have rolled the edge on your serger, you can scallop it by stitching over it with the blindstitch on your sewing machine. Allow the zigzag portion of the stitch to swing just off the edge, pulling the edge in and forming the scalloped edge. (Since most machines "zig" to the left, you'll have to use the mirror image button or place the rolled edge under the needle with the gown to the *right* of the needle.)

Picot, Shell, or Scalloped Edge

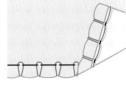

This finish can done on a conventional machine or on a serger. See page 136.

Machine Scalloped Edge

Some machines have a built-in decorative scallop stitch. TEST on a scrap to be sure this finish will work with your fabric. You will need a ¼"-wide hem allowance. Using machine embroidery or rayon thread, stitch ¼" away from the raw edge. Trim close to the stitching, using a very sharp scissors and taking care not to clip the stitches. A dab of Perfect Sew™ along the edge of organza or chiffon will stabilize it while you stitch (page 48).

Lined-to-the-edge Finish

Choose this hem finish when your fabric is too bulky for a folded (double-layer) ruffle or it won't roll nicely (velvet or heavy bridal satin).

1. Cut one layer of the ruffle from the fashion fabric and another from organza or lining fabric. The lining will show in circular ruffles so the colors should match. (Join ruffle strips as needed to create a ruffle of the required length.) Cut it the desired finished width plus 1¼" (two ⅝" seam allowances).

2. Stitch the lower edge of the ruffle and lining *with right sides together*, using a ⅝"-wide seam. Trim to ¼" from the stitching.

3. Understitch through the lining and the seam allowance so that the lining will roll naturally to the underside of the finished ruffle. Turn and press from the wrong side. (If velvet, steam from the wrong side rather than pressing.)

4. With *right sides together*, stitch the short ends of the ruffle. Trim to ¼".

5. Press the seams open over a point turner. Turn right side out and press flat along the seam edges.

6. Baste the upper edge of the ruffle and lining together, then handle as one to gather and attach to the gown.

Lace Edging

You may want to add lace to the edge of a ruffle or to a collar edge. This can be done on the sewing machine or the serger.

On the sewing machine:

1. Finish the edge that will have lace added with pinking (weakest) or turn under and edgestitch, or serge.

2. Lap the lace ¼" over the edge on the *right* side of the ruffle. Edgestitch or zigzag in place.

On the serger:

1. Adjust the serger for 2- or 3-thread flatlocking.

2. Press under the hem allowance at the bottom edge of the ruffle.

3. Follow the flatlocking directions on page 83, being careful not to cut the fabric fold or the lace.

NOTE: You can add lace trim to a lined-to-the-edge ruffle by inserting it between the ruffle and the lining when stitching the edges together. Use the process illustrated at right for attaching a pre-gathered lace ruffle to a collar. If you are attaching lace to a bias edge, be careful not to stretch the edge as you sew.

Attaching a Ruffle to the Bodice Neckline

1. Complete the bodice and the bodice lining. Set the lining aside. Insert the back closure before attaching the ruffle (see "Closures," beginning on page 111).

2. Pin the ruffle to the neckline edge of the bodice *with the underside of the ruffle against the right side of the fabric.*
   Adjust the gathers evenly to fit the neckline. Baste in place along the gathering line (to avoid making unsightly tucks in the ruffle).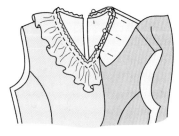

3. *With right sides together* and raw edges even, pin the lining to the bodice with the ruffle between the two layers.

4. Stitch from the bodice side, exactly on top of the basting line.

5. Clip the seam, trim, grade, and press, taking care not to press the ruffle to avoid flattening the gathers.

6. On the right side, edgestitch just inside the bodice neckline seam, keeping the ruffle free.

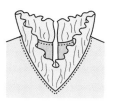 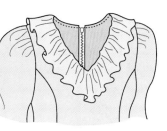

Attaching Lace to a Collar

To attach lace to a collar, choose the method below that best suits the type of lace you are using in your gown. Some techniques will be done prior to constructing the collar, some prior to sewing the collar to the bodice, and some on the completed collar.

Ruffled Lace Trim

If collar edge is a fold, topstitch or handstitch the lace in place over the folded edge (or under it if you prefer). *If the collar edge is a seam,* catch the lace in the seam when sewing the collar layers together by machine, as shown below with a pre-gathered ruffle.

Pre-Gathered Ruffle
With right sides together, stitch the organza strip to which this gathered ruffle is attached to the seamline of the upper collar. Complete the collar assembly.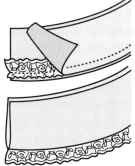

Ruffle with a Header
Attach after constructing the collar but before attaching it to the neckline edge. Lap the lace over the finished edge and stitch, following the gathering stitch in the ruffle heading. Make sure that you catch the edge of the collar in the stitching.

Galloon or Double-Edged Lace Trim
To attach galloon or double-edged trim, topstitch or hand stitch in place after the collar is attached to the bodice.

Edging Lace Attached to a Single-Layer Collar

Edging lace has one straight and one decorative edge. To attach:

1. *With right sides together,* pin the lace to the outer curved edge of the collar with the straight edge just over the seamline and the decorative edge against the body of the collar.

2. Stitch in place, using a short, narrow zigzag stitch.

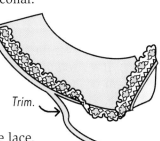

Trim.

3. Cut away the *collar* fabric close to the stitching underneath the lace.

4. Press the seam allowance toward the collar so the lace extends past the outer edge of the collar.

Lace Motifs

Machine zigzag or hand stitch individual lace motifs in place on the completed collar. If machine stitching, do prior to attaching to bodice. If hand sewing, it may be done after attaching to the bodice.

Lace Cutouts

Use net as the undercollar to maintain the sheer effect. Machine zigzag or hand stitch lace in place on upper collar. Cut fabric away under lace (page 82) and complete the collar.

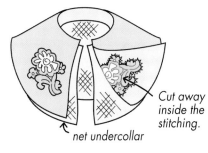

net undercollar

Cut away inside the stitching.

Tip for a Dressmaker

Keep a record of ruffles and other special techniques that you "figure out" (measurements, gathering ratio, etc.) in a notebook. (I tuck my samples into plastic sleeves that are closed on three sides and fit into a three-ring binder.) The next time I have a similar project, I refer to my samples so that I can spend less time "figuring out" and more time creating a beautiful gown.

Victorian Collars

These elegant collars can be made with lace, fabric, or a combination of the two. A Victorian collar is usually attached to a jewel neckline. For added body without unnecessary bulk, use organza for the interfacing in this type of collar.

The finished collar should equal the circumference of your neck, plus 1" for wearing ease and comfort. The collar depth depends on how long your neck is and the look you wish to achieve. If you have a short neck, this is not your best choice.

The collar is usually slightly curved to the neck. Cut the collar and interfacing on the bias—it will curve around your neck with a smoother line than a collar cut on the straight of grain.

Victorian collars are generally fastened with buttons and loops (see page 113). If you are using self-fabric loops, baste them onto the left end of the collar prior to stitching the seam. (Be sure to position them so the loops lie on the collar fabric and will be caught in the center back seam but not in the neckline or upper edge seams. When you turn the collar, they will face toward the center back and fasten over the buttons on the right end of the collar.)

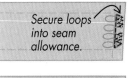

Secure loops into seam allowance.

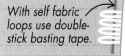

With self fabric loops use double-stick basting tape.

Ready made loops

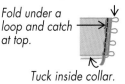

Fold under a loop and catch at top.

Tuck inside collar.

If you are using purchased elastic or non-stretch bridal loops, you may apply them after completing the collar.

If the bodice back closure is a zipper, you could apply the zipper up to the top of the collar. You may need to buy YKK's zipper-by-the-yard to find one long enough.

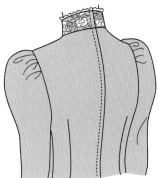

TIP: For a better looking collar, cut ⅛" off the ends of the undercollar at the neck edge before sewing it to the upper collar. Because it is the inside circle around your neck, it takes up less room than the upper collar. Match edges when stitching.

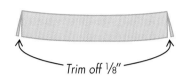

Trim off ⅛"

Victorian Collar Construction Basics

1. Construct the collar, trim and grade the seam allowance, turn right side out, and press. Understitch the seam along the top edge of the collar to help it roll under and lie smoothly.

2. Carefully press from the undercollar side to shape the collar and prevent the undercollar from rolling to the outside.

3. Complete the bodice and sew the collar to the neckline.

4. Complete the back closure (zipper or loops).

A Shaped, Stand-up Collar

This Victorian collar is often made of a lace upper collar and a sheer undercollar.

1. With right sides together, stitch along the upper edge of the collar. Trim the seam allowance to ¼" and clip curves as needed.

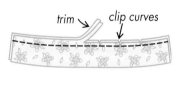

trim   *clip curves*

NOTE: If you are using a button-and-loop closure, with self-fabric loops, baste them in place and stitch the collar ends at this point. If you are using elastic loops, or a zipper closure, proceed as shown below.

2. Turn right side out and press, rolling the seam slightly to the underside. Baste the raw edges together.

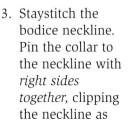

basting

3. Staystitch the bodice neckline. Pin the collar to the neckline with *right sides together*, clipping the neckline as necessary. Stitch the collar in place. Press the seam toward the collar.

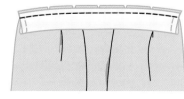

4. On the *outside*, topstitch ⅛" from the seamline through all layers. On the *inside*, carefully trim the seam allowances close to the second stitching.

5. Insert zipper or loops at center back. (Zipper or buttons-and-loops extend to the top edge of the collar.)

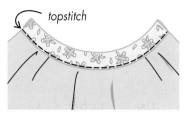

topstitch

A Stand-up Lace Collar on a Sheer Bodice

Use two layers of the same sheer fabric for the upper and undercollar layers. Then cover the collar with lace. Add button looping (page 107) before sewing the collar layers together if desired.

1. Turn under and press the seam allowance along the bottom edge of the undercollar. Trim allowance to ¼".

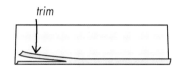

trim

2. *With right sides together*, stitch the upper collar to the undercollar along the upper edge and the two short ends. Trim seams and clip corners. Press the seams open over a point presser before turning the collar right side out.

upper collar

3. Turn and lightly press along the seam edges.

4. Staystitch the bodice neckline edge.

5. With right sides together, pin the collar to the neckline, clipping the bodice neckline only as necessary so collar fits.

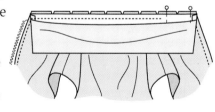

6. Stitch. Trim the seam to ¼" and press the seam toward the collar.

7. Slipstitch the undercollar to the seamline on the inside of the bodice.

8. Cover the collar with lace, sewing it in place by hand.

A Stand-up Fabric Collar

Use the fashion fabric for the under and upper collars. Use a lightweight interfacing and follow the assembly steps described on page 108.

If you want ruffled lace trim along the upper edge of the collar, position it on the upper collar and baste it in place *before* sewing the upper and under-collars together.

Fast Serger Stand-up Collar

Use this technique *for opaque fabric collars only* or those collars you'll be covering with lace or other trim. If you do not use trim and your collar is sheer, the seam will show through to the outside.

1. Apply interfacing to the upper collar and to the undercollar.

2. *With right sides together*, serge the upper collar to the undercollar along the upper edge. Press the seam toward the undercollar and understitch.

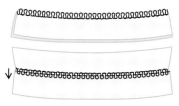

3. *With right sides together*, serge the short ends, allowing the understitching to offset just slightly. This keeps the undercollar rolled to the inside of the finished collar).

4. Turn the collar right side out and press from the undercollar side. Baste the raw edges together along the seamline.

5. Pin the collar to the neckline edge, clipping the neckline as needed. Place the pins to the left of and parallel to where you will be serging.

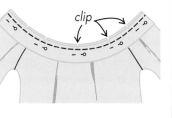

6. Serge, trimming away the excess seam allowance. For a soft seam next to your skin, use woolly nylon in the loopers. Press the seam toward the bodice.

Designing Collars

It's always easier to buy a commercial pattern with the desired collar shape, but there are times when you just can't find exactly what you want. For example, the covers of the original bridal book, ***Sew a Beautiful Wedding***, featured two fabulous gowns from Alicyn Wright, the bridal designer for The McCall Pattern Company.

They were gorgeous and readers loved them, particularly the necklines. But, patterns eventually get discontinued. So, what do you do?

If you love a pattern, buy it as soon as possible and keep it for later mix and matching.

Here are some collar design basics that will help you create your own designs.

◆ If the collar is exactly the same shape as the tissue, it will lie flat on the dress.

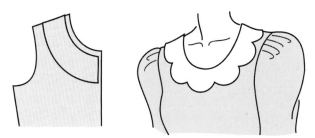

◆ If the collar has less curve than the dress neckline, it will stand up.

♦ If the collar has more curve than the bodice neckline, the outer edges will ruffle.

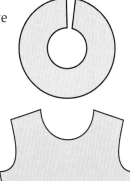

Alicyn's Draped Collar

A draped collar like the one on Alicyn's dress must follow the neckline shape so an understay is created to fit the shape of the neckline. The draped, gathered piece is sewn to the stay.

Alicyn's pattern pieces look like this:

The stay is in 3 parts, two backs and a shaped front.

The drape is cut in 4 parts with seams at the center front and shoulders so it can be gathered at these places.

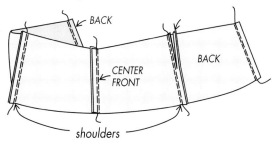

The drape is seamed using a long stitch length gathered to fit the stay. Then they are sewn *right sides together* and turned to form the collar.

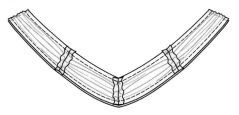

Then the completed collar is tacked to the neckline, covering the raw edge or allowing a lace-finished edge show.

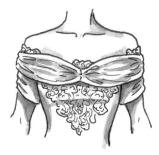

NOTE: Alicyn is one of the best bridal designers for sewers. Because she sews bridal gowns herself and writes the instructions for McCall's bridal patterns, you won't get any better help anywhere. She also has bridal sewing tips on her web page (page 155).

Crisscross Collar

Another collar style that we see occasionally is the crisscross style. The left collar is the length from the center back to the center front, plus seam allowances. The right collar is the same, *plus the crossover*—from the center front to the side seam. The right collar generally overlaps the left; as the designer, of course, you can change this as you wish.

Prepare the collar and attach as described for Alicyn's draped collar, remembering to leave an opening in the bodice side seam where the right collar will be inserted.

Gridded Pattern Paper Makes Re-designing Easier

For any redesigning or designing you want to do, use Perfect Pattern Paper (page 61). Pati Palmer designed it for McCall's as a fitting tool, but it also is perfect as a design tool. All the lines and the grid will help you in accuracy, grainline, and matching. Cut a collar out of this tissue and try it on your pattern to see how it looks and to see if it is accurate. Have fun!

CHAPTER 15

Closures

Generally, wedding gowns have a zipper and/or buttons and loops. You usually insert the zipper *after* attaching the bodice to the skirt. Here are a few sanity-saving tips.

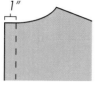

- A lapped zipper looks more professional than a centered one and is especially important when there is a lace overlay. The lace designs can lap over the left edge, hiding the zipper. An invisible zipper is another good choice.

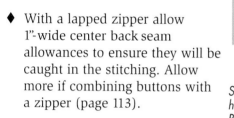

- With a lapped zipper allow 1"-wide center back seam allowances to ensure they will be caught in the stitching. Allow more if combining buttons with a zipper (page 113).

Stop sewing here. Backstitch.

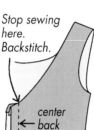

center back

- When applying a zipper in a deep V-back, stitch the neckline of the bodice to the center back, leaving the seam allowances free to the edge. Finishing the inside will be easier.

- If the skirt has an overskirt, insert the zipper in the underskirt *only*, leaving the overlay free (page 132.)

- When possible, such as in a gown without a waistline seam, insert the back zipper *before* you sew the side seams so you can work on flat pieces.

- If you have a piped waistline or neckline, eliminate bulk before applying the zipper. Pull out the filler cord and cut off ⅞" from the left back and ¾" from the right back. Turn under the seam allowance and apply the zipper.

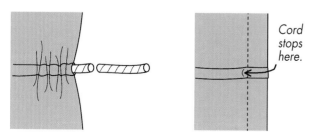

Cord stops here.

Lapped Zipper

1. If the bodice neckline is lined to the edge, complete the neckline *before* applying the zipper.

2. Turn under ⅞" on the right back and press. Turn under 1" on the left back and press.

1" ⅞"

TIP: Use a synthetic coil zipper 1" longer than the opening so the tab will be out of the way of your topstitching. You may need to use YKK's zipper-by-the-yard to get one long enough.

3. Apply ⅛"-wide double-stick basting tape to the right side of zipper, next to the edge of the zipper tape. Peel off the protective paper.

basting tape

paper

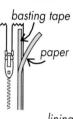

4. Place the fold on the right back next to the zipper teeth with the zipper tab above the neckline seamline. Stick in place. Using a zipper foot, stitch next to the folded edge.

lining

5. Stick basting tape next to the fold on the overlap (left) side. Remove the protective paper. Stick to the right back, just covering the zipper stitching.

basting tape

6. Place ½"-wide Scotch Magic Transparent Tape along the fold. (Test first to make sure it won't damage your fabric.) Stitch next to the tape, then remove it. Remove basting tape from the edge of the overlap.

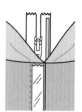

7. Unzip the zipper. Cut off some of excess tape at the top. Fold the remaining excess zipper tape down and catch to the seam allowance.

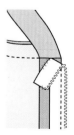

8. On the inside, turn under the lining edges and slip-stitch to the zipper tape.

111

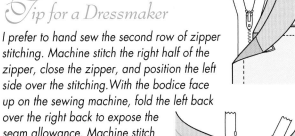
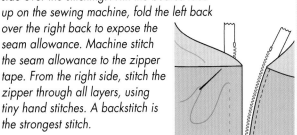
NOTE: There will be instances when you will need to finish the entire bodice and insert the zipper *before* attaching the skirt, even though the zipper extends into the skirt. In this case, leave 3" above the waistline seam unstitched. Then complete the remainder of the bodice, complete the skirt, sew the skirt to the bodice, and complete the zipper.

Leave 3" unstitched.

Invisible Zipper

Invisible zippers are particularly appropriate for the back closure of a wedding gown in fabrics such as brocade, velvet, and sequins. Insert this zipper after attaching the skirt to the bodice, but *before* stitching the center back seam in the skirt. Use a ⅝" center back seam allowance.

1. Unzip the zipper. From the wrong side, press, using the tip of the stream iron to push the coil flat.

2. Apply ⅛"-wide double-stick basting tape to both edges of the zipper. Peel off the protective paper from only the right zipper tape.

3. Position the zipper *face down on the right side of the right bodice back*, with the lining out of the way and the top of the zipper coil ⅜" below the *finished* neckline seam. Position so the edge of the zipper tape is along the edge of the fabric.

4. With the special foot for invisible zippers, stitch close to the zipper coil. Stop sewing when the zipper foot touches the slider. (After sewing both sides of the zipper and zipping it up, decide if you need to go back and sew closer to the teeth.)

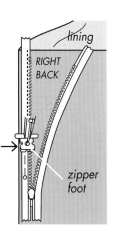

lining

RIGHT BACK

zipper foot

NOTE: If the waistline seam is bulky, don't stitch too close to the zipper in this area—it will pop open. Trim as much bulk out of waistline seam as possible.

5. Remove the protective paper from the left half of the zipper and position zipper on the left bodice as shown. Stitch in place as described for the right back.

LEFT BACK

RIGHT BACK

6. Zip the zipper.

7. Stitch the remainder of the garment seam, using a zipper foot and beginning 3 or 4 stitches above the end of the zipper stitching. Pull threads through and tie to secure.

TIP: Lower the needle exactly where you want it *with presser foot up and zipper standing on its edge. Then lower presser foot and begin stitching.* Pull threads through and tie to secure.

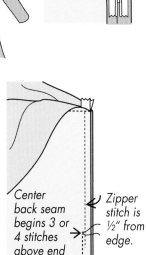

Center back seam begins 3 or 4 stitches above end of zipper stitching.

Zipper stitch is ½" from edge.

8. Stitch the lower ends of the zipper tape *to the seam allowances only* with a regular zipper foot.

9. Hand sew the lining to the zipper tape on the inside. Hide the tab with lace at the neckline if you wish.

NOTE: Even though you are stitching the invisible zipper only ½" from the edge, the turn of the cloth when the coil is closed takes up the full ⅝" seam allowance.

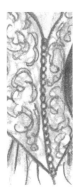

Buttons/Loops

Make self-fabric loops or use one of the ready-made versions.

TIP: To prevent raveling, leave an extra one to two loops at each end to fold under and tack to the seam allowance.

Self-fabric Button Loops

1. Cut a *true-bias* strip no more than ¾" wide and about 18" long.

2. Fold the strip in half lengthwise and stitch, using *very short stitches.* Begin stitching at an angle, coming in to about ⅛" from the fold. Leave a long thread tail at the end.

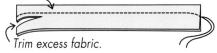
1/8"
Trim excess fabric.

3. Use a blunt-end tapestry needle to draw the thread tails through the loop. Pulling gently, turn the loop right side out.

4. For thin, flat loops, pin one end to the ironing board and steam press while stretching the bias. Pin the other end to board and leave until cool.

5. Press under the the left bodice back to mark the center back seamline. Open it out.

6. Stick ⅛"-wide double-faced basting tape on the seam allowance next to the crease. For even loop spacing, pin a strip of graph paper or Perfect Pattern Paper along the other side of the crease.

basting tape
strip of graph paper along seamline

basting tape

7. Remove the protective paper from the basting tape. Stick loops in place with the first loop ⅜" below the neckline seam. Using a zipper foot positioned along the left edge of the tape, stitch loops in place. An alternate method is to sew loops to paper first, then stitch in place, using a regular presser foot instead of a zipper foot. Remove the basting tape.

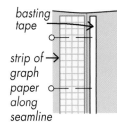

8. Turn under the seam allowance and edgestitch to hold the loops in place. Hand sew the lining in place over the the loops.

9. Press under ½" on the right back. Lap left over right ½", matching centers; sew buttons opposite loops, knotting securely after each button. Go on to next button without cutting threads, but burying thread between the layers.

TIP: To hide under garments and add strength to button area, sew an underlay to right back, then press it under and attach buttons opposite the loops.

underlay

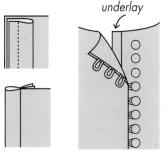

Button the dress using a crochet hook to pull the loops over the buttons.

Zipper with Buttons and Loops

Attach buttons to the overlap of a lapped zipper for an elegant look combined with the security of a zipper. Cut 1⅝"-wide center back seam allowances for this method.

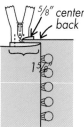
5/8" center back
1⅝

1. Sew the bodice to the skirt, then press under 1⅝" on the overlap side (left back) and ⅝" on the underlap side (right back).

2. Stitch the center back seam, backstitching at the mark for the zipper opening.

3. Stitch loops to the left back as previously described.

4. Stitch the zipper to the underlap.

5. With the zipper closed, match center back lines and pin along the fold of the overlap.

6. Flip the overlap to the right over the zipper and stitch the zipper to the seam allowance only.

7. Sew buttons in place opposite the loops.

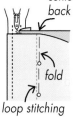
center back
fold
loop stitching

NOTE: There is no need to topstitch the zipper to the left back since the buttons and loops will keep it lapped over the zipper.

Closures in Illusion Necklines

Edgestitch.

lapped zipper

A button-and-loop closure in an illusion back yoke (page 98) is customary. The first method shown below is the one Alicyn recommends in her patterns for McCall's. The other methods must be done *before* sewing the neckline or shoulder seams.

Loops and Lace

1. Zigzag loops in place just inside the left center back.

2. Position narrow lace trim *right side down* on top of loops with the straight edge ⅜" from the raw edges and the upper end extending ⅝" above the collar or binding and below the yoke seam. Stitch in place along center back. Trim the illusion seam allowance to ¼".

Trim.

LEFT BACK

3. Turn the lace toward the seam allowance, turning under the ends. Understitch, then turn under along the center back and edgestitch.

RIGHT BACK

4. Add finishing lace to right back in the same manner.

NOTE: If you choose one of the following two methods, you will finish the shoulder and neckline *after* completing the closure.

Loops Sandwiched Between Layers of Illusion

1. Insert loops between outer and lining layers of illusion on left back.

2. Turn and press, leaving full seam allowance width.

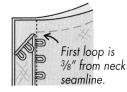

First loop is ⅜" from neck seamline.

LEFT BACK

3. To reinforce both back edges, tuck horsehair braid between the lining seam allowance and the lining and edgestitch in place. Stitch buttons in place opposite loops.

horsehair braid

LEFT BACK

Susan's New Method for Loops in Sheers

Susan's method makes strong loops in sheers.

1. Sew a strip of sheer fabric the length of the back plus 1" for each loop as shown on page 113.

2. *With right sides together* and using a 3mm-long stitch, stitch the illusion to the lining along the center back seam. Do not trim the seam allowances. Press the seam open.

3. Place the loop strip under the seam. Pull loops through with a fine crochet hook, making them all the same size.

4. Stitch on the inside next to the original stitching line to secure the loops.

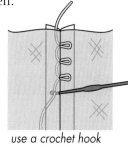

Catch loops.

use a crochet hook

original seamline

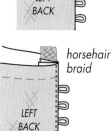

¼"
¼"

QUICK TIP for a **faux button closure**: Attach buttons to the overlap of a lapped zipper for a super fast method of "buttoning" the back of your gown.

Covered Snaps

Cut a circle of fabric that is twice the diameter of a size 3 snap. Sew running stitches around the circle, ⅛" from the edge. Place the "female" half of the snap face down *on the wrong side* of the circle, draw up the stitches and anchor the fabric around the snap. For the protruding ("male") half, create a small hole in the center of the circle with an awl first and apply seam sealant to prevent fraying, then cover.

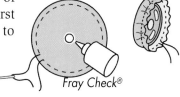

Fray Check®

Covered Buttons

You can purchase satin bridal buttons, cover your own, or have them covered professionally. If the metal shows through the fabric or the fabric ravels, fuse a lightweight fusible interfacing to the wrong side of the fabric.

Tip for a Dressmaker

You may want to invest in a professional button covering machine to make beautiful bridal buttons with cloth shanks.

114

CHAPTER 16

Sleeves

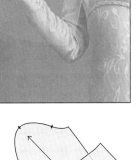

As with all design elements, sleeve styles come and go in popularity. You can create, re-create, change, and design any type of sleeve you want for your gown. Whatever style you choose, it should be in keeping with the overall style of the dress and a shape and size that will flatter your figure proportions. Room for movement is another factor to consider. Active dancing isn't possible in a dress with fitted sleeves, even with a gusset (page 116). If you really want movement, choose a less fitted sleeve, a sleeveless style, or make fake "sleeve-gloves."

Interchanging Sleeves

Many brides combine patterns to get the look they desire. It is relatively easy to interchange most set-in sleeves, but, if the sleeves are dramatically different you'll need to trace the armhole of "A" onto "B" before you can use the sleeve of "A" on bodice of "B."

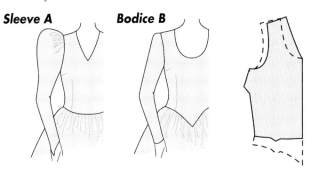

Sleeve A   **Bodice B**

Modifying for A Better Fit

You can modify sleeves for a more comfortable fit by cutting them on the bias, adding elbow ease, or adding a gusset.

Cut Sleeves on the Bias

Cutting long, fitted sleeves on the bias makes them hug the arm without being uncomfortably tight. Bias-cut sleeves also create a more slender silhouette. This is particularly effective in heavy fabrics such as bridal satin, velvet, and brocade. Long full sleeves also drape better when cut on the bias.

To change to bias grainline:

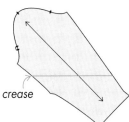

1. Fold the sleeve pattern tissue so that the grainline forms a 90° angle. Crease along the fold.

2. Open the tissue and use the crease as the new grainline when laying out the sleeve.

3. Cut the sleeves single layer, *taking care to flip the pattern* when cutting the second sleeve.

NOTE: **_Do not_** cut sleeves on the bias when using sheer, lightweight fabrics and lace.

Add Elbow Ease

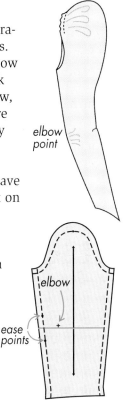

Long, fitted sleeves are very traditional in formal wedding gowns. Most patterns for long sleeves allow ease for the elbow along the back seam. However, some very narrow, fitted sleeves may need a bit more ease, especially if you have heavy arms.

NOTE: If your pattern does not have ease, first mark your elbow point on the sleeve tissue (page 31).

1. Draw a line perpendicular to the grainline halfway between the ease points (notches). This should be the elbow point.

Alicyn Exclusives© courtesy of The McCall Pattern Company

115

2. Cut the pattern on the elbow line *to but not through* the front seamline. Cut the front seam allowance *to but not through* the seamline to make a "hinge."

3. Spread the pattern no more than 1"; more than that will distort the pattern too much. The seam allowance will overlap at the "hinge."

4. True the grainline as shown.

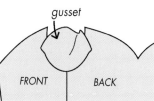

5. Do a row of easestitching in the elbow ease area. When stitching the sleeve seam, draw up the ease and distribute evenly. For lace, you can cut around a motif and overlap to take up the ease.

Make a Gusset

Raising your arms to dance could be tricky in a very fitted sleeve! Add a gusset under the arm for movement. If a gusset is not included in your pattern, create a pattern using the bodice front and back pattern pieces.

1. Lap the front and back bodice pieces with seamlines matching. Place a piece of tissue paper on top.

2. Draw a straight line across the armhole from notch to notch. Mark dots where the line crosses the seamline.

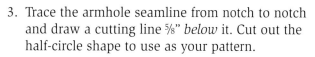

3. Trace the armhole seamline from notch to notch and draw a cutting line ⅝" *below* it. Cut out the half-circle shape to use as your pattern.

4. Place the straight edge of the pattern on the fabric fold and cut 2 gussets.

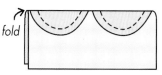

5. Open out each gusset and mark dots at the fold line ⅝" from the edges.

6. Stitch the bodice and sleeve underarm seams and press them open.

7. Staystitch the sleeve and bodice under-arms from dot to dot. Clip to the stitching.

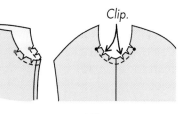

8. *With right sides together* and matching dots, pin the gusset to the bodice underarm. Stitch from dot to dot.

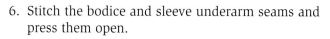

9. *With right sides together*, pin the sleeve to the other edge of the gusset, matching dots. Stitch from dot to dot.

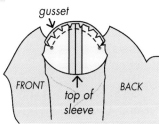

10. Stitch again ¼" from first stitching and trim seam allowances to ⅜".

11. Insert the remainder of the sleeve into the bodice armhole, stopping the stitching *exactly* at the dots. If the sleeve has no cap, finish as you would an off-the-shoulder sleeve.

Hemming Sleeves

Choose one of the following methods to hem the bottom edge of a long sleeve.

♦ Lining and hairline seam

♦ Faced with button and loop closure

♦ Narrow lace trim along raw edge

♦ Rolled edge

♦ Wide lace or ruffle

♦ Narrow handstitched hem

If you hem before you insert the sleeve into the armhole, fit carefully to accurately determine the final length. You won't be able to change it later!

Closures on Long Sleeves

Because long bridal sleeves are generally quite narrow, they need to be open near the wrist so you can get your hand through the bottom of the sleeve. Use the same type of button-and-loop closure as you plan for the bodice (pages 113-114). Lace requires special finishing (page 118).

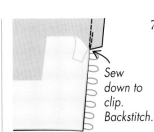

Faced Sleeve with Button-and-Loop Closure

1. Using small stitches, staystitch along the seamline 1" above and below the top of the wrist opening. Clip to the stitching.

clip

1"
1"

staystitch

WRONG SIDE

2. To mark the seamline for loop placement, press under ⅝" along the edge of the sleeve at the wrist opening.

3. Open out the pressed edge and pin loops just inside the seam allowance along the crease. Baste in place.

   Zigzag one or two extra loops to the seam allowance to ensure that end loops won't pull out with use.

fold back

clip

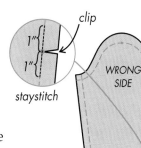

staystitching

RIGHT SIDE

hemline

crease line

4. Pin the facing in place. If your pattern does not have a facing create a 2½"-deep facing. Be sure to extend the facing up ⅝" above the opening.

5. With short stitches, sew the facing to sleeve from clip to clip, catching the loops in the stitching. Trim the seam.

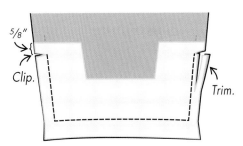

⅝"

Clip.

Trim.

6. Turn and press.

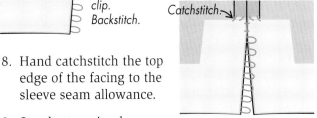

Sew down to clip. Backstitch.

7. Fold the top edge of the facing out of the way and stitch the sleeve seam. Press.

Catchstitch.

8. Hand catchstitch the top edge of the facing to the sleeve seam allowance.

9. Sew buttons in place opposite the button loops, positioning them so the edges of the opening just meet.

Buttons and Loops for Lightweight Lace Sleeves

With this method, you attach the sleeve and lining along the bottom edge, then treat the lining as an underlining.

1. Mark lace along the sleeve opening edge. Staystitch along the seamline for 1" on each side of the opening edge to stabilize. Clip to the stitching as shown.

Clip.

2. Press under ⅝" on the back edge of the sleeve along the wrist opening to mark the seamline as shown at left.

3. Zigzag loops to the seam allowance, making sure they extend beyond the pressed edge.

4. *With right sides together* and the lining on top, stitch a hairline seam (page 66) around the wrist opening and lower edge.

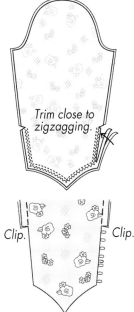

Trim close to zigzagging.

5. Turn the lining to the inside and press. Baste the lining to the lace sleeve along all raw edges.

Clip.   *Clip.*

Long Sleeves with Pointed Hems

Sleeves with pointed hems are usually slim and require an opening. With most fashion fabrics, a faced opening works best. For sheer sleeves with a pointed hemline, roll the hem by hand or machine. For lace, follow the steps on the next page.

Moving the Point

Traditionally, the point of this style sleeve points to the ring finger. If you do not like the shape of the point over your ring finger, you can adjust the pattern so that it is centered on the hand. Simply shift it about 1" toward the front. Adjust the facing to match.

Pointed Hems in Lace Sleeves

Lace sleeves with a pointed hem require some special handling. However, because lace does not ravel, the sleeve edges do not need to be faced. Choose from the following hem finishing methods:

Lined and Embellished with Lace Scallops or Lace Motifs

1. Place lace and lining sleeves *right sides together* with lower raw edges even. Stitch with a hairline seam (page 66), taking care not to stretch the bias edge. Trim. Clip curves.

2. Turn the lining to the inside and press the edge.

3. Position loops for wrist opening if there is one.

4. Pin scalloped-edge lace or motifs cut from lace yardage along the finished sleeve edge and opening as shown, allowing the scalloped edges to

extend slightly beyond the finished edge of the sleeve (but don't hide your ring!). Miter the lace at the point (page 86) and hand sew the mitered fold in place. Turn wrist opening seam allowances to the inside. Trim seam allowance. Handstitch lace to cover raw edges.

Narrow Lace Trim Finish

1. Clip seam allowances at at top of closure. Pin lace over the loops and along the button edge of the sleeve with the straight edge of the lace along the seamline from the top of the wrist opening to the lower edge. Turn under the raw edges at the top and bottom ends of the lace. Stitch in place. Turn under seam allowances.

2. Place lace on the right side of the lower edge of the sleeve with the straight edge just inside the ⅝" seam allowance. Miter at the point (page 86.) Stitch close to the straight edge of the lace, pivoting at the point.

3. Trim the sleeve seam allowance under the lace to ¼".

4. Turn the lace to the inside of the sleeve along the seamline and hand sew in place, mitering the point as needed.

Tips for Long Lace Sleeves

◆ For an all-over lace pattern, cut as you would other fabrics. If design motifs are large, position the sleeve pattern with a full motif in the center of the sleeve. Flip the pattern to cut the second sleeve, making sure to center the motif in the same location on the second sleeve.

◆ Since underarm seams are seldom scrutinized, a conventional seam is appropriate and takes less time than a lapped seam in lace sleeves.

◆ Since lace does not ravel, facings are not needed.

◆ Apply appliqués, beads, or sequins while the lace sleeve is flat, keeping all embellishments at least 1" away from all raw edges so they won't be caught in the seamlines.

◆ Underline fitted lace sleeves with a layer of net, organza, or chiffon for support.

◆ Underline full lace sleeves with chiffon for a better drape.

◆ For a couture finish on a sleeve seam in very lightweight lace or a sheer, use a French seam (page 60). Since the underarm seam is not as noticeable as other seams, this seam finish is not necessary, but it is a mark of quality.

Completing Lace Sleeves

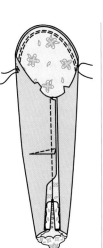

1. To gather the sleeve cap, machine-baste ½" and ⅝" from the raw edge between the front and back notches marked on the pattern. (Most ease will end up between the circles marked on the pattern.)

2. Stitch the underarm sleeve seam from the upper edge to the opening. Backstitch.

3. Press the seam allowances open, (continuing to press finishing lace to the inside if you used it; slipstitch it to the underlining).

buttons

4. Sew the buttons in place opposite the loops.

Finger Loops

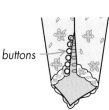

You may want to hold your sleeve closer to your hand with a finger loop. You can make one by crocheting a length of single chain in perle cotton thread to match your fabric color. Or, you can use a leftover loop from those made for the bodice closure—purchased elastic loops, serged chain loops, or self-fabric loops. Baste the loop to the point before finishing the hem edge, making sure that it fits easily over your finger before stitching permanently. Then finish the bottom edge of the sleeve as desired.

Hemming Short Sleeves

Proportioning Short Sleeves

It's important that short sleeves be proportioned to your particular body type. If you have a full bustline, be careful to cut the sleeve so that the finished edge will be *above or below* the fullest part of your bust to avoid adding undesirable visual width.

Line to the Edge

You can create a shaped hem edge on short sleeves and finish them by lining to the edge. Refer to **Couture, The Art of Fine Sewing** (page 158) for directions for designing petal and other interesting sleeves for your gown.

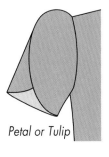

Petal or Tulip

Scalloped, Faced Short Sleeves

1. Draw the scallop stitching lines so they are at the desired finished length of your sleeve. (See page 100 for more information on creating scallops.) Add a seam allowance.

Scalloped

2. For a facing, place the scalloped sleeve pattern on a flat surface and lay tissue paper on top. Tape in place. Measure up about 2½" and draw a line across the tissue. Trace along the bottom and sides of the sleeve.

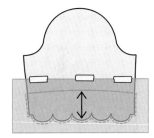

3. Cut the facing from fashion fabric unless your fabric is very heavy—velvet or brocade, for example. For heavy fabric use lining fabric or organza for the facing.

4. Finish the straight, upper edge of the facing by pinking, serging, binding, or clean finishing (turn under ¼" and edgestitch).

5. *With right sides together,* stitch the facing to the sleeve up to the underarm stitching line. Trim, clip and notch as needed.

NOTE: Piping (pages 52-53) is a nice finish for the scalloped edge. Baste in place along the scallops before applying the facing.

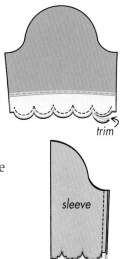

trim

sleeve

6. Turn the facing to the inside and press.

7. With the facing opened out, stitch the underarm seam.

8. Fold the facing up and hand sew to hold in place.

facing opened out

Lace Sleeves Underlined to the Edge

For a sheer look, underline short lace sleeves with net. Then finish the lower edge in one of the following ways.

- ◆ Outline stitch, following the lace design. Trim to the stitching.

Trim netting close to the stitching.

- ◆ Cut sleeves so the the hemline is along the scalloped edge of the lace.

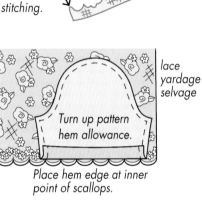

lace yardage selvage

Turn up pattern hem allowance.

Place hem edge at inner point of scallops.

- ◆ Finish the raw edge with trim. (Trim could be cut from lace yardage.)

Lap lace over raw edge of sleeve cut to finished length. Hand or machine stitch in place.

Short Pleated Sleeve

For a slimmer-looking, short puffed sleeve, change gathers at the bottom edge to a center pleat.

1. Draw the pleat stitching lines on the pattern at the desired width. Test the pattern on your arm to determine the placement of the stitching lines for a comfortable fit.

2. Transfer the pleat lines to the wrong side of the sleeve. With right sides together, stitch along the lines for about 2" (adjusting for the desired look).

3. Press into an inverted box pleat.

Sleeve Support

Cap Sleeves

These need no special treatment unless they are exaggerated. To give the sleeve more body, underline with net or crinoline. Use a large shoulder pad, covered with lining fabric to shape the cap.

Puffed Sleeves

Puffed, Leg o'mutton, Victorian, Bishop, and Gibson sleeves are all treated much the same—gathered at the top or bottom or both—and require support and shaping in the sleeve cap.

Short, full puffed sleeves should be completely underlined to help them retain their "pouf" and prevent dips and hollows. It also helps the sleeve to stand out from the arm.

Organza is a good underlining for most sheer fabrics. For medium-weight fabrics, try organdy. For a heavy satin sleeve, which may also require a sleeve head, use crinoline or net.

Making a Sleeve Head

A sleeve head supports and lifts the cap of a gathered sleeve. It is a football shape, generally about twice the width of the sleeve cap.

If the pattern you are using does not provide a pattern piece for a sleeve head, you can make your own pattern and cut it from crinoline or net.

1. Trace the top portion of the sleeve cap pattern between the gathering dots. Cut out the shape.

gathering dots

2. Cut the shape in half crosswise and spread it to double its original length.

x″   x″+ x″   x″

3. Cut out the sleeve head, placing the straight edge on the fold of the sleeve-head fabric. (If sleeves are unlined, cover crinoline or net sleeve heads with organza or English net for sheer sleeves or lining for sleeves of other fabrics—so the sleeve head won't be uncomfortably scratchy.)

4. Machine baste ½" and ⅝" from from the curved edge. Draw up the gathers to fit the head of the sleeve and pin in place.

soft, unpressed edge

5. Holding the sleeve up and supporting the shoulder area with your hands, check the drape, fullness, and overall effect. Adjust as needed, considering the following:

   ♦ If the sleeve cap is too puffy, the sleeve head is too full. Cut a smaller one and test again.

   ♦ If the sleeve doesn't stand up the way you want it to, the sleeve head may not have enough depth or fullness; or, you may need to use a heavier fabric for the sleeve head. (For example, if you used net, switch to crinoline; if you used crinoline, try two layers for added lift.)

   ♦ If the edge of the sleeve head is making stiff marks on your fashion fabric, pull the sleeve head apart at the fold. This softens the fold area and should eliminate the problem.

   ♦ If the above trick doesn't work, try underlining the sleeve with organza (if you haven't already). If you cannot get rid of the sleeve head edge marks, decide whether you can live with it or if you want to try a different fabric for the sleeve head.

   ♦ If neither net nor crinoline work for a sleeve head with your fabric, try fusing a heavy interfacing to your fashion fabric.

   ♦ If a net sleeve head is too stiff, try bridal tulle. It's softer.

   ♦ If you haven't underlined your sleeve and you find it is too droopy, you may need to underline after all.

6. *If the sleeve is lined*, baste the sleeve head to the sleeve prior to setting the sleeve into the bodice. Then baste the lining so the sleeve head is sandwiched between the fashion fabric and the lining. Set the entire unit into the bodice.

   If the sleeve is not lined, set the sleeve into the bodice first. Then pin the sleeve head in place, centered over the top of the sleeve. Sew from the bodice side *exactly on top of* the sleeve stitching lines.

Making a Sleeve Stay

Another way to help puffed sleeves hold their shape, long or short, is to add a *sleeve stay*—a fitted undersleeve that hugs your arm inside the full outer sleeve. The outer sleeve is underlined and the sleeve stay is basted to the underlining at the point where they are still the same size. (For an off-the-shoulder sleeve stay, see page 122.)

fashion fabric | *stay*

1. For the sleeve stay, use a pattern for a fitted, set-in sleeve. If your gown pattern does not include one, find one in your pattern stash or buy a new pattern. Make sure that the sleeve will fit the armhole of your gown. (See "Interchanging Sleeves" on page 115.)

2. Cut the full outer sleeve from the fashion fabric and underlining (crinoline or net for support). Baste the underlining to the outer sleeve.

3. Cut the sleeve stay from organza, lining, or other lightweight fabric to avoid unnecessary bulk in the finished sleeve.

4. *For a long sleeve*, lay the sleeve stay on top of the underlining and pin in place. Catchstitch the stay to the outer sleeve, *catching just the underlining*, at the point where the outer sleeve is wider than the stay.

underlining | *stay*

   For a short sleeve, it is not necessary to catchstitch.

5. Gather the outer sleeve cap until it is the same size as the stay. Baste a sleeve head in place, if needed (see previous section).

6. Baste the two sleeve caps together.

7. Baste the lower edges and hem together.

8. Stitch the underarm sleeve through all layers and press the seam open. Finish the seam edges and hem as desired.

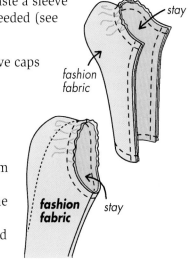

stay | *fashion fabric* | *fashion fabric* | *stay*

Off-the-Shoulder Sleeves

Sleeves for an off-the-shoulder neckline can either hug the shoulder or stand away from it. They can be made of fashion fabric, lace, organza, or a combination of any of these.

Fitted Off-the-Shoulder Sleeves

1. Sew a casing ⅝" from the top edge of the wrong side of the lining using twill tape. Cut elastic the exact width of the casing. Insert and stitch to anchor one end. Pull elastic out ½" to 1" at other end of the casing and stitch to anchor. (The sleeve should not look gathered.)

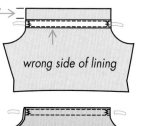

2. Sew lining to the top edge of the sleeve with right sides together. Trim the seam, turn, and press.

3. *Right sides together,* sew the underarm seam in the lining. Right sides together, sew the underarm seam in the sleeve. Press seams open.

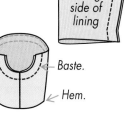

4. Turn right side out. Hem the sleeves.

5. Baste the lining and sleeve together at the armhole.

6. Sew the sleeve to the armhole of the bodice, *right sides together.*

7. Trim the seam allowance to ¼" and bind with a bias strip of your bodice fabric or a fabric that blends with it. (See page 124.)

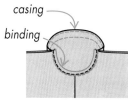

Off-the-Shoulder, Stand-Away Sleeves

For added support, stitch a length of 2"- to 6"-wide horsehair braid between the fashion fabric and the underlining near the top of the sleeve, prior to construction.

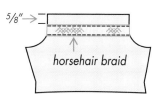

Instead of sewing a casing to the top of the sleeve lining, make a separate, loose casing filled with elastic. Baste one short end of the casing to the front sleeve seam allowance just below the finished top edge. Pin the other end to the back sleeve seam so it can be adjusted during fitting.

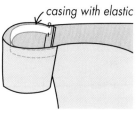

Off-the-Shoulder Poufed Sleeve

1. Cut a fitted sleeve from lining. Add a casing ⅝" from the top edge for elastic as shown at the left.

2. For the pouf part, cut your fitted sleeve pattern in half and spread until it is 2 to 3 times the width of the original sleeve.

3. Cut one layer from your fabric and another from net. Baste the layers *wrong sides together* and gather until the top and bottom edges match the edges of the fitted sleeve lining.

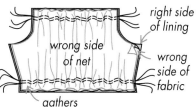

4. Sew pouf to lining *right sides together* along the top and bottom edges. Trim seams and turn.

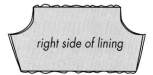

5. Sew the underarm seams and set in the sleeve following directions at the left.

NOTE: For a more finished (but awkward to sew) underarm seam, sew the lining to lining and fashion fabric/net to fashion fabric/net (see step 4 on the next page). Press seam allowances open before turning right side out.

Off-the-Shoulder Lace Sleeves

If lace doesn't have two scalloped edges, finish raw edges with trim.

Sew a casing at the top edge and narrow hem the lower edge of organza underlining.

Place underlining on wrong side of lace with hem and casing away from lace. Baste together. Insert elastic and finish as shown on page 122.

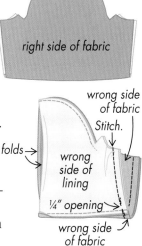

organza

Sleeves with a Strapless Bodice

Some bridal designs feature a strapless bodice with a sleeve set into the underarm, then held in place on the shoulder with elastic. You can wear this style with the sleeves pushed down over the arm for a peasant look or with the sleeves over the shoulder for a little more coverage.

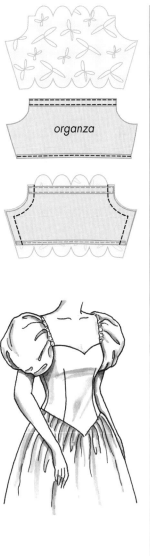

1. Machine stitch along the seamline of the sleeve cap for ½" on each side of the dots that mark the points where the sleeve will be joined to the bodice. Clip to, but not through, the stitching at the dots. Repeat on the lining.

clip   *clip*

1"   *1"*

right side of fabric

2. With the sleeve and the lining *right sides together,* stitch the cap between the dots. Stitch the hem. Trim the seams to ¼".

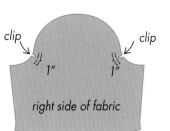

trim

wrong side of fabric

trim

3. Turn and press.

4. Place *lining to lining* and *fabric to fabric,* right sides together (this requires turning it inside out—a tricky maneuver, but necessary). Sew the underarm seam. Leave a ¼" opening at the hem edge of the lining seam for threading elastic through the casing. Backstitch at both ends of the opening.

right side of fabric

wrong side of fabric

Stitch.

folds →

wrong side of lining

¼" opening

wrong side of fabric

5. Press seam allowances open before turning to the outside through the opening at the underarm.

6. Topstitch the edge of the sleeve cap and the hem to form casings for the elastic, stitching the width of the elastic plus ⅛" from each edge.

casings

right side of lining

opening

7. Insert elastic in the cap and hem casings. Pin ends to hold them in place until fitting

8. Pin the sleeves to the bodice. Try on the dress and adjust elastic for a comfortable fit over the shoulders and around the upper arm.

9. Stitch through the shoulder elastic and bodice at the ends of the casing to secure elastic.

10. Lap the ends of the elastic in the hemline casing and topstitch to secure. Slipstitch the opening in the lining closed if you choose (although it's not necessary since no one will see it).

11. With right sides together, stitch the underarm seam of the bodice to the sleeve.

12. Trim the underarm seam to ¼" and encase with binding.

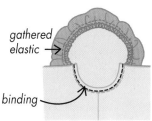

gathered elastic →

binding

Ruffled, Layered Sleeve

This sleeve is attractive and attention getting and deceivingly simple to make. It's bound to draw such comments as, "You really made that?"

Rows of ruffles are stitched to a base sleeve of organza or gown fabric, which is then attached to the actual sleeve. You can make the ruffles from organza, chiffon, or even a lightweight satin. To make them, you'll need fishline and a serger that can do the rolled edge hem.

TEST this technique on bias and crosswise-grain ruffle strips to decide which looks best. You can finish one edge of the ruffle and gather the other or you can finish both edges of the ruffle and stitch it to the base sleeve through the center of the strip.

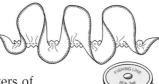

1. Decide how many layers of ruffles and how full you want them. Cut the ruffle strips the desired finished width, plus ¼" for each edge that will be rolled. Cut the strips 2 to 3 times the width of the sleeve, depending on the fabric weight and the desired fullness. (The softer the fabric, the longer the ruffle strip can and should be to avoid a skimpy look.)

2. Cut a strand of 12- to 25-pound fish line 1½ times the length of the ruffle strip. (Test on the fabric. Read "Helpful Hints" above right.)

3. Set the serger for a short, rolled-edge stitch. Use Woolly Nylon in the loopers and attach a cording foot, or a beading and pearl foot if available, to help guide the line along the fabric edge. First serge over 2" to 3" of the fish line. Then place the fabric under the presser foot and continue serging the edge, catching the line under the stitching while trimming away some of the fabric. Leave a long tail of fish line at the end.

4. After serging, stretch the edge firmly to spread the fabric over the fish line. Gather the other edge of the ruffle and stitch it in place on the base fabric. Stitch the ruffled base sleeve to the garment sleeve.

Helpful Hints

♦ Experiment with fish line. Finer line produces a more ruffled, curlier edge; heavier line makes a more flared edge.

♦ On a bias fabric ruffle, allow very long fish line tails at the beginning and end so you won't run out when you spread out the bias edge. To be sure you have enough fishline, you can stretch already serged sections before serging the next section.

♦ Serge slowly to avoid hitting the fish line with the needle—it will break the needle!

Finishing the Armhole Seam

The most common method for finishing the armhole seam allowance is serging. This is fine for regular fabric sleeves/bodices. If the sleeve head irritates your skin, bind the armhole with lining fabric or a piece of satin. (Seams Great™ is too thin to protect you from scratchy sleeve heads).

The seam allowance generally shows through sheer sleeves attached to the bodice so you'll want to bind the entire seam allowance with fashion fabric—it carries the bodice out to the shoulders and gives quite a nice finish.

1. Cut bias strips about 1" wide.

2. Machine stitch to the seam allowance of the armhole, using a ¼"-wide seam.

3. Turn the binding over the seam allowance and slipstitch the other seam, folding under a ¼"-wide seam allowance on the binding.

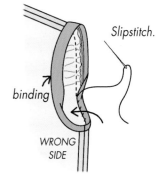

Slipstitch.

binding

WRONG SIDE

CHAPTER 17

Skirt Basics

Designs

There are only a few basic skirt styles for wedding gowns: slim and fitted, A-line, princess-seamed, gored, or full with gathers, tucks, or pleats at the waist. It's the fabric choice and train style that make the difference.

Skirts can be cut from all-over lace or fabric, may be lined or unlined, have lace motifs or lace trim, no train or sweep-, chapel-, or cathedral-length trains, removable trains, overskirts of lace, organza, or tulle—and any other combination that you may design.

Alicyn Exclusives© courtesy of The McCall Pattern Company

Skirt Sewing Order

Assemble the skirt after you have completed the upper half of the gown.

1. Stitch the seams of the skirt, skirt overlay if there is one, and lining separately. Press each one. If the skirt is not fully lined, finish the raw edges.

2. If your design calls for them, apply lace motifs to the outermost layer.

3. If necessary, gather, tuck, or pleat the waistline seams of each layer, separately or together.

4. Hem the overlay and baste it to the skirt at the waistline seam with large stitches so you can adjust the gathers, independently as necessary when you attach the skirt/overlay to the bodice. Baste the skirt lining in the same manner.

5. Baste the skirt unit to the bodice.

6. Permanently stitch the skirt, overlay, and lining to the bodice, after assessing the fit, position, and appearance of any gathers, tucks, or pleats.

7. Turn the waistline seam allowances up toward the bodice. Trim. Cover with finishing lace.

8. Finish the back closure.

9. Hem the skirt and lining.

10. Add any trims that couldn't be added prior to hemming.

11. If it has a train, bustle the skirt.

Stand back and admire your handiwork!!

Layout, Cutting, and Marking

For a sheath gown with a slim, fitted skirt, follow the bodice chapter for assembly. Except for a completely lace skirt, there are no special tricks for this portion of a slim skirt on a wedding gown.

For all other types of skirts, layout can be tricky. Many bridal gown skirts are so full that you may not be able to lay the pieces on doubled, folded fabric as you normally do.

1. To fit the pattern pieces onto the fabric without having to piece the fabric, you will need to lay them on the full fabric width.

2. To ensure that all pieces are cut in the same direction to avoid color and shading differences, mark arrows along the selvage of the entire length of fabric.

3. Cut across the fabric creating two pieces, each long enough to accommodate a skirt piece. Place the pieces *right sides together* with arrows in the selvage *pointing in the same direction.*

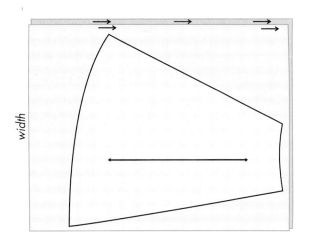

4. Position all pattern pieces with the hem edges pointing in the same direction.

If your fabric is not quite wide enough for the pattern piece, you will need to make a decision:

♦ If the skirt is extremely full, you might be able to take out some of the fullness without losing the overall design effect of the skirt. Do this by taking a large tuck lengthwise down the pattern piece, tapering to a narrower tuck or to nothing at the waistline so that you affect the waistline fullness as little as possible. Refer to the illustration, above right.

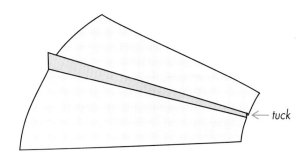

If you'll be trimming the skirt with lace, you may be able to create a seam that can be covered with the trim in one of the following ways:

♦ If your fabric is textured (brocade, velvet) a seam may not show. For a brocade or jacquard fabric, match the pattern precisely. Make the seam in an inconspicuous area—near the side of the lower portion of the skirt, for example.

♦ If the skirt has a lace or organza overlay, an extra piecing seam won't show anyway—don't worry about it.

♦ You may be able to add an extra panel to the back of the skirt if it is too wide to fit on your fabric.

5. Cut out the skirt. To make long, straight cuts, use a rotary cutter if at all possible. It will make your job faster and more accurate and is less stressful on your hands. Be sure to use an acrylic straight-edge ruler as a guide and place a cutting mat underneath. You can slide the cutting mat under your fabric as needed to the area you are cutting. If cutting with scissors, purchase two cardboard cutting boards and lay them on the floor. (See **Dream Sewing Spaces**, by Lynette Ranney-Black, for more ideas for cutting spaces.)

6. Snip mark notches and centers.

Seams, Seam Finishes, and Pressing

Long seams on bridal skirts should be stitched *with* the grain. To determine the correct direction, run your finger along the raw edge of the seam. Short fibers will stand straight up if you are rubbing against the grain. They'll stay flat along the cut edge if you are rubbing with the grain. Think of a cat—don't make the kitty's hair stand on end!

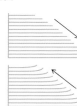

♦ To keep the underlayer of fabric from creeping while you sew, place pins in the seam allowance while the pieces are on a large, flat surface.

♦ When stitching, hold the fabric at about 12-inch intervals and let the fabric feed naturally under the feed dogs without dragging in front of or behind the machine. Easier said than done, I admit, but crucial to avoid stretching the seam unnecessarily! If seams are on the straight of grain, use "taut sewing." Pull equally on the fabric in front of and behind the needle to prevent puckers.

♦ For extra support when stitching large pieces, set up the ironing board next to your sewing table and adjust it to the same height as the table. Rest the bulk of the skirt on the ironing board. Or, move your sewing machine to your dining room table so you'll have the support you need.

Tip for a Dressmaker

When pressing the long seams in full skirts, first press them flat, then place a dowel (from the hardware store) or the long Seam Stick (which is flat on one side) underneath to prevent seam edges from making a visible impression on the right side of the garment. Place a smooth dish towel over the seam stick or dowel before placing the seam on top—it will absorb the moisture from the steam.

♦ The same extra support strategy can be used for pressing. Rest the skirt on the dining room table, for example, while pressing the seams. It's important to support the weight so it doesn't drag on the skirt causing unwanted stretching.

♦ For most gowns, finish the seams according to the type of fabric: serge, pink, bind with Seams Great® or Seams Saver,® or leave unfinished if the fabric does not ravel or if you are lining the skirt.

Tip for a Dressmaker

I finish the seams on a skirt. Though they probably won't ravel with one wearing, it gives the dress a custom look.

Lining

The skirt lining is cut the same as the skirt unless you want to cut down on bulk at the waist.

♦ Full skirts may need to be underlined and lined for enough body to create the desired look.

♦ Narrow skirts should be underlined and lined to help them skim over the body. The lining takes the wearing strain, instead of the gown fabric.

♦ If you are making a lace overskirt, use your fashion fabric as the underskirt and line it for a finished look.

For a *very heavy dress fabric,* eliminate bulk by changing the lining pattern to a fitted A-line style.

1. Measure the lower bodice seamline.

2. Beginning at a point just above your knee level, taper the side seams to meet the measurement at the bodice waistline. Allow for 1"-wide seam allowances. Tissue-fit (page 31) the new pattern to make sure it fits your hips. The adjusted lining will still have the original fullness at the hemline.

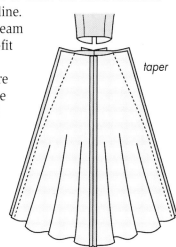

taper

- The lining is usually hemmed at floor length, even when the skirt includes a train, unless the unprotected train will catch on the floor surface.

- Hem with a narrow machine rolled hem (page 134).

- For a super fast hem, serge-finish the lining to the appropriate length.

- For fully-lined skirts, a horsehair hem is the nicest (page 133).

Techniques for Full Skirts

Traditional wedding gowns have full skirts attached to the bodice. These skirts can be gathered, tucked, or pleated to fit the bodice.

Gathering

Gathering techniques are described in the "Tip for a Dressmaker" on the bottom of page 103. Following are some additional pointers for skirts.

- When attaching a skirt to a pointed bodice, place the skirt on a flat surface to make matching the edges and the points easier.

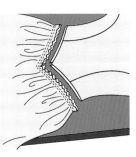

- To make the gathers lie properly, tug on them until the angle of the gathered edge matches the angle of the bodice.

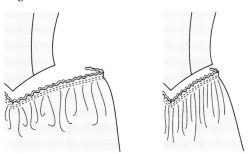

- Start and end the basting stitches for the gathers at each seamline, but lap lines for about ½". Pulling on shorter lengths of stitching lessens the probability of breaking—very annoying when gathering long expanses!! Or, use a heavy-duty thread and go all the way around.

- Baste the skirt and lining together and gather as one unit if the circumference is the same.

Tip for a Dressmaker

Baste the skirt and bodice together for a fitting. Often, the bride will be surprised at the fullness of the actual skirt (yes, even after they've seen a trial run in the muslin fitting shell!) and will want some of the fullness removed. Or, the bride will be dismayed at how "hippy" she looks in the full skirt. Try moving the gathers forward and backward from the side seams to remove some of the fullness from that area. This will often correct the "problem." You can also mark the finished hemline at this time.

- For more fullness, gather the skirt and lining separately—even if they are the same circumference.

- To help alleviate bulk, press gathers flat in the seam allowance only.

- If you have an exceptionally heavy fabric such as bridal satin, Duchesse satin, silk satin, or brocade, consider pleating your skirt instead. Heavy fabrics are very difficult to gather successfully.

Tip for a Dressmaker

You may not be able to convince your customer that tucks or pleats will do the trick. If they insist on gathers, you'll have to persevere! (You could sew a small test sample to make your point more visual.)

Tucks and Pleats

The vertical lines of tucks and pleats have a slimming effect near the waistline.

To convert gathers to pleats, measure the bodice and skirt waistlines, front and back. If the bodice is 14" and the skirt is 28", you will need to pleat out 14" in the skirt so it will match the bodice. It's a good idea to test the conversion in paper and muslin first before you get to the "real" dress.

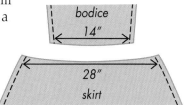

Decide where you want the pleats.

♦ On both sides of the center front.

♦ One deep pleat at the center front.

♦ Pleats evenly space all the way around.

If you want pleats at both sides of centers, you need to eliminate 7" in each area.

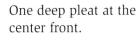

Pin the skirt to the bodice at the center and sides. Pleat one side with 2 to 4 pleats until you get a nice look.

Take the skirt off and mark the pleat folds with snips. Fold the skirt in half and make snips on the other side so the pleats are in the same place on both halves of the skirt.

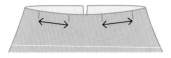

center front

Tucks are generally stitched down from the waistline for a few inches, especially if you are placing lace trim on the waistline seam.

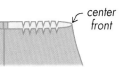

Press tucks in one direction or press them with the stitching line centered as for box pleats.

tucks pressed in one direction

stitching line centered (like a box pleat)

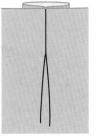

Preventing "Full-Skirt Droop"

Sometimes the weight of a full skirt can cause the skirt to droop at the waistline seam, especially on medium- to heavy weight fabrics. To prevent this, add a supporting ruffle.

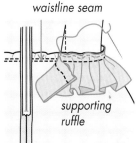

waistline seam

supporting ruffle

1. Cut a 4"- to 5"-wide strip of organdy (or any other crisp, lightweight fabric), making it 2 to 3 times the waist measurement.

2. Fold the strip in half lengthwise.

3. Gather the raw edge along the seamline, distributing the gathers evenly.

4. Pin to the waistline seam allowance, distributing the gathers evenly.

5. Machine stitch to the waistline seam allowance, being careful that the organdy doesn't interfere with any closures.

Attach the supporting ruffle to the waistline seam allowance *between* the skirt and the lining to keep it from scratching your skin.

Techniques for Slim Skirts

Narrow, floor-length skirts require "walkability." This can be added in several ways: adding fullness to the back at the hem; tapering to nothing at the waist (with or without a train); adding a godet; or adding a walking slit.

Add Fullness to the Back

If you don't like the look of a walking slit in a narrow skirt, add walking room in the back with this simple pattern alteration.

For a straight skirt without a train:

Add to the center back seam for a little extra walking room.

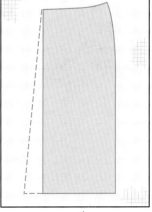

tissue paper or Perfect Pattern Paper

For a straight skirt with a train:

Add fullness to both the center back and to the side seams to provide more walking room in a skirt with a train.

Place the back pattern piece under a larger piece of Perfect Pattern Paper (page 61).

Add the train length. Add width to the center back seam, then add to the side back seam, curving along the lower edge to blend in with the train.

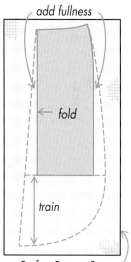

Perfect Pattern Paper

Adding a Godet

A godet is a pie-shaped piece of fabric stitched into the seam (usually at the center back or along princess seams in the front or back).

A godet adds fullness for movement to the bottom edge of the skirt without affecting the overall look of a narrow silhouette.

1. To make the pattern piece, measure from the knee to the hemline. (Starting at the knee ensures that you'll have the walkability you need. You can, of course, adjust when it's basted in place.)

2. Decide how full you want the godet. This depends on: 1) how much drape your fabric has—a heavy satin will stick out if the godet is too full; conversely, a soft fabric such as rayon will look skimpy if not full enough; 2) how much walking room you need—a factor of how pegged (narrow) the skirt is and the length of your normal stride; and 3) your preference.

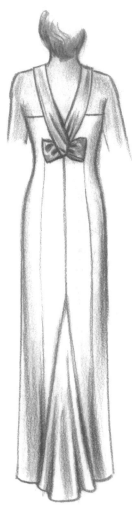

NOTE: You may want to make a test godet. Pin it in place and check to be sure the fullness and drape please you. Adjust as needed for the look you want.

3. On Perfect Pattern Paper (page 61) or tissue paper, draw a straight line (A) the length of the seam from the knee to the hem.

4. At the bottom, measure out one-half the additional desired bottom-edge fullness to each side of Line A. Mark these two points and connect them to line A. Lines A, B, and C should be the same length.

5. With a French curve, connect the ends of the three lines.

6. Add seam allowances at B and C and a hem allowance at the lower curved edge. The center line is the straight-of-grain.

SKIRT BACK

← godet insertion point

7. To insert the godet, stitch the appropriate seam to, but not through, the godet insertion point. Backstitch.

8. Mark the seam intersection at the point of the godet.

9. Pin the godet to the skirt, *right sides together*, matching the seamline intersection to the last stitch in the seam at the godet opening.

10. With the skirt on top (the godet edges are cut on the bias and will stretch), put the needle into the fabric *exactly* at the insertion point. Lower the presser foot. Stitch the seam. Stitch the other side in the same manner.

godet

11. Hem the skirt and godet, using the appropriate hemming technique for your fabric and gown. (See "Hems," beginning on page 133.)

Adding a Walking Slit

Adding a walking slit to a slim skirt is the easiest way to make walking more comfortable.

1. If your pattern does not have a walking slit extension, add one as shown, making it 1⅝" wide. On the lining, stitch small reinforcing stitches ⅝" below the top edge of the extension and 1⅝" from the edge. Clip to the stitching at the corner.

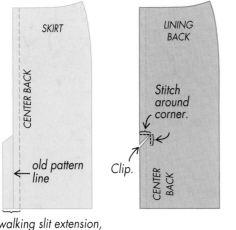

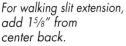

For walking slit extension, add 1⅝" from center back.

2. Stitch the center back seam to ⅝" below the top edge of the extension. Backstitch. Press open and hem the skirt.

3. Turn up the lining hem so it is shorter than skirt by ½". Turn under ⅝" around the extensions on the lining and pin. Slipstitch the folds to the extensions.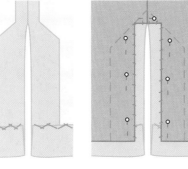

4. Hem the lining.

Skirt Overlays

Skirt overlays are usually made of lace or a flowing fabric such as organdy, chiffon, or organza. You can make an overlay as full as you like; attach rosettes, lace motifs, or lace trim; use several layers to make a flowing, opaque skirt; or make layers of ruffles for a fairy-tale princess look.

♦ You would generally use an overlay for a ballroom-style gown that does not have a train.

♦ To create an overlay for your gown when the pattern does not include one, use the pattern pieces from the skirt.

♦ Stitch the seams of the overlay and press. Since the overlay is made of a lightweight fabric, use French seams (page 66). For a lace overlay, use an invisible lapped seam (page 81).

♦ For a full, gathered overlay over a gathered skirt, gather each layer separately at the waistline.

♦ Hem the overlay before attaching it to the bodice.

♦ A net overlay needs only to be trimmed to the correct length. Or, edge the net in the same manner as your veil is edged for a complementary and coordinated look.

♦ Attach any embellishments *before* gathering the overlay; it's easier to work flat. When embellishing, place the overlay on a large flat surface and position the trims at pleasing intervals. Pin in place, then stitch.

Attaching Skirt and Bodice

When your gown has a pointed bodice, you'll need to take special care when attaching the skirt. If the skirt is gathered, refer to "Gathering" on page 128, before proceeding.

1. Mark the ⅝" stitching line very lightly with pencil at the center front. Stitch with a short stitch just inside the stitching line for 2" to 3" on each side of the center front to reinforce the point. Clip *to but not through* the stitching. Mark the stitching line on the bodice in the same manner, but do not staystitch.

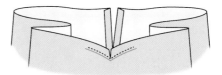

2. Gather or pleat the top edge of the skirt.

3. Matching seamlines and points, carefully pin only the right skirt front and back to the bodice *with right sides together.*

4. With the bodice on top and starting at the center back, stitch the bodice to the skirt. When you are ½" from the center front point, shorten the stitch length to 18 to 20 stitches per inch. Stitch *exactly* on the seamline as marked, *ending precisely at the intersection* of the two seamlines. Backstitch. Remove the gown from the machine.

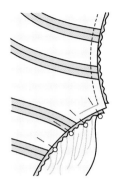

5. Check the gathers and the point. Restitch if necessary to remove unwanted tucks.

6. Pin the remaining half of the skirt to the bodice, pinning carefully at the center front point where the stitching ended. *Starting exactly at the center front where you ended*, stitch from the center front to the center back.

7. Check the seam and correct if necessary. Press the seam allowance toward the bodice. Press only the seam allowance if the skirt is gathered to avoid flattening the gathers. To reduce bulk at the center front, trim the seam allowance diagonally across the point, ¼" from the stitching.

If your skirt has a center front seam, stitch the seam *up to but not past* the waistline seamline. Backstitch. This creates the same effect as clipping to the point in step 1, on previous page. Continue as above, *keeping the center front seam free of the stitching* so you can easily see the last stitch in the center front seam and to avoid bulk.

Complete the Skirt Closure

In "Bodice Construction Basics" (page 95), I recommended that you leave the last 3" of the zipper unstitched in the bodice until after you stitched the bodice to the skirt. To complete the closure, simply complete the stitching of either the zipper or the buttons and loops.

When sewing a zipper into a lined dress with a sheer overskirt:

1. Sew through both layers of the underlined bodice, but only the lining of the skirt.

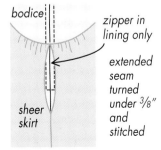

bodice

zipper in lining only

extended seam turned under ⅜" and stitched

sheer skirt

2. Turn under and stitch the seam allowance on the fashion fabric or sheer lace seam edges. This is easier to achieve if you cut a 1"-wide center back seam allowance for inserting the zipper as recommended on page 111.

Waistline Stay

A waistline stay is one sign of a custom-made gown. It holds the gown at the waist, so that the weight of the skirt doesn't drag the bodice down. (This is especially important on strapless gowns!)

1. Cut a piece of 1"-wide grosgrain ribbon the length of your waist plus 3".

2. Pin it around your waist so that it's snug, but comfortable. Mark with pins where it overlaps.

3. Pin the stay into the dress at the waistline, placing the pins on each side of the zipper. Try the gown on to double-check the stay placement. Adjust if necessary, so the stay rests at your natural waistline. This is very important.

4. Sew the stay to the gown by catchstitching the bottom edge of the stay to the seam allowance next to the waistline stitching. Leave the ends loose so you can sew hooks and eyes in place and still be able to hook them before the dress is zipped or buttoned.

5. Turn the stay ends under and stitch them in place. Attach hooks and eyes to fasten the stay ends inside.

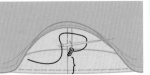

Tip for a Dressmaker

Make thread chains to connect skirt layers at the center back and side back seams about ¾" up from lower edge.

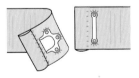

CHAPTER 18

Hems

The hem in a bridal gown is an important detail. You can ruin a beautiful gown with an ugly hem. If improperly hemmed, the gown won't "walk" well, creating a disturbance all the way down the aisle!

Helpful Hints for Hems

♦ Most bridal fabrics should hang *at least* 3 days before hemming. Bias-cut skirts and those that are extremely flared or cut from lightweight or very drapey fabric require several weeks if you have the time.

♦ *Always* wear your wedding shoes when having the hem marked as heel height affects the length. High heels also change posture, thereby affecting the fit and final hem length as well.

♦ The more flared the skirt, the narrower the hem should be. The following guidelines should help.

Straight skirt . . . 2"-3" Flared hem . . . . . ½"
A-line . . . . 1"-2" Circular hem . . . . ¼"

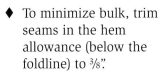

♦ To minimize bulk, trim seams in the hem allowance (below the foldline) to ⅜".

♦ On enclosed seams, clip *to but not through* the seam stitching at the hemline. Turn the seam allowances in opposite directions.

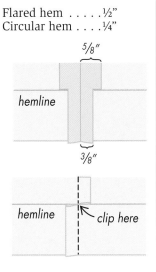

♦ Lightly press the hem fold before stitching.

♦ Be sure to use the same hemming technique on the skirts and sleeves of all the bridesmaids gowns. All hems should be the same distance from the floor.

♦ Finish the raw edges of the hem according to the fabric you are working with and the seam finish treatments used throughout the rest of the gown. Choices include: serging, pinking, stitching and pinking, straight stitching ¼" from the edge, or doing a Hong Kong finish (page 70). Do not use hem tape or lace as these add unnecessary bulk.

Tip for a Dressmaker

Refuse to pin the hem of a bridal gown or bridesmaid's dress without the proper shoes! You will save yourself and the customer a lot of grief!

Hemming Techniques

Before deciding on the hemming method for your gown, read through the possibilities below. TEST your chosen technique on a scrap of fabric that is at least 12" long and the same shape as the lower edge of the skirt.

Horsehair Braid Hem

Horsehair braid adds body to a hem edge and helps keep the hem flared. It is available in widths from as narrow as ⅝" to as wide as 6". Consider the fabric, style of skirt (full or narrow), and the desired look to determine the appropriate width. If the skirt is narrow, you may want to use up to a 3"-wide braid; if the skirt is full and made from a soft, flowing satin you may choose a ⅝" width. Heavy bridal satin may need 1"- to 2"-wide horsehair braid in the hem to hold a flare.

1. Turn up and press the hem. *Be sure the hem is the correct length. It can't be lengthened when completed!*

2. On the right side, place the horsehair braid ⅛" from the hemline fold.

3. Topstitch very close to the edge of the braid, being careful not to stretch the braid as you sew. (Lap ends ¾".)

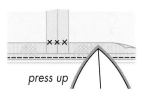

4. Trim the hem allowance to ¼" and press the braid to the wrong side of the gown. Tack at the seam allowances or sew to the lining or underlining. On a long, full skirt, topstitch in place; the stitching will be barely visible.

NOTE: Horsehair hems, especially those on long trains, can "catch" on carpets. To prevent this, cover the horsehair with slightly wider satin ribbon. Topstitch the ribbon in place over the horsehair braid. After turning up the hem, tack it at the seams to secure.

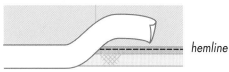

Cover horsehair braid with satin ribbon.

Catchstitched Hem

This "invisible" hem is sewn by hand. The flexibility of the stitches prevents unsightly "pulls" on the right side of the gown. It is often used for a deep, traditional hem on a slim skirt. It's nice on velvet as well.

1. Turn up the skirt at the desired length and press.

2. Trim the hem to the desired finished depth.

3. Finish the raw edge using the method of your choice.

4. Stitch the hem, using loose X-shaped stitches as shown. Catch only a thread or two of the garment and take a longer stitch in the 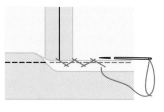 hem allowance for security. At the seams, catch the *seam allowances only* in the hemming stitches.

NOTE: Fold just the hem edge down as you stitch. Don't fold the hem back against the right side of the gown as you work as this creates a crease on the outside along the stitching line that may be difficult to remove.

For narrow, lined skirts, fold the hem over the lining and catchstitch to the lining only. This hem treatment completely eliminates the problem of the hem stitches showing on the right side.

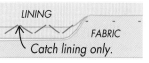

Double Hem

A double hem finish adds weight to a straight hem edge, especially in lightweight, sheer fabrics. *Do not use for a flared edge (A-line for example).*

1. Allow double the hem allowance depth (from 4" to 12") when cutting out the skirt pieces. After stitching the skirt seams and marking the hem, grade the seam allowances as shown at right.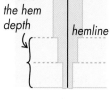

2. Turn up half the hem allowance. Turn up the same depth again, enclosing the raw edge. Press.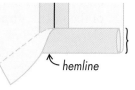

3. Blind hem, topstitch, or slipstitch (lace fabric) the hem in place. Press again.

4. You can cover the stitching line on the outside with ribbon, lace, or other trim if appropriate for your gown design.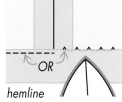

Machine Rolled Hem

This is an easy finish for flared skirts. You will need a ⅝"-wide hem allowance.

1. Turn up ½" and edgestitch very close to the fold.

2. Trim hem close to the stitching.

3. Turn up ⅛" and edgestitch again.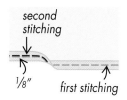

Hand Rolled Hem

This is a beautiful, albeit time-consuming method, for finishing the hem of your gown.

1. To stabilize the edge, stitch ⅛" outside the hemline fold (in the hem allowance). (Make sure you try on the gown to ensure the hemline is accurate.)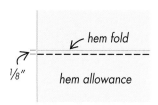

2. Carefully trim the hem allowance away ⅛" from the stitching.

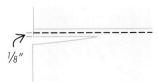

3. Use a new, fine hand sewing needle (size 9) and a single strand of fine silk or cotton embroidery thread. Make a tiny knot in the end.

4. With your fingers, fold the fabric along the stitching line (⅛") and take the first stitch into the fold. Come out of the fold, go straight to just beyond the raw edge of the hem and pick up only a thread of the skirt fabric. Bring the point of the needle straight back into the fold and along the fold for ¼". Bring the needle out again and pick up a thread of the fabric. Continue this sequence for approximately 2".

5. Pull gently on your thread until the fabric rolls and the stitching "disappears."

Pull thread gently to roll the edge.

6. Continue sewing in this manner in 2" segments until the hem is done. Press gently.

Lace Hem

Rather than hem the raw edge, you can cover the edge with lace.

1. Trim the skirt to the desired *finished* length.

2. Cut pieces of leftover gown lace or narrow lace edging long enough to trim the lower edge of the dress. If the edge is flared, allow extra for easing.

3. Pin the lace in place just over the lower edge of the dress, easing or cutting and lapping along curves. To join lengths of lace, turn under one end and lap over the raw edge of the next piece of lace. Stitch in place by hand or machine.

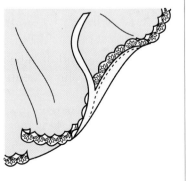

4. On the *inside*, trim the *skirt* fabric close to the stitching.

Serged Hem

This hem treatment is a good choice for full skirts and for linings.

1. Serge the bottom edge of the skirt or lining. If possible use a 2-thread stitch—it's less bulky than the traditional 3-thread overlock stitch.

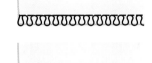

2. Turn up and press the lower edge along the serging; edgestitch.

Serged Rolled Hem

This method is even faster than a machine-rolled hem. Just make sure that your serger, thread, and fabric are compatible. Some fabrics don't roll at all; some sergers roll only very lightweight fabrics; and some threads don't cover as well as others.

1. Follow your serger instruction manual for a rolled edge. If your serger can do a 2-thread rolled edge, use it on lightweight fabrics such as bridal veil net and chiffon. Tighten the lower looper tension on a 3-thread serger or the needle tension on a 2-thread. Depending on your fabric, use regular thread, woolly nylon, or decorative thread in the loopers and regular serger or clear nylon thread in the needle. TEST on a scrap.

A shorter stitch length is usually used for a rolled edge. However, it is best to start with a 2.0mm stitch length and gradually shorten the stitch until you achieve the look you want. Sometimes a stitch that is too short will cause the rolled edge to fall off, especially along the bias or cross-wise grains in lightweight fabrics. Check the durability of your test sample. Any stitch length is fine if it gives you the look you want. In fact, a longer stitch length (3 to 4mm) is often used to hem ready-made scarves.

2. Serge slowly, making sure that the fabric is rolling properly, the thread is covering the edge, and stitches are not pulling away from the fabric edge. If the skirt hem is curved, make a curved edge sample first.

If you have trouble serging a rolled edge, try lengthening the stitch a bit to reduce bulk. Also, try the left needle position. Check your manual *before* trying this solution—not all sergers can do a rolled hem with the left needle.

Picot Hems

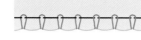

You can add a picot edge (lightly scalloped) to a hem edge using your sewing machine or your serger. TEST on fabric scraps first.

For a conventional machine:

Use a thread that blends or try a metallic thread for some sparkle.

1. Turn and press the hem allowance in place.

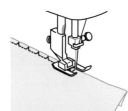

2. Set your machine for a blind-hem stitch. On the right side, stitch along the hemline fold edge.

3. Trim the hem allowance close to the stitching on the wrong side.

For a serger:

This finish can also be done on the serger by lengthening the stitch to 5mm, 6mm, or 7mm (rolled hems are commonly set at 2mm). Use taut sewing (page 65) as you serge to create this edge finish.

Lettuce Leaf Hem

This hem can be done on your sewing machine or your serger. The amount of ruffling will vary.

◆ Stretchy fabrics, such as single knit and jersey knit, ruffle well.

◆ Lightweight fabrics ruffle more than heavy-weight fabrics.

◆ Bias edges in wovens stretch more, as do edges cut on the crosswise direction of knits.

◆ The shorter the stitch length, the more lettuce effect you will get.

◆ To increase ruffling, increase the presser foot pressure.

For a conventional machine:

1. Set your machine on a medium to wide, short zigzag stitch.

2. Trim the hem allowance to ½" and turn it under.

3. Begin stitching, stretching the edge in front of and behind the presser foot. The more you stretch the edge, the more it will "lettuce."

4. Trim the hem allowance to the stitching.

For a serger:

To serge a lettuce leaf hem, set your serger for a narrow, rolled hem as described on page 135 and stretch as you serge.

Lined-to-the-Edge Hems

When lining to the edge, pin the lining to the skirt at the lower edge *with right sides together*, matching centers and seams. Baste, then try on to make sure that the layers are hanging evenly. Remove basting threads and re-pin as needed. Stitch. Trim the seam to ¼". Turn and press. Understitch if desired.

Faced Hem

Choose a faced hem when you want to eliminate bulk but don't want to line to the edge—on a sequined fabric, for example.

1. Trim the bottom edge ¼" below the desired finished hemline. Remove sequins or beads within 1" of the raw edge (see page 49). You will replace them down to the finished edge after completing the hem.

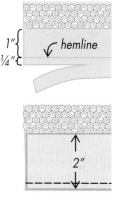

2. *With right sides together*, stitch a 2"-wide bias strip of lightweight fabric to the hem edge along the hemline.

3. Turn the facing toward the seam and press.

4. Turn the facing to the inside and turn under the raw edge. Slipstitch or catchstitch in place.

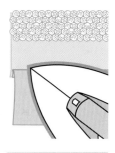

5. Replace sequins or beads down to the finished edge.

CHAPTER 19

Trains & Bustling

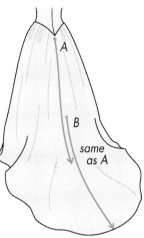

Bustling a Train

If your gown has a long train, you'll need to bustle it to get it out of the way for the reception. *Overbustling* is the most common (and the quickest) bustling method. The train is lifted up to the waistline in folds, over the back of the skirt and is fastened with hooks and eyes or snaps or with buttons and loops.

Underbustling brings the train to the waistline by folding the fabric and fastening it *under* the skirt with ribbon loops and ties as in the gown illustrated below. While the less common of the two methods, this nevertheless creates a unique look and can be stunning when executed properly.

The method you choose depends on your taste, the style of the gown, the weight of the fabric, and the length of the train. Before bustling, the gown must be completed, including the hem.

underbustle

Overbustling

Put the gown on with all of the proper undergarments, petticoat, and shoes.

1. Measure the center back seam of the skirt from the waistline seam (A) to where it hits the floor.

2. Measure from edge of the train up along the center back seam the same distance. Mark with a pin (B).

3. Bring point (B) up to point (A). Pin securely.

4. Pull up and arrange the sides of the train in a pleasing manner until the rest of the skirt back is floor length. Pin in place at even intervals, at enough points to hold the train securely.

5. Sew loops or hooks in the train at the pinned points.

6. Put buttons or eyes at the back waist. If your gown fastens with buttons and loops at the back, you can use the bottom loop for the center bustle point.

- ◆ Try to hide the loops on the skirt. Blend them into lace motifs or trim if the skirt has any. If not, use a thread that matches the skirt exactly and finger crochet the loops (page 138).

single motif with loop

interfacing on wrong side

  - ◆ Before sewing each loop in place, cut a small circle of non-fusible interfacing with your pinking shears. Position on the underside of the skirt at each location where you will sew a loop. (Pinking helps prevent the interfacing edges from showing on the outside of the gown.)

◆ To make finger crocheted loops, thread a needle with strong thread (buttonhole twist works well) and insert it through the interfacing and the train, next to the seamline. Take a small backstitch from the right side of the train. Pull the thread and leave a 1" to 2" loop. Insert your fingers through the loop, grab the thread, and pull. Repeat until you have a chain of the desired length. Sew the other end of the chain in place where you started.

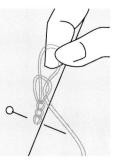

Tip for a Dressmaker

Don't make the loops too strong; if someone steps on the bride's dress, the fabric could rip. Try to ensure that the loop will break instead. It may be necessary to repair a couple of loops before the gown is cleaned and stored, but that's a lot easier than repairing ripped fabric!

Underbustling

An example of this bustling style is illustrated in the fashion drawing on page 137.

1. Measure the train as you did for overbustling (step 1 on page 137). Bring point (B) up to point (A) *between the skirt and the lining*. Pin the train in place. Pin mark the waistline and the train where they meet.

2. Pull under and arrange the sides of the train in a pleasing manner until the rest of the skirt back is floor length. Pin in place at even intervals, adding enough points to hold the train securely.

3. Hand stitch 15"-long pieces of narrow grosgrain ribbon to the waistline at the pin marks between the skirt lining and the train.

4. Fold 2½"-long pieces of grosgrain ribbon into loops and hand sew to the

lining

skirt

pin-marked points on the train, stabilizing the fabric at each loop location with a small piece of interfacing as shown on page 137.

5. To bustle, pull the train up from the underside, tying the loops with the ribbon at the waist. Adjust the folds.

Wrist Loops for Your Train

(Also see page 154.)

1. Cut a piece of ⅜"-wide satin ribbon 11" to 14" long. Fold the ribbon in half and baste raw edges together.

ribbon

2. Turn under ½" on the ribbon raw edges. Pin this edge to the wrong side of the train along the back center seam, high enough above the hem so it won't peek out. Hand sew securely in place.

Detachable Trains

A detachable train is a beautiful accent for the ceremony but allows you the flexibility of making your dress a little more casual and comfortable for the reception. It also eliminates the bustling that an attached train requires—something to think about if you don't want all the extra fullness that a bustled train creates (at your reception).

You may be able to find a pattern with a detachable train like those shown on page 139 or you can use the method described below to add a simple train to almost any gown. Just be sure that your dress is as finished underneath the detachable train as it is with the train attached. Otherwise, it will look like something is missing from your dress after you remove the train.

Your detachable train should match the overall design and feeling of the rest of the gown. Make it from the fashion fabric, lace, organza, chiffon, or bridal illusion.

1. Using the back skirt pattern, modify it to add the desired fullness and train length as shown in the illustration on page 139. Cut it from muslin and test the fullness, length and shape, adjusting as needed for the desired effect.

2. Cut one train of fashion fabric and one of lining fabric.

3. When cutting the train from your fabric, place the center back seam on the fold for all but very full trains. For a very full train, you may need to modify it as shown for skirts on page 130.

← fold

Adjust train to desired length.

NOTE: If you are using lace appliqués cut from your lace fabric, use organza or netting for the lining.

4. Apply any lace trim or appliqués, at this point. Do not extend lace into seam or hem allowances.

5. *With right sides together*, stitch the lining to the train, being careful not to stretch the seams as you sew.

6. Trim the seam, clip curves, and understitch. Turn the train right side out and press lightly from the wrong side.

NOTE: If you are trimming the edge of the train with lace trim, simply arrange the two layers with wrong sides together, then serge them together. The lace trim will cover the serging.

7. Baste the upper edges together, then gather or tuck according to your design.

Attach a Train Around the Waist

Determine where you want the train to end—at the center front, off-center, or the side or side back. To attach, follow the directions on page 140.

To finish the upper edge of the train, decide how you will attach it to the gown and consider these three distinctive alternatives. Make sure the train style is compatible with the dress design. For example, you wouldn't want to attach a train around the waist of gown with a dropped waistline. Where the train will be attached is a function of the design as well as the weight of the finished train.

around the waist

at the sides

at the center back

1. Measure your waistline and add 6" for ease, underlap, and gown fullness under the waistband of the train.

2. Decide on the desired finished width of the waistband. Cut a strip of fabric that is the length determined above and twice the finished width plus two seam allowances. For example, if you want a 1½"-wide finished belt and your waist measures 28", you would cut a fabric strip 4¼" wide and at least 34 long. You will trim any excess length later.

3. Stabilize the fabric strip with monofilament waistband interfacing (see **Pants for Anybody** [page 157] by Pati Palmer and Susan Pletsch for a super method) or insert elastic later.

4. Put your gown on. Fold the fabric strip in half lengthwise and wrap it around your waist so that if feels comfortable. Don't make it too tight as you don't want it to crush your gown and you will need *at least* 1" of "breathing room" in the finished band. If the train is made of heavy satin and is to be gathered to the band, allow 2" to 3" of breathing room. The weight and thickness of the gathered fabric will take up some of this ease.

5. Pin mark the waistband center back and the points at which the train will end.

6. *With right sides together,* stitch the waist band to the train. Clip into the seam allowance of the band where the stitching ends.

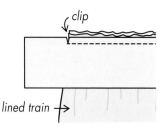

clip

lined train →

7. Fold the band *with right sides together* and stitch the ends and the lower seam up to the edge of the train. Trim corners.

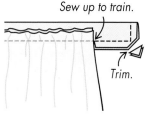

Sew up to train.

Trim.

8. Turn right side out. Turn under the waistband seam allowance and handstitch in place along the inside edge.

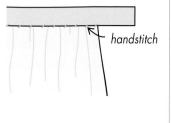

handstitch

TIP: Serge one long edge of the waistband before sewing it to the train, then stitch in the well of the seam from the right side to catch the seam allowance instead of turning it under.

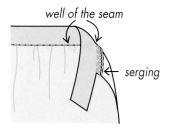

well of the seam

serging

11. Attach a hook-and-eye closure.

12. Trim as desired—with rosettes, bows, or lace, for example.

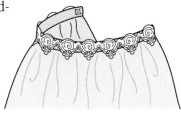

Attach a Train at the Sides

To attach a train at the sides, choose from one of two methods:

♦ Modify the waistband so that the train can be attached with clear snaps or fabric-covered snaps (see page 114 for covered snaps).

♦ Bind the top edge of the completed train with a length of grosgrain ribbon, self-fabric or a contrasting fabric. Cover the bound edge with trim. Sew clear snaps to the binding and to the appropriate positions on the gown.

Attach a Train at the Center Back

Plan the the trim along the top edge of the train so that it is integrated with trim on the bodice. For example, if you are trimming with rosettes, attach them to the dress and the train waistband so that they alternate and fit together to create one long row of rosettes when the train is attached.

Roses on dress will fit between roses on train.

CHAPTER 20

Slips

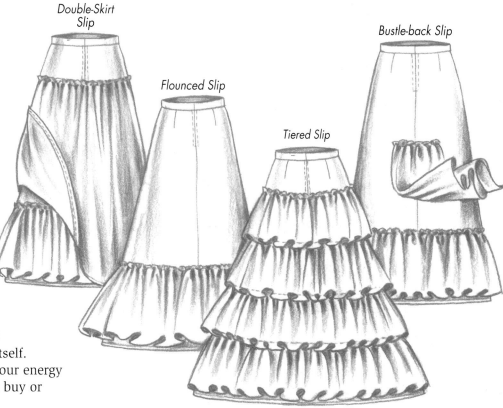

Double-Skirt Slip

Flounced Slip

Tiered Slip

Bustle-back Slip

If you have created a slim, fitted gown, the lining will act as a slip and give you a perfect fit and the gown will "walk" beautifully. For full skirts, a petticoat is a must for additional shaping. Full slips are easy to make. Some bridal patterns include sewn-in slips as part of the gown design. A separate slip, made in the following manner, won't add weight or bulk to the gown itself. On the other hand, if all of your energy went into the gown, you can buy or rent slips from bridal shops.

Making the Basic Slip

Although there are several slip style variations, each begins as a basic A-line skirt. Use a smooth polyester lining, Ambiance rayon, lightweight satin taffeta or, for the tiered style, a medium-weight fabric to add extra body.

1. Use an A-line skirt pattern in your size and adjust to fit as needed. (If one is not available, use a straight skirt and flare it from the waist so it is about 5" larger than your hips and continues flaring to the hemline.)

2. Using extra tissue paper or Perfect Pattern Paper (page 61), extend the skirt to full length (1" shorter than your gown, plus hem allowance).

3. Measure the hemline. It must be at least 60" around for easy walking.

4. Sew a centered zipper in the center back seam.

5. Fit, then sew the side seams.

6. Bind the waistline seam with lining fabric. Sew hooks and eyes to ends.

7. Turn up the hem and machine top-stitch in place.

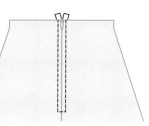

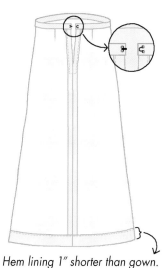

Hem lining 1" shorter than gown.

Tip for a Dressmaker

You may want to have a basic A-line skirt pattern in multiple sizes on hand to use for the slip pattern when one is not included with your bride's pattern. It saves you time and saves the bride the expense of another pattern. Or, buy slips for fittings and sell them to your brides.

The Flounce Slip

This slip is worn with A-line or princess silhouettes. The flounce style skims the hip area, but adds fullness at the hem. You will need 1½ yards of 72"-wide crisp net for the flounces in addition to fabric for the basic A-line slip as described on page 141.

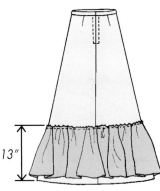

1. Cut net sections as shown and make the basic A-line slip as shown on page 141.

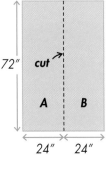

2. Stitch the short ends of the ruffle together, using a ½"-wide seam allowance. Press the seams open.

3. Fold the ruffle in half lengthwise right sides toegether and machine baste the raw edges together. Gather the raw edges by zigzagging over buttonhole twist (page 68), taking care not to catch it in the stitches. (You can serge over cord instead of zigzagging). Draw up the twist and adjust the gathers. Instead of gathering over buttonhole twist, you can serge and pull up on the needle thread to gather.

4. Place the top edge of the gathered ruffle about 13" above the finished edge of the slip. Distribute gathers evenly and pin in place.

5. Stitch the ruffle to the slip.

The Double Skirt Slip

This slip should be worn under fuller princess silhouettes and soft gathered skirts. You will need 3½ yards of 72"-wide net and 4 yards of 1"-wide horsehair braid in addition to fabric for the basic A-line slip.

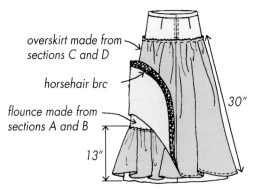

1. Cut the net sections as shown and make the basic A-line slip following the directions on page 141.

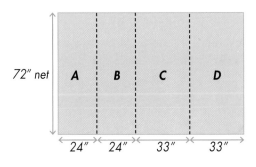

2. Add a flounce to the bottom of the basic slip, using net pieces A and B and following the directions for the flounce flip at left.

3. Stitch the short ends of C and D together, using ½"-wide seam allowances; press seams open.

4. Trim fabric ¼" below the finished hem length.

5. Place horsehair braid on the right side, overlapping the edge ¼". Stitch close to the edge. Turn up along the hem edge and stitch through all layers to hold the braid in place.

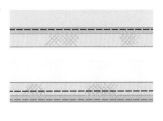

6. Gather the remaining edge of the overskirt and pin to the slip over the bottom ruffle about 30" above the bottom edge. Align the overskirt and slip hems and distribute gathers evenly. Stitch the ruffle to the slip using a long stitch.

The Tiered Slip

This is perfect under bouffant silhouettes. You will need 4¾ yards of 72"-wide net in addition to fabric for the basic A-line slip.

For a very elegant slip, make this style in Chantilly lace—expensive, but lovely!

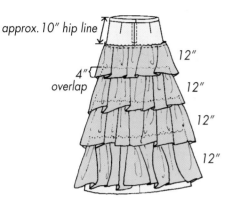

1. Cut net sections as shown below.

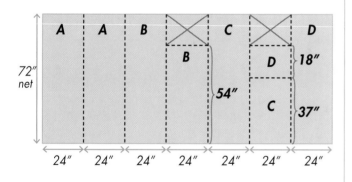

2. Make the basic A-line slip as shown on page 141.

3. Stitch together the short ends of each net piece (A to A, B to B, C to C, D to D) as shown. Press the seams open.

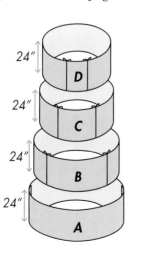

4. Fold each section in half lengthwise, gather, and sew to the basic slip as directed for the flounce slip on page 142. Position on the basic slip at the intervals shown above.

The Bustle-Back Slip

This slip is, of course, great for bustled gowns, but also works well when worn under one with an extended train. The net bustle holds the train away from the body. You will need 2¾ yards of 72"-wide net in addition to fabric for the basic A-line slip.

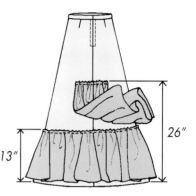

1. Cut net sections as shown.

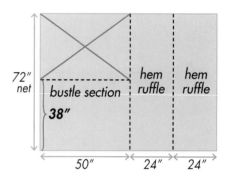

2. Make the basic A-line slip as shown on page 141 and add the hem ruffle as shown to the flounce slip on page 142.

3. Fold the bustle section in half to form a 38" x 25" piece. Machine baste along the 38"-long edge. Draw up gathers until the edge is 10" wide.

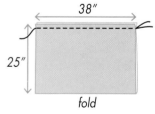

4. Position the gathered bustle over the center back seam, about 26" above the hem edge, as shown above. The net hems should be even with the finished bottom edge of the basic slip.

5. Machine stitch in place.

The Headpiece

Your headpiece is the finishing touch to your bridal ensemble, drawing attention to your face. Even if you don't sew anything else for your wedding, consider making the headpiece and veil.

Headpieces require minimal time and simple sewing skills with amazing savings in relation to ready-made headpieces, which usually retail for well over $100. The materials you will need to duplicate even the most elaborate ones will cost a fraction of what you would pay. You can create a stunning headpiece with simple materials—plus a little imagination and bridal glue.

Read through this chapter, then choose the treatment that will coordinate with the theme of your wedding and add the finishing flourish to your wedding attire.

Tip for a Dressmaker

Your client may ask you to define the "proper" headpiece and veil for her gown. Assure her that whatever style she chooses is the right one for her and help her coordinate the headpiece and veil with her gown as you did when you helped her design her gown. (See pages 12-16 for questions.) It's a good idea to have on hand a catalog of veil and headpiece styles for your clients to peruse for ideas. Encourage your client to bring pictures from bridal magazines (just as she did for her gown) and help her "design" her own headpiece and veil.

CHAPTER 21

Headpieces, Hats, & Veils

Headpiece Style Selection

If you look through bridal magazines, you'll probably notice that some headpieces are definitely "in fashion" during a particular bridal season. Be careful, however, to choose a headpiece style and veil length that is compatible with your overall wedding design—one that is flattering to you and your planned hairstyle and one that enhances your gown—even if it's not the style that seems to be the current trend.

With your hair styled as you will wear it for your wedding, try on ready-made headpieces, veils, and hats. You may want a hat, a veil, or a simple decorated frame, or a combination of all three. Some brides decide to wear no headpiece at all and some add a flower or ribbon to their hair. For some, a special hairdo with no added adornment is the crowning touch to their special look.

Headpiece Frames

The bridal headpiece begins as an inexpensive frame made of buckram or wire—a variety of styles are available. You can also fashion your own frame using milliner's wire, available at craft stores or through mail-order sources.

Fabric stores usually carry buckram or fabric-covered frames in their bridal departments. Craft stores and catalogs are likely to carry a wider selection of uncovered wire frames. Try on frames to find the one that best suits your facial structure and the style of your gown.

You can use leftover lace and fabric scraps, appliqués, or beads to embellish your frame. Glue or stitch them to the frame. Remember that a covered frame can be a headpiece in itself—veiling is not a must. Wire frames are especially nice for lace and flower headpieces.

Common Frame Styles

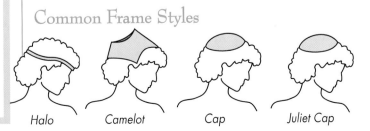

Halo   Camelot   Cap   Juliet Cap

Remember that these are basic frame shapes. They are each available in a variety of *sizes* and *widths* so that you can select the one that is most flattering to your face and head size and shape.

Cover a Wire Frame

1. If the frame is narrow (1" across or less), try florist's tape (available in white). Wrap the florist's tape around the frame, stretching it slightly to activate the slightly sticky surface of the tape.

2. Cover the frame with fabric as shown above right and embellish as desired.

Cover Wider Frames with Horsehair Braid

1. Purchase 6"-wide horsehair braid and cut a piece 2" longer than the frame. Glue the uncorded edge of the braid to the wider side of the frame. Allow to dry.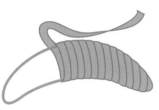

2. Pull on the cord on the remaining edge of the braid to shape it to the frame. Glue the braid to the remaining edges. After it has dried, trim away the excess.

Band   Wreath   Tiara

Cover the Frame with Fabric

1. Purchase the frame and gather necessary supplies —fabric, appliqués, beads, veiling fabric.

2. Press the fabric to remove any wrinkles. Roll the frame along the bias line of the fabric and use tailor's chalk to trace around it, allowing a ½"-wide seam allowance all around.

3. Cut out along the marked lines.

4. Dot the edge on the underside of the frame with glue. Allow to dry for a minute or so.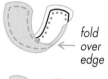

5. Starting at the center of the frame, attach the wrong side of the fabric seam allowance to the glue. Work from side to side, stretching the fabric across the frame so that it is taut and wrinkle-free.

fold over edge

6. Trim away any excess fabric and add extra glue where necessary.

7. Cover the underside with a piece of fabric cut ⅛" smaller than the frame. Glue in place.

8. To finish, position narrow lace trim or ¼"-wide satin ribbon over the raw edges; glue in place.

NOTE: See page 153 if you want to make your veil detachable.

Embellish the Headpiece

Now get ready to have some fun! To make trimming your headpiece easier, purchase a styrofoam head from a beauty supply house (the kind used for storing wigs), and pin your headpiece in place on it. This allows you to view the headpiece from a distance, identify holes that need filling, and judge how the headpiece is shaping up. It also makes it easier to glue embellishments in place.

In addition to lace, beads, and appliqués, you can use artificial flowers, petals, and leaves to embellish your headpiece. These are often packaged in groups of leaves and flowers and are available at crafts and fabric stores and through mail-order sources. It's easy to separate them as needed. Leave wire stems in place; they come in handy when attaching them to the frame. You can trim away excess later if desired. Instead of artificial flowers, you may want to embellish your headpiece with roses made from your gown fabric (see page 45) or with lace motifs cut from fabric scraps.

Decorating Guidelines

- Use odd numbers of embellishments—1, 3, 5—in groups. Even-numbered groups of 2 or 4 of the same flower or leaf will look too contrived and too balanced.

- Strive for a 1 to 3 to a 2 to 3 balance—not 50/50. Start in the center of the headpiece and decide what the focus will be. One large flower? A set of three small rosebuds? Or a cluster?

- Place the focal point a bit off center— placing it dead center is uninteresting. An asymmetric arrangement is always more visually appealing.

- The design should have movement—it should flow from one end to the other or curve. Don't arrange the leaves and flowers in a straight line; it's boring.

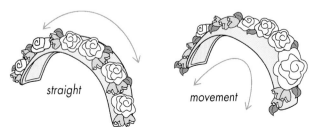

straight   *movement*

- Begin by positioning the largest embellishment first, working from the main focal point out to the ends and edges of the frame.

- Cover the entire frame, extending the leaves and other decorations over the edges to hide them.

- Combine small buds with whole flowers, small leaves with larger leaves, etc. Experiment with placement before gluing pieces in place.

- When you are pleased with the effect, stand back from the headpiece and look for "bald" spots. Fill in with small flowers and buds.

- Add beads and sequins for extra sparkle if desired.

- Secure embellishments with a bridal glue. It is flexible and dries quickly. (Craft glue is runny and doesn't dry fast enough to hold the flowers.)

- When you've decided you're finished, run a bead of glue all the way around the underside edge of the frame to help solidify the headpiece.

- To attach the headpiece to your hair, use either a comb with loops and bobby pins or a barrette. To secure with a comb and button loop, cut a length of button looping slightly longer than the hair comb. Glue it to the inside of the frame near the front, with the loops facing the *back* of the rame. Glue one loop of button looping at the sides of the headpiece, as shown.

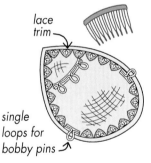

lace trim

single loops for bobby pins

- To secure your headpiece with a barrette, purchase a barrette frame, available at fabric stores and in craft shops. Stitch the barrette to the underside of the headpiece. To give the barrette better holding power, wrap the catch spring with white florist's tape. It's just sticky enough to hold to the hair; but not so sticky that it will disrupt your hairdo.

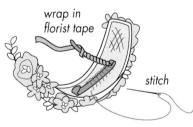

wrap in florist tape

stitch

The Allure of Hats

Whether it's a classic pillbox, a glamorous derby or a charming picture hat, the wedding hat makes a fashion statement. Getting married outdoors? A picture hat will keep the sun off your freckles!

Hats can add elegant sophistication to your gown ensemble or reflect a casual mood, depending on how they're decorated.

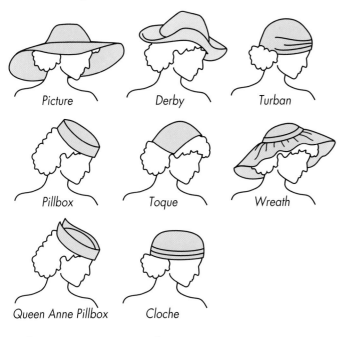

Picture   Derby   Turban

Pillbox   Toque   Wreath

Queen Anne Pillbox   Cloche

Choosing a Hat Style

It's important to choose a hat size and shape that flatters your facial size and shape and suits the overall mood of your wedding. If you are adding a veil, you must also consider the length and shape to make sure it will be in balance with the hat and your gown. A small hat looks best with a small veil or with a wisp of facial veiling only. Experiment. It's easy to get overwhelmed with veiling when

matching it to a hat. Some of the most intricate and detailed headpieces and veils look best when worn with very plain gowns. Conversely, very elaborate gowns look best when worn with plain headpieces. Your gown and headpiece should complement each other, not fight each other for attention.

Cover a Hat

You can purchase hat bases already covered with satin (called "semi-finished frames" in mail-order catalogs) or you can cover your own with leftover scraps from your gown, then trim as desired with lace motifs, silk flowers, or net, as described for a headpiece on the previous page.

The Pillbox Hat

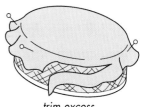

1. Cut a fabric circle 1" to 2" larger than the crown of the hat.

trim excess

2. Center the fabric circle on top of the hat and smooth the excess fabric over the sides. Secure with pins.

3. Glue the fabric in place along the side, using bridal glue. Allow glue to dry thoroughly, then trim away excess fabric.

4. To make a pleated cover for the sides of the hat, cut a bias strip of fabric twice the width of the sides plus 1" (to wrap inside) and 1" longer (for overlap) than the length around. Press desired pleats in place.

5. Glue the pleated strip to the crown, folding under one end and lapping it over the raw edge of the other end.

6. Wrap the lower edge of the fabric to the inside; glue in place.

raw edge

7. Glue lace trim over the raw edge inside the completed hat. Attach veil if desired (page 148-153).

A Picture Hat or Derby

1. Place the hat on the wrong side of the fabric and mark from the edge of the brim a distance equal to the width of the brim plus 1" all the way around the brim.

width of brim plus 1"

2. Measure the inside diameter of the crown from the center front to center back and from side to side as shown. Trace the circle in light pencil on the wrong side of the fabric. Cut a hole in the fabric ³⁄₈" or more *smaller* than the marked inner circle. Snug the fabric down over the crown and onto the hat brim.

3. Wrap the fabric over the edge of the brim at center front and pin in place; repeat at the center back and then at the sides.

4. Begin pleating the fabric, working around the brim and making pleats so the folded edges face the center back. Pin the pleats in place.

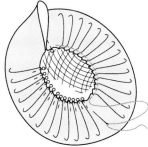

5. Adjust pleats as needed for the desired effect, then glue or hand stitch in place. Trim away excess fabric.

6. Cut a piece of fabric on the bias, making it slightly larger than the crown. Smooth the fabric over the crown, taking small tucks as necessary to distribute the fullness.

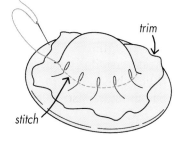

trim

stitch

Or, you may pull all fullness to the back as shown in the photo at left. Stitch or glue in place at the base of the crown and trim excess fabric close to the base of the crown.

7. Cover the raw edges inside and out with narrow lace trim.

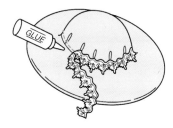

The Veil

The custom of wearing a bridal veil started during the days when matchmakers arranged marriages between total strangers. The bride was delivered to the ceremony hidden by the veil and the groom was not allowed to unveil his bride until they were husband and wife.

Since then, veils have evolved into wedding fashion, very much a part of the classic bridal look. Veil choices abound so it's a good idea to try on several in order to choose the best style to make for your wedding.

Luckily, pattern companies now offer veil patterns with a variety of styles in one package. Veil patterns provide ideas as well as measurements and tips on how to work with lace and illusion. For most veil styles, you need only dimensions and general shape guidelines to create the crowning touch to your ensemble.

You can also purchase ready-made veils at fabric stores or through mail-order sources. These veils are cut in pre-measured lengths and have gathering threads already stitched in. You can modify the shape and length of to suit your taste.

To experiment with veil styles, use the "Traceable Veil" figure on the next page in conjunction with your tracings made from "The Traceable Bride" on pages 19-22.

Veil Fabrics

The most commonly used veil fabrics are illusion and tulle. Illusion is the softest, most drapable, and most versatile because of its width (up to 144" wide). Other choices and their most common characteristics and uses are also included in the chart.

Traceable Veils

Combine with your choice of frame or hat if desired as discussed on the previous pages.

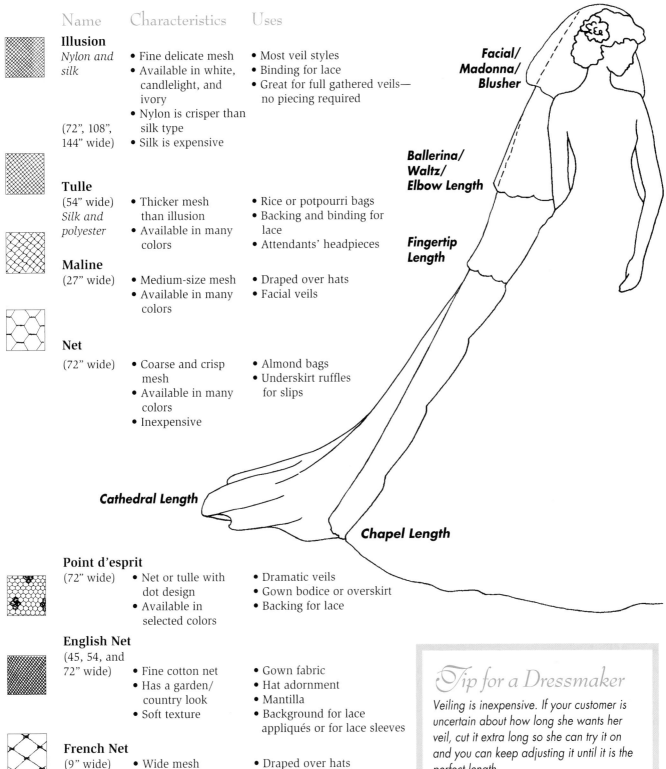

Name	Characteristics	Uses
Illusion *Nylon and silk* (72", 108", 144" wide)	• Fine delicate mesh • Available in white, candlelight, and ivory • Nylon is crisper than silk type • Silk is expensive	• Most veil styles • Binding for lace • Great for full gathered veils—no piecing required
Tulle (54" wide) *Silk and polyester*	• Thicker mesh than illusion • Available in many colors	• Rice or potpourri bags • Backing and binding for lace • Attendants' headpieces
Maline (27" wide)	• Medium-size mesh • Available in many colors	• Draped over hats • Facial veils
Net (72" wide)	• Coarse and crisp mesh • Available in many colors • Inexpensive	• Almond bags • Underskirt ruffles for slips
Point d'esprit (72" wide)	• Net or tulle with dot design • Available in selected colors	• Dramatic veils • Gown bodice or overskirt • Backing for lace
English Net (45, 54, and 72" wide)	• Fine cotton net • Has a garden/ country look • Soft texture	• Gown fabric • Hat adornment • Mantilla • Background for lace appliqués or for lace sleeves
French Net (9" wide)	• Wide mesh • Limited color selection	• Draped over hats • Facial veils

Facial/ Madonna/ Blusher

Ballerina/ Waltz/ Elbow Length

Fingertip Length

Cathedral Length

Chapel Length

Tip for a Dressmaker

Veiling is inexpensive. If your customer is uncertain about how long she wants her veil, cut it extra long so she can try it on and you can keep adjusting it until it is the perfect length.

Veil Lengths

Shoulder-length veil touches the shoulders and is usually worn with an informal gown. If combined with other veils, a shoulder-length is appropriate for semi-formal and formal weddings.

Facial is a blusher-length layer that covers the face and is later lifted and pushed back over the other veil layers. A **flyaway** blusher veil has multiple layers.

Elbow length touches the elbows when arms are straight and is usually worn with short and/or informal gowns.

Fingertip length touches the finger-tips when the arms are straight at the sides. It is worn with semi-formal and formal wedding gowns.

Ballet or Waltz length falls to the ankles and is worn with semi-formal and formal gowns.

Chapel length (about 2½ yards long) falls to the floor from the headpiece, trails slightly on the floor, and is worn with semi-formal and formal gowns.

Cathedral falls about 3½ yards from the headpiece and is worn with formal gowns.

Veil Styles

Follow the patterns given for your particular length and fullness desired. Refer to page 152 for instructions for attaching the veil to the headpiece.

Mantilla, (pronounced MAN TEE YA), is tradition-ally made of lace and is worn with a classic gown with simple, elegant lines. Mantillas can also be made of veiling with a wide lace edging. A mantilla is usually attached to the hair with combs or hair pins rather than attached to a frame. If a frame is used, it is usually worn under the mantilla for added height. Camelot and Juliet frames (see page 144) are most commonly used under a mantilla.

Sew by hand to small hair combs or to a frame if used.

Mantilla Pattern

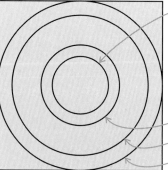

36"—waist length

NOTE: Mantilla style veils are seldom cut smaller than 36" in diameter.

48"— fingertip length

80"-90"— chapel length

108"— cathedral length

◆ To wear a mantilla, drape it over the crown of your head and secure with bobby pins or stitch a comb to the center of the mantilla instead.

◆ If attaching the mantilla to a frame, hand stitch it to the frame after you have covered it with fabric.

"Pouf" Veil is a veil that is very full through the crown. Many short brides like this style because it adds height. Cut short, this style can be a "blusher" or facial veil. You can incorporate a pouf into any veil style.

Simply add two times the height of the pouf (plus 1") to the length of your veil. Fold the pouf over and do a row of machine basting stitches 1" from the raw edge.

♦ Attach a pouf to the headpiece and a separate, single-layer veil under it; or use a double-layer veil with the pouf attached at the top.

♦ To "pouf" the veil, pull apart the veil layers at the sides.

Pouf Pattern

Fabric Width Required:
gathered – 72"
full – 108"
very full – 144"

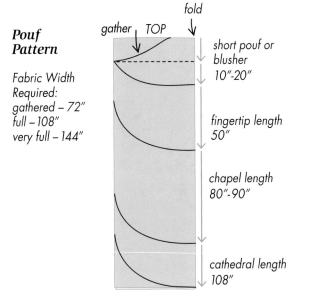

gather | TOP | fold

short pouf or blusher 10"-20"

fingertip length 50"

chapel length 80"-90"

cathedral length 108"

Basic Drape Veil is the most popular of all the veil styles. It is less gathered through the crown than the pouf veil and can be attached to any frame or hat.

Basic Drape Pattern

TOP | fold
gather

fingertip length 50"

chapel length 80"-90"

cathedral length 108"

Fabric Width Required:
gathered – 72"
full – 108"
very full – 144"

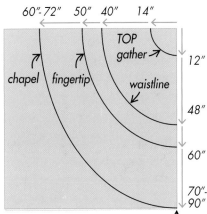

60"-72"   50"   40"   14"

TOP gather

chapel | fingertip

waistline

12"

48"

60"

70"-90"

Cascade Pattern

fold & center back

Fabric Width Required:
waistline – 108" illusion
fingertip – 108" illusion
chapel – 144" illusion

Cascade Veil is less full than the basic drape veil and is longer at the back than the sides. You can make a cascade veil with a double tier (see below) and/or combine it with a pouf veil or with a blusher.

Double-Layer or Tiered Veil has fewer gathers so it drapes or hangs down, rather than adding height. This style can also be frameless by simply attaching it to hair combs or a barrette. Because it is made of a double layer of illusion, this style can look "whiter" and heavier than a single-layer veil. Try the look before actually making the veil to decide if you like it. The top tier of this style is generally made shorter than the bottom tier in a 1 to 2 ratio. Adjust for your personal taste.

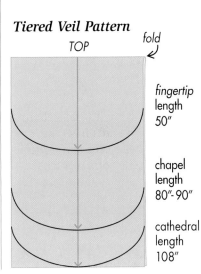

Tiered Veil Pattern

TOP | fold

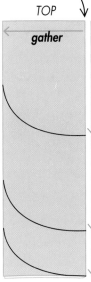

fingertip length 50"

chapel length 80"-90"

cathedral length 108"

NOTE: This style is also used when making a blusher.

Fabric Width Required:
gathered – 72"
full – 108"
very full – 144"

General Instructions for Veils

1. Cut veiling to the desired length and fold in half *lengthwise*. Cut rounded corner at the lower edges, using a rotary cutter or scissors. For a double-layer veil, fold the veil in quarters before cutting the corners.

2. Apply trim to edges (see below).

3. Gather your veil as desired (see below right).

4. Attach to the headpiece (see below right).

Trimming Veil Edges

Before gathering, finish the veil edge as desired and attach any other trim—lace motifs, pearls, beads, sequins. Choose from the following edge finishes.

Plain Edge

Since veil fabrics do not ravel, it is not necessary to finish the edge. An untrimmed veil will be "pouffier" because it doesn't have trim on the edge to weigh it down. Use a rotary cutter and an acrylic rotary ruler to avoid cutting unsightly jagged edges on your veil.

Edge Tracing or Pencil Edging

This finish creates a defined, delicate edge. Stitch around the edge using one of theses methods.

♦ Using a short, wide zigzag stitch, stitch so the needle goes over the edge into the veiling about ¼" on the left swing and then off the edge on the right swing. The wide stitch will pull the veiling in creating a thin, delicate edge.

♦ Zigzag or serge with a narrow stitch over buttonhole twist or pearl cotton ¼" from the edge; trim close to the stitching.

♦ For a curly edge, stitch over 12- to 25-pound fish line using a narrow zigzag stitch or the rolled-edge on your serger.

Lace Edge

A lace edge is lovely on a veil, but take care when choosing this finish. Sometimes adding yards and yards of lace around the outside edge of a veil can make it too busy. TEST first by pinning the lace trim around at least half of the veil edge. Try on with your gown and check in front of a mirror. Is this the look you want?

Lap the wrong side of the lace over the right side of the veil edge. Then topstitch, using a long, straight stitch, taking care not to stretch the veil.

Stitch.

Ribbon Edge

Ribbon trims the edges of Cindy's and Sheila's veils (pages 40-44). Use narrow ribbon (⅛"-wide) so it will lie flat and curve smoothly around the veil. Place ribbon ¼" from the lower, outer edge of the net and zigzag or straight stitch it in place. Trim away the excess veiling close to the stitching. A wider bias band of satin is a pretty edging for a veil worn with a simple gown.

Pearl Edging

Ready-made pearl edging can be applied using a *pearls 'n piping* foot. Just follow the instructions that come with the foot. You can also serge pearl trim using a special pearl or cording presser foot and the rolled-edge stitch (page 53). For a speedier application, you can glue pearls with bridal glue.

NOTE: Pearl trim may be too heavy for shorter veils. Test first on a sample or the actual veil.

Gathering the Veil

For a single-layer veil, stitch ¼" from the raw edge; for a double-layer veil, stitch ¼" from the fold.

♦ Do two rows of basting spaced ¼" apart **OR**

♦ Stitch over buttonhole twist with a long, narrow zigzag stitch.

Then pull the bobbin threads or the buttonhole twist to gather. Secure both ends.

Attaching Your Veil

Attach the veil permanently to a headpiece by hand stitching it to the underside. For a cap or small hat, attach your veil to the underside toward the back.

Sew the combs to gathered edge with long whipstitch.

Sew gathered veil to a frame under back edge.

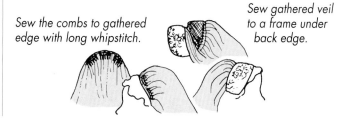

Making a Detachable Veil

I prefer to make the veil detachable so the bride can remove it at the reception, without having to remove the headpiece. (Veils get in the way when dancing and can be a nuisance at other times during the reception.)

cut ribbon this length

1. Gather the veil so it fits the space on your headpiece where you plan to attach it.

2. Cut a piece of ½"-wide satin ribbon or sturdy lace the length of the gathered edge of the veil. Pink the ends or apply a seam sealant such as Fray Check. Stitch one-half of each clear plastic snap down the center of the ribbon, spacing them about 1" apart. (I usually use 5 snaps.)

3. Attach the other half of each snap to the inside edge of the headpiece.

4. Permanently stitch the ribbon trim to the top edge of the veil on top of the gathering stitches, stitching along each edge of the ribbon. Snap the veil to the headpiece. Easy on, easy off!

TIP: Velcro works well and is easier than sewing hooks and snaps.

Embellishment Ideas

♦ Embellish your veil with lace appliqués from your gown as shown on this lovely double-layer veil.

♦ Copy your lace pattern by embroidering it onto your veil.

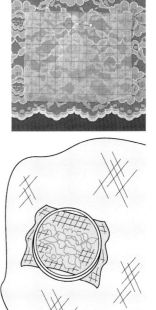

1. Trace the lace motif onto Perfect Pattern Paper or tissue.

2. Place tracing over net or tulle and secure it in an embroidery hoop. (Netting should be larger than the final piece so you can place designs with a little freedom.)

3. Using rayon, metallic or matching thread in the needle, and clear monofilament nylon or matching thread in the bobbin, stitch over the traced lines using a narrow satin stitch or other embroidery stitch. Loosen thread tension by 1.

4. Unhoop and tear away the tissue.

CHAPTER 22

Finishing Touches

Lingerie Straps

Prevent bra and slip straps from peeking out during the ceremony or reception with lingerie straps.

1. Cut a 1½"-long piece of ½"-wide satin ribbon, the color of your gown, for each shoulder.

2. Position as shown and hand stitch for about ½" at the shoulder seam. Sew a snap to the end of the ribbon and to the shoulder seam allowance. Catch straps inside when you put your gown on.

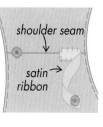

shoulder seam

satin ribbon

Take the Weight Off

The weight of yards and yards of fabric or heavy beading can put potentially damaging strain on the shoulder seams when your gown is hanging. Hanging loops alleviate the problem.

1. Cut two pieces of ⅜"-wide seam tape or ribbon twice the length of the bodice front from the waistline to the shoulder plus 1" (for two ½"-wide seam allowances).

2. Fold each piece in half and sew to the waistline seam allowances at the side seams.

3. Slip the loops over a padded hanger. They will hang under the skirt when you wear the gown.

Tip for a Dressmaker

I provide a padded hanger with each of my gowns. It helps the dress hang better and is a "value-added" service to the customer. Purchase these from your local fabric store or lingerie shop or make from leftover gown fabric following the techniques in Chapter 24 of **Couture, the Art of Fine Sewing** *(page 156).*

Garter

A garter is a wonderful finishing touch and can be made from leftover fabric and lace from your gown. Make two—one to throw, one to keep!

1. Measure your thigh where you expect to wear the garter. Cut a length of your leftover fashion fabric 4" wide by twice this measurement.

2. Trim half the fabric with leftover lace or lace trim. *With wrong sides together,* serge the long edges. Hide the serged edge with lace.

4. Cut ¾"-wide elastic the measurement of your thigh minus 1". Insert into the fabric tube, overlap the ends, and stitch to secure.

5. Slipstitch ends together.

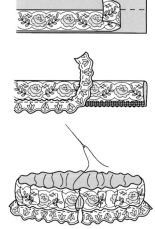

Wrist Loops

If you decide not to bustle your train, try *wrist loops* (page 138). Your hand slips through the loops, lifting the train off the floor.

NOTE: Pin the wrist loop in place before stitching and give it a "test run." When carried in this manner, the weight of some trains can drag on the sleeve and bodice too much (too revealing).

Resources

Some of the products mentioned in this book may be difficult to find. Look first at your fabric store, but if the item is unavailable there, contact the distributor or manufacturer in the list below.

Alicyn Wright, from Utah, designs exclusively for The McCall Pattern Company. She designs and sews the bridal wear featured in her patterns and writes the guidesheets. Her instructions are excellent—she holds your hand throughout the project. Her technical advise on this book was invaluable. Thanks Alicyn!!

Photos of her designs can be seen throughout this book. For more information, visit Alicyn's web site at www.sewbridal.com.

Bridal Couture by Susan Khalje

Couture Sewing School,
4600 Breidenbaugh Lane
Glenarm, MD 21057
(410) 592-5711 phone,
(410) 592-6913 fax
www.sewnet.com/Susan Khalje

To go beyond the basics covered in *Bridal Gowns* and add couture touches and techniques to your works of art, you won't want to be without *Bridal Couture*, by Susan Khalje. The section on boning for support is particularly impressive and Susan walks you through the construction of several gowns she has created.

Students from all over the world attend her sewing school to study the art of sewing custom bridal and evening wear. If you are a dressmaker, she is an invaluable source.

Check your favorite book or fabric store for her book, or contact Susan to order her book and to inquire about her school.

Things Japanese
9805 N.E 116th
Kirkland, WA 98034-4248
Phone: (425) 821-2287
Fax: (425) 821-3554
thingsjapanese@seanet.com

The pre-cut bias silk charmeuse is invaluable for bridal sewing. It saves so much time as it is far more accurately cut than you can do yourself with this slippery fabric! Use it to bind seams, make roses, cover buttons, edge veils, and make piping and spaghetti straps.

Things Japanese also offers TIRE silk threads in 5 weights and 171 colors and a high-quality, very fine 100-weight silk thread in white.

COLORHUE instant set silk dye and LUMIERE fabric paint were used for the hand painting featured on page 42. Write for a free catalog of products and instructional guides and kits for dyes and paints.

Metric Conversions

1/16 inch	=	1.6mm
1/8 inch	=	3.2mm
3/16 inch	=	4.75mm
1/4 inch	=	6.35mm
3/8 inch	=	9.5mm
1/2 inch	=	1.25cm
5/8 inch	=	1.6cm
3/4 inch	=	1.9cm
7/8 inch	=	2.25cm
1 inch	=	2.54
1/8 yard	=	11.5cm
1/4 yard	=	23cm
3/8 yard	=	34.5cm
1/2 yard	=	45.75cm
5/8 yard	=	57.25cm
3/4 yard	=	68.5cm
7/8 yard	=	80cm
1 yard	=	91.5cm

inches	x 25.4	=	millimeters (mm)
	x 2.54	=	centimeters (cm)
	x .025	=	meters (m)
yards	x 91.44	=	centimeters
	x .9144	=	meters

Listed below are some mail order bridal sources for boning (mostly plastic); looping—elastic and soutache braid; laces, trims, etc.; cloth shank or metal back bridal buttons, and headpiece supplies

Greenberg & Hammer
212-246-2835
1-800-955-5135
24 W. 57th St.
NY, New York 10019

Bridal's International
1-800-752-1171 (orders)
1-315-655-8555 (inquiries)
45 Albany Street
Cazenovia, NY 13035

Washington Millinery Supply
P.O. Box 5718
Derwood, MD 20855
1-800-368-2753 (ordering)
1-301-963-4444 (inquiries)

Milliners Supply Company
911 Elm Street
Dallas, TX 75202-3164
1-800-627-4337 (ordering)
1-214-742-8284 (inquiries)

The following is a source for machine embroidery designs and equipment.

Criswell Embroidery Designs
(800) 308-5442
www.criswell-emb.com

These sewing machine companies are also sources for embroidery designs and equipment:

Baby Lock
(800) 422-2952
www.babylock.com

Janome America, Inc.
(800) 631-0183
www.janome.com

Bernina
(800) 405-2739
www.berninausa.com

Pfaff
(800) 997-3233
www.pfaff.com

Brother USA
(800) 422-7684
www.brother.com

Singer
(800) 474-6437
www.singersewing.com

Elna USA
(800) 848-3562
www.elnausa.com

Husqvarna Viking
(800) 631-0001
www.husqvarnaviking.com

Index

Alençon lace 78, 86
all-over lace 77, 78
alterations (see fitting)
appliqués 78, 80, 82, 88, 107, 153
assembling a bodice 95
assembly order 89
attendants, color 25; styles 26-27
Basque waistlines 20
basting tape 62, 111-112
bead and pearl foot 46, 48, 53, 62
beaded fabric 71, 88
beading 47-49
beeswax 61
beveling 65
bias binding
    armholes/necklines 73,
       101-102, 124
    piping 52-53
    precut silk charmeuse 40, 62
    roses/rosettes 44-45
    sleeves 115
blood stains 61
bodice
    applying lace to 86
    assembling 89, 95
    shaping 90
    styles 20
boning 61
    for shaping a bodice 92-93, 96
borders 75
bows
    embellishing 52
    placement 49
    sewing 50-52
bra carriers 154
bra cup size 29
bridal consultants 28
bridal glue, for beads 47
bridesmaids
    color 25
    style 26
buckram 144
bust
    altering 31-32, 34, 37-38
    full 17
bustling trains 137-138
button loops 61, 113
    on illusion necklines 114
    on sleeves 114, 117
    with zippers 113
buttons 61, 113, 114
    buttoning with crochet hook 113
cap sleeves 120
chantilly lace 78
chiffon
    embroidering on 40
children 27
Cindy 32-35, 39, 40
circular roses 46
closures 111-114

buttons and loops 113
    completing in skirt 132
    covered buttons 114
    invisible zippers 112
    lapped zippers 111, 112
    zippers with buttons and loops 113
    snaps 114
collars 102-110
    designing 109, 110
    ruffled 103-106
    sewing 102
    styles 21
    Victorian 107
color 25, 27
computerized embroidery 42
convertibility 26
cording foot 46
corset 92
crinoline 90
    with scallops 100
cutting tips 62, 63-64,
    cutting special fabrics 70-76
    skirts 57, 126
darts 95
    in lace 86
designing
    collars 109, 110
    gown 19-24
    sleeves 115
    veil 149
dressmakers 4, 5
dyes 42, 47, 155
ease 65
    in sleeves 115
ease plus 65, 94
edge finishes (also see trims)
    blindstitched scallops 105
    French binding 101
    lace 84, 85, 105, 107, 114, 118,
       120, 135, 147, 148, 152
    lined-to-edge 96, 105, 136
    pearl 53
    picot 105
    piping 52, 53
edge stitch foot 40
embroidery 40-42
    computerized 42
eyelet fabric 75
fabrics 50-59
    chart 58-59
    preparation 63
    sewing 69-76
    suggested 7-13
facings
    eliminating 92
    sleeves 117
fasteners (see closures)
figure
    flattering styles for 14-18
    full 14, 16
    short 14
    tall 15

fish line
    on bridal veils 152
    on rosettes 46
    sleeves 124
Fit For REAL People book 37, 158
fitting 29-38, 89
    alteration tissue 30
    sleeves 115-116
flounce lace 78
flowers 28
French binding 101
French seams 66, 73, 99, 118
galloon lace 78
garter 154
gathering 67, 68
    foot 62
    glue baste 91
    skirts 128
glue, bridal 47
    for headpieces 145-148
godets 130
grainline 63
    change to bias 115
    sewing with the grain 127
grosgrain 132
guipure lace 78
gussets 116
hairline seam 66, 116
hanging gown 154
hats 147, 148
headpieces 144-146
    embellishing 41, 44
heirloom sewing 55
    sleeves 116-120
hems 133-136
    double 73, 134
    faced 136
    lettuce 136
    picot 136
    rolled 104
Hong Kong seam finish 70
horsehair braid 61
    for bodice shaping 93
    for buttons 114
    for headpieces 145
    for hems 133
    for off-the-shoulder sleeves 122
illusion necklines 21, 98, 99
illusion net 149
insertion lace 78
interfacings 44, 94
interlining 92, 96
Juliet sleeve 22
knits 59, 76
lace 58, 77-88
    appliqué 80, 82, 88, 107, 153
    applying to bodice 86, 87
    beaded/sequined 88
    closures 114
    darts in 86
    heirloom yardage 84

hems 83, 87, 135
lapped seams 81
layout and cutting 80, 81, 87, 88
marking 81
mitering 84
on necklines 85, 87
sewing 81
sleeves 118-120, 123
trim 84, 85, 105, 107, 114, 118,
  120, 135, 147, 148, 152
types 77-79
lining 91, 92, 95, 96
  sheer sleeves, to-the-edge
    96, 105, 136
  skirts 127-128
loops and buttons 61, 113
maline veiling 149
mantilla 150
marking 64, 65
Moiré taffeta 72
muslin test garment 35
napped fabrics 72-75
necklines 21, 97-102
  binding 101, 102
  illusion 98, 99
  lace 85
  styles 21
needle threader 60
needles 60
  for machine embroidery 42
net 90, 122, 149
  for slips 142-143
notions 60-62
off-the-shoulder
  collars 102, 110
  sleeves for 122
organdy 59, 61
organza 61, 90
overbustling, trains 137
overlock (see serger)
pearl cotton, on bridal veils 152
pearl edging 48
  necklines 53
  veils 43, 44, 152
pearl piping 53
pearls 47
  by hand 48, 49
  by machine 48, 53
  foot 62
  gluing 47
Perfect Fuse Interfacings 44, 94, 160
Perfect Pattern Paper 30, 35, 61, 80,
  110, 113, 117, 153, 160
Perfect Sew 61
  for beading 48
  for butterflies 41
  embroidering georgette 40, 42
  in computerized embroidery 42
  on polyester satin 43
  pins 60, 63

Perfect Sew Needle Threader
  60, 160
petticoat (see slips)
pins 60, 63
pintucks
  conventional 54
  double-needle 54-55
  serger rolled edge 55
piping 52, 53
  waistlines 43
pleats 128, 129
point d'esprit net 149
preshrinking 63
pressing 68
princess seams
  fitting 32
  sewing 65, 94
recycling a gown 55
ribbon
  dyed silk embellishment 47
  loops on train 138
  on bridal veils 41, 152
Rigalene 61
rolled edge 66, 134, 135
roses and rosettes 44-47
ruffles
  collars 102-106
  sleeves 124
  support under full skirt 129
satin 70
scallops 100, 101, 119
Schiffli lace 78
scissors for lace 61
seam finishes 67
seams 65, 66, 69-76
Seams Great 62, 70
sequins 48, 49
  sequined fabric 71, 88
Sew Fit cutting tables 64
sewing order 89, 125
shaping the bodice 90-94
sheers 59, 60, 72, 73, 114
Sheila 36-39, 43, 44
silk charmeuse, precut bias 62
silkies 69
size (also see fitting) 29
skirts 125-132
  altering 31
  length 19
  overlays 132
sleeve heads 120, 121
sleeves 115-124
  altering 31, 34, 38
  closures 117
  finishing armhole 124
  off-the-shoulder 122-123
  ruffled 124
  stays 121
  styles 22
  with strapless bodice 123

slips 141
spaghetti straps 101
stabilizers, for embroidery 42
stabilizing neckline 97
Sta-Tape 61, 97, 98
strapless bodice
  boning 93
  sleeves for 123
styles of gowns 6-13
  flattering 14-18
supplies 60-62
surplice necklines 21
sweetheart neckline 21
taffeta 72
taut sewing 65
test garment 35
Thread Heaven 61
thread tracing 64
thread chain 132
tissue-fitting 29-38
traceable bride 19, 20, 149
traceable veil 149
trains 24, 130, 137-140
  bustling 137-138
trims, suggested for styles 7-13
trims, neckline 43
tucks 128, 129
tulle 149
underbustling 138
underlining
  bodice 90, 91
  bows 50
understitching 66
veils 144, 148-153
  designing 149
  pearl edging 44
  ribbon edging 41
velvet 59, 60, 74, 75
Venice lace 78
Victorian
  collars 107
  neckline 21
  sleeve 22
  style 10
waistlines
  stays 132
  styles 20
  traceable 20
wrist loops 138, 154
zippers
  invisible 112
  lapped 111
  with buttons and loops 113
  with sheer overskirt 132

Palmer/Pletsch
PRODUCTS

These ready-to-use, information-filled sewing how-to books, manuals and videos can be found in local book and fabric stores or ordered through Palmer/Pletsch Publishing (see address on last page).

8½ x 11 BOOKS

❏ **Creative Serging for the Home and Other Quick Decorating Ideas** *by Lynette Ranney Black and Linda Wisner, 160 pages, $19.95* Color photos and how-to's of dozens of rooms to help you transform your home into the place YOU want it to be.

❏ **Looking Good—A Comprehensive Guide to Wardrobe Planning, Color and Personal Style Development** *by Nancy Nix-Rice, 160 pages, $19.95* Everything women need to look their personal best—not by following what fashion dictates, but by spotlighting their best features to create the most flattering, effective look possible.

❏ **The BUSINE$$ of Teaching Sewing,** *by Marcy Miller and Pati Palmer, 128 pages, $29.95* If you want to be in the BUSINESS of teaching sewing, read this book, a compilation of Palmer/Pletsch information from 20 years of experience, plus Miller's innovative ideas on: Appearance and Image; Getting Started; The Lesson Plan; Class Formats; Location; Marketing, Promotion & Advertising; Pricing; Teaching Techniques; and Continuing Education—Where To Find It.

❏ **Dream Sewing Spaces— Design and Organization for Spaces Large and Small,** *by Lynette Ranney Black, 128 pages, $19.95* Make your dream a reality. Analyze your needs and your space, then learn to plan and put it together. Lots of color photos!

❏ **Couture—The Art of Fine Sewing,** *by Roberta C. Carr, 208 pages, $29.95* How-to's for couture techniques and secrets, brought to life with illustrations and dozens of garments photographed in full color.

❏ **Sewing Ultrasuede® Brand Fabrics— Ultrasuede, Ultrasuede Light, Caress, Ultraleather,** *by Marta Alto, Pati Palmer and Barbara Weiland, 128 pages, $16.95* Color photo section, plus the newest techniques to master these luxurious fabrics.

❏ **Fit for Real People: Sew Great Clothes Using ANY Pattern** *by Marta Alto & Pati Palmer, 256 pages, $24.95* The authors write from 25 years of hands-on experience fitting thousands of people. Their practical approach is explained in simple, logical style. Finally, learn to buy the right size, and hen learn to tissue fit to determine alterations. Special sections include fitting young teen girls, the history of sizing, and fitting REAL people.

❏ **Bridal Gowns—How to Make the Wedding Dress of Your Dreams** *by Susan Andriks, 160 pages, $19.95* Sewing bridal gowns is popular because of the great cost savings, superior fit, and originality. This book will help you design that dream dress, select and combine patterns, get the perfect fit the easy way, and sew with satins and laces. Also, learn how to make trains, veils, and headpieces. The author specializes in sewing custom-made wedding gowns.

These books are all softcover. They are also available with coil binding: $3.00 additional for large books, $2.00 for small.

5½ x 8½ BOOKS

❏ **Sew to Success!—How to Make Money in a Home-Based Sewing Business,** *by Kathleen Spike, 128 pgs., $10.95* Learn how to establish your market, set policies, price your talents, and more!

❏ **Mother Pletsch's Painless Sewing**, *NEW Revised Edition, by Pati Palmer and Susan Pletsch, 128 pgs., $8.95* The most uncomplicated sewing book of the century! Lots of tips on how to sew FAST!

❏ **Sewing With Sergers— The Complete Handbook for Overlock Sewing,** *Revised Edition, by Pati Palmer and Gail Brown, 128 pages, $8.95* Learn easy threading tips, stitch types, rolled edging, and flatlocking.

❏ **Creative Serging— The Complete Handbook for Decorative Overlock Sewing,** *by Pati Palmer, Gail Brown and Sue Green, 128 pages, $8.95* In-depth information and creative uses of your serger.

❏ **Sensational Silk— A Handbook for Sewing Silk and Silk-like Fabrics,** *by Gail Brown, 128 pages, $6.95* Complete guide for sewing with silk and silkies— great for blouse and dress sewing.

❏ **Pants For Any Body,** *Revised Edition, by Pati Palmer and Susan Pletsch, 128 pages, $8.95* Learn to fit pants following clear problem-and-solution illustrations.

❏ **Easy, Easier, Easiest Tailoring,** *Revised Edition, by Pati Palmer and Susan Pletsch, 128 pgs., $8.95* Learn four different tailoring methods, easy fit tips, and timesaving machine lining.

❏ **Sew a Beautiful Wedding,** *by Gail Brown and Karen Dillon, 128 pages, $8.95* Bridal how-to's from choosing the most flattering style to sewing with special fabrics.

❏ **The Shade Book,** *Revised Edition, by Judy Lindahl, 152 pages, $9.95* Everything you need to know to make six major shade types.

MY FIRST SEWING BOOK KITS

My First Sewing Books, *by Winky Cherry,* are available packaged as kits with materials for a first project. With a Teaching Manual & Video, they offer a complete, thoroughly tested sewing program for young children, 5 to 11 years old. They'll learn patience, manners, creativity, completion, and how to follow rules—all through the enjoyment of sewing. Each book follows a project from start to finish with clever rhymes and clear illustrations. *Each book, 8½" x 8½", 40 pages, $10.95, each complete kit $14.95*

❏ **My First Sewing Book**
Children as young as 5 can learn to hand sew and stuff a felt bird shape. Also available in Spanish.

❏ **My First Embroidery Book**
Beginners learn the importance of accuracy by making straight stitches and using a chart and gingham to make a name sampler.

❏ **My First Doll Book** Felt dolls have embroidered faces, yarn hair, and clothes. Children use the over-stitch and skills learned in Levels I and II.

❏ **My First Machine Sewing Book** With practice pages, then a fabric star, children learn about the machine, seam allowances, tapering, snips, clips and stitching and turning a shape right side out.

❏ **My First Patchwork Book**
Children use a template to make a Fourpatch block and can make the entire Alphabet of patchwork flags used by sailors, soldiers, pilots, and astronauts.

❏ **My First Quilt Book** Children machine stitch a quilt pieced with strips and squares and finish it with yarn ties or optional hand quilting.

❏ **Teaching Children to Sew Manual and Video,** *$29.95* The 112-page, 8½" x 11" **The Teaching Manual** shows you exactly how to teach young children, including preparing the environment, workshop space, class control, and the importance of incorporating other life skills along with sewing skills. In the **Video,** see Winky Cherry teach six 6-to-8-year olds how to sew in a true-life classroom setting. She introduces herself and explains the rules, then shows them how to sew. Then, see close-ups of a child sewing the project in double-time. (Show this to your students.) Finally, Winky gives you a tour of an ideal classroom setup. She also talks about the tools, patterns and sewing supplies you will need. *1 hour.*

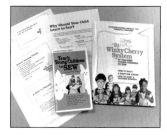

❏ **Teacher's Supply Kit,** *$49.95* (a retail value of $65.00) The refillable kit includes these hard-to-find items: 50 felt pieces (9" x 12") in assorted colors; balls of crochet thread in 6 colors; 12 needles with large eyes; 2 pincushions; pre-cut felt for 12 birds (six large, six small); and printed patterns for the shapes.

159

Teach Young Children to Sew is part of the training package described on the previous page.

VIDEOS

According to Robbie Fanning, author and critic, "The most professional of all the (video) tapes we've seen is Pati Palmer's *Sewing Today the Time Saving Way*. This tape should serve as the standard of excellence in the field." Following that standard, we have produced 8 more videos since Time Saving! *Videos are $19.95 each.*

❏ **Sewing Today the Time Saving Way.** 45 minutes. Features Lynn Raasch & Karen Dillon sharing tips and techniques to make sewing fun, fast, and trouble free.

❏ **Sewing to Success!** 45 minutes. Features Kathleen Spike presenting a wealth of information on how to achieve financial freedom working in your home as a professional dressmaker.

❏ **Sergers Basics.** 1 hour Features Marta Alto & Pati Palmer teaching about stitch tension, stitch types and their uses, serging circles, turning corners, gathering, and much more.

❏ **Sergers Basics II.** 1 hour. Features Marta Alto & Pati Palmer discussing in-depth how-to's for rolled edging & flatlocking as well as garment details.

❏ **Creative Serging.** 1 hour. Features Marta Alto & Pati Palmer discussing how to use decorative threads, yarns, and ribbons on your serger. PLUS fashion shots!

❏ **Creative Serging II.** 1 hour. Features Marta Alto & Pati Palmer showing more creative ideas, including in-depth information on creative rolled-edge applications.

❏ **Two-Hour Trousers.** 1 hour, 40 minutes. Features Kathleen Spike with fit tips using our unique tissue-fitting techniques, the best basics, and designer details.

❏ **Sewing Ultrasuede® Brand Fabrics—Ultrasuede®, Facile®, Caress™, Ultraleather.™** 1 hour. Features Marta Alto & Pati Palmer with clear, step-by-step sewing demonstrations and a fashion show.

❏ **Creative Home Decorating Ideas: Sewing Projects for the Home.** 1 hour. Features Lynette Ranney Black showing creative, easy ideas for windows, walls, tables and more—a great companion video to *Creative Serging for the Home.*

FOR PERFECT SEWING...

Perfect Sew	**Perfect Sew Needle Threader**	**Perfect Pattern Paper**
See index in this book for ways to use this stabilizer.	for hand and machine needles.	See index in this book for uses.

INTERFACINGS

Ask about our new, extra-wide fusible weft **PerfectFuse™ Interfacings**. Available in four weights, they come in 1-yard packages in both charcoal black and ecru-white. Call for more information and pricing.

PALMER/PLETSCH WORKSHOPS

Our "Sewing Vacations" are offered on a variety of topics, including *Pant Fit, Fit, Tailoring, Creative Serging, Ultrasuede, Couture* and a special *Sewing Update/ Best of Palmer/Pletsch* session. Workshops are held at the new Palmer/Pletsch International Training Center near the Portland, Oregon, airport.

Teacher training sessions are also available on each topic. They include: practice teaching sessions; hair styling, make-up, and publicity photo session; up to 300 slides and teaching script; camera-ready workbook handouts and publicity flyer; and the manual *The BUSINE$$ of Teaching Sewing.*

Call or write for schedules and information:

Palmer/Pletsch School of Sewing
P.O. Box 12046
Portland, OR 97212
(503) 294-0696
info@palmerpletsch.com

Check your local fabric store or contact Palmer/Pletsch Publishing, P.O. Box 12046, Portland, OR 97212-0046. www.palmerpletsch.com (503) 274-0687 or 1-800-728-3784 (order desk) or fax (503)274-1377